Don't Shoot the Manager

Don't Shoot the Manager

THE REVEALING STORY OF
ENGLAND'S SOCCER BOSSES

Jimmy Greaves

with

Norman Giller

B⬚XTREE

First published in Great Britain in 1993 by Boxtree Limited

Text © Jimmy Greaves and Norman Giller 1993
Illustrations © Roy Ullyett 1993

The right of Jimmy Greaves and Norman Giller to be identified as
Authors of this Work has been asserted by them in accordance with the
Copyright, Designs and Patents Act 1988.

1 3 5 7 9 10 8 6 4 2

Designed by Penny Mills

Printed in England by Clays Ltd, St Ives plc

for

Boxtree Limited
Broadwall House
21 Broadwall
London SE1 9PL

A CIP catalogue entry for this book is available
from the British Library.

ISBN 1 85283 414 5

Picture Acknowledgements:
Front cover photograph reproduced by courtesy of
Action Images Sports Photography
Photographs in plate sections reproduced by courtesy of
Sport and General photographic agency

Dedication

The authors dedicate this book to the memory of their much-mourned pal Bobby Moore, the Master of football, who graced 108 England matches with his skill, great dignity and sportsmanship.

Acknowledgements

Jimmy Greaves and Norman Giller wish to thank the backroom team at Boxtree Publishing who made this book possible, and in particular our main motivator Susanna Wadeson, her editorial colleagues Jenny Ridgwell and Nicola Paris, production manager Christine Corton, and publicist Nichola Motley; thanks also to designers Penny and Tony Mills, Sport & General librarian Paul Kurton, statistician Michael Giller for his computer skills, and, of course, thanks to the artistic genius who always draws a good crowd, the doyen of sports cartoonists Roy Ullyett, of the *Daily Express*.

It would be impossible to compose an all-embracing book such as this without dipping frequently into the waters of wisdom that flowed through previous works, and the authors would like to acknowledge in particular the compilers of the following books which were invaluable in helping them get their facts right:

Captain of England by Billy Wright (Stanley Paul), *Soccer at Home and Abroad* by Neil Franklin (Stanley Paul), *It's All in the Game* by Johnny Haynes (Arthur Barker), *Banks of England* by Gordon Banks (Arthur Barker), *Soccer in the Fifties* by Geoffrey Green (Ian Allen), *Book of Football* (Marshall Cavendish), *Talking Football* by Alf Ramsey (Stanley Paul), *A Century of English International Football* by Morley Farror and Douglas Lamming, *England Football Fact Book* by Cris Freddi (Guiness Publishing), *Against the World* by Kevin Keegan and Mike Langley (Sidgwick and Jackson), *Peter Shilton* by Peter Shilton and Jason Tomas (World's Work), and *The Book of Football Facts and Feats* by that walking record book from Essex, Jack Rollin (Guiness Publishing).

Thanks most of all to the seven managers featured in the following pages: Sir Walter Winterbottom, Sir Alf Ramsey, Joe Mercer, Don Revie, Ron Greenwood, Bobby Robson and Graham Taylor. We could not have managed without them. And we just wish that the 'Manager of Managers' Brian Clough could have had a shot at the job before his deserved retirement.

Contents

Introduction

Roy Ullyett.

This is two books in one. First of all I give an honest and searching appraisal of each of the men who have managed the England football team since the war. Then I hand over to my co-author Norman Giller for a breakdown summary of every match England have played during that time.

When I set out with Norman to research this book, some of the in-built prejudices I had against the managers gave way to sympathy as I began to get some idea of the pressure they have faced. Even the Prime Minister does not experience the sort of stress and strain an England manager is put under by the fans in general and the media in particular. Everybody, but everybody, thinks he (or she) can do the job better, and my old playing partner Bobby Robson summed it up when he told me: 'If I fielded every player the press were pushing for I would have to send about twenty players on to the pitch each time England played.'

There is nobody in any profession who takes as much stick as an England manager. When the team wins, the players get the praise. When they lose, a mountain of abuse falls on the manager. Yet it remains the job every manager wants, even though – like Graham Taylor – you have to put up with being called 'Turnip Head' or – like Ron Greenwood – you have to face headlines that scream, FOR GOD'S SAKE GO! In the following pages we try to get under the skin of the men who have managed England – and it has to be extremely thick skin for them to stand up to the poisoned darts of criticism fired at them from all angles. We study their personalities as well as their performances, and we have endeavoured to flesh out their stories with little-known anecdotes that give them more of a human face.

I feel that I am well qualified to assess the England managers. Walter Winterbottom, the first official England manager, awarded me twenty-five caps, and I won another thirty-two when the one and only Alf Ramsey was in charge. I got to know Joe Mercer and Don Revie on the club circuit, and I played for Ron Greenwood at Under-23 level and then for West Ham United when, as you will learn, we had a bit of a bust up. I have tried not to let any personal feelings get in the way of my judgement, just as I have not allowed the close friendship I had with Bobby Robson in our playing days to colour my view of his reign as England manager.

Graham Taylor is the one England manager I have not had the experience of knowing in a professional capacity. My assessment of him has been made on the evidence of what I have seen from the teams he has selected, and I have not been greatly impressed. When I have met him I have found him a charming man, but he would not have been my choice as England manager. It is one of the scandals of English international football that the man best suited to the job of managing the team has never been given a chance. I refer, of course, to the old bulldog Brian Clough, who, at his peak, would have made the perfect England boss. But the duffers who run our game were frightened of his bite.

Don't shoot the manager. Shoot the men who pick the man to do the job.

CHAPTER ONE

Walter Winterbottom

(1946–1962)

THE SHACKLED MASTER

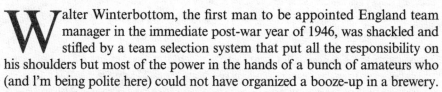

Walter Winterbottom, the first man to be appointed England team manager in the immediate post-war year of 1946, was shackled and stifled by a team selection system that put all the responsibility on his shoulders but most of the power in the hands of a bunch of amateurs who (and I'm being polite here) could not have organized a booze-up in a brewery.

It was Winterbottom who awarded me my first England cap, and so I will always have a soft spot for him. He also has my sympathy for having had to do the job with his hands tied while answerable to football club chairmen blinded by vested interest and who had never kicked a ball in their lives. The farcical situation throughout most of his sixteen years in charge was that he *managed* the team but did not *select* it.

In the first half of his reign, Winterbottom was given access to arguably the greatest English footballers of all time. The names of the prominent players of that era echo like a roll-call of footballing gods: Stanley Matthews, Tom Finney, Tommy Lawton, Raich Carter, Len Shackleton, Wilf Mannion, Nat Lofthouse, Stan Mortensen, Jackie Milburn, Frank Swift, Billy Wright and a poised and purposeful right-back called Alf Ramsey.

With players of that quality to call on, England should have cemented their traditionally held reputation as the masters of world football. It is an indictment of the overall system rather than Winterbottom's management that even with all this talent on tap English football went into a decline. Our game was in the throttling grip of the barons of the Football League, the club chairmen who put club before country at every turn. Winterbottom was lucky if he got his players together a day before an international match, and often they would arrive just a few hours before the kick-off. It was nothing unusual for England team-mates to meet each other for the first time in the dressing-room shortly before going out to play.

Despite the stature of his job, Winterbottom managed to keep a low public profile. The only time he used to make it into the headlines was after an England defeat, when the football writers would line up like a firing squad. It was a standing joke in Fleet Street that the sports desks of the national newspapers had WINTERBOTTOM MUST GO! headlines set up for every match. He would shrug off the searing criticism and get on with his job as if nothing had been said, and he would greet the journalists who had been sniping at him with friendly courtesy. I would have kicked them in the shins.

His influence on post-war English football is greater than almost anybody's, yet to the man in the street (and on the terraces) he was a little-known figure. It was as a coach that he made his most telling contribution, combining the role of England manager with what he saw as the more important job of the Football Association's Director of Coaching. In fact it was made clear to him right from the outset that he was the FA coach first and England manager second. Sir Stanley Rous, the forward-looking secretary of the Football Association who first spotted the potential of Winterbottom, said:

> Most of the FA councillors did not want a national team manager, but I persuaded them to rather reluctantly appoint one. They gave Walter the responsibility, but saw to it that they retained the power. Anybody assessing what Walter achieved for English football must think of him first and foremost as a coach and an organizer extraordinaire.

I have never tried to disguise my distrust of coaches. It is a purely personal view that too many of them squeeze out the natural skills of young players and turn them into faceless robots. Having said that, I accept that I am in the minority with my opinion, and those who plead the case for coaches will tell you that Winterbottom was the 'father' of English coaching. He set up a nationwide network of FA coaching schools, and among his many disciples you will find outstanding coaches such as Ron Greenwood, Bobby Robson, Dave Sexton, Malcolm Allison and Don Howe. Who am I to argue with such respected brains of the game?

Winterbottom himself, as modest a man as I have ever met in sport, would give the credit for the success of his coaching scheme to Sir Stanley Rous, who later became President of the world-governing body, FIFA. He had been impressed by Winterbottom when they met on an experimental course that the visionary Rous had set up in 1937. It was a meeting that was eventually to lead to the appointment of Winterbottom as the man with all the responsibility for England's international football teams but none of the power.

Winterbottom,
THE MAN AND THE MANAGER

Born in Oldham in 1913, Winterbottom was an outstanding footballer while at Oldham Grammar School, but elected to study at Chester College rather than start a career as a professional. At college he met Eddie Lever, a Portsmouth professional who was catching up on studies while recovering from injury. It was Lever, later manager of Portsmouth, who first opened his mind to the theory and tactics of the game. Winterbottom left college with a teacher's diploma, and while working as a schoolmaster in Oldham played as a centre-half for Royston Amateurs and Mossley. He was spotted by Manchester United's famous scout, Louis Rocca, and was persuaded to turn professional on the understanding that he would be given time off to study at the Carnegie College of Physical Training.

Winterbottom made his League début against Leeds United in 1934, but a spinal injury interrupted his career and he joined the college staff as a sports lecturer. Then, on the outbreak of World War II, he became a wing commander in the RAF and was seconded to the Air Ministry where he was appointed Head of Physical Training. He resumed his playing career as a guest for Chelsea and was twice called up as an England reserve for wartime international matches, understudying master centre-half Stan Cullis. He had arranged to return to teaching after the war when he got the call from Sir Stanley Rous inviting him to take over as the supremo of English football, responsible for the development of the game at all levels.

Winterbottom was a brilliant organizer, and it was he who introduced the idea of Under-23 and youth team matches and an annual summer tour that brought the England squad continuity and a stronger foundation. But he was continually frustrated by the grandfathers who infested the Football Association. They all meant well, of course, in their roles as unpaid FA selectors, and I recognize that they all willingly tried to put a lot into the game, but what they saw as duty to club and country amounted to little less than meddling and interference on a grand scale. It was a committee that is said to have come up with the camel when designing a horse, and the selectors must have often given Winterbottom the hump, although he was much too dignified a gentleman to ever make public his feelings.

Sir Stanley Rous, who was one of the greatest of all football administrators and a raconteur much in demand on the after-dinner speaking circuit, once had me literally in tears of laughter when he gave this blow-by-blow account of a typical selection committee meeting, using a different regional accent for each selector:

> Walter would hand in a list of recommended players to the chairman, and then a dozen selectors would tug and pull at his nominations like dogs fighting over a bone.
>
> Chairman: 'Right, gentlemen, in goal our manager recommends Frank Swift. Those in favour ...' Eleven hands go up. The Rovers' chairman Bloggs, a retired baker, keeps his hand down. Chairman: 'Who's your nomination, Joe?'

Bloggs: 'Our lad Jones had a blinder against United on Saturday. He's in the best form of his life.'

Chairman: 'But you were beaten three-nil.'

Bloggs: 'Aye, and it were a bloody robbery. Two of the goals were offside and Jones had a forward standing on his toes when t'third goal went in.'

Following a ten-minute discussion on the merits of Jones versus Swift, Bloggs would climb down after a promise that Jones would get serious consideration for the next match.

Chairman: 'Our manager suggests Ramsey for right-back. Those in favour ...'

Nine hands would go up, and there would be a twenty-minute debate on the strengths and weaknesses of three other nominations. And so it would go on, with only a handful of Walter's nominations receiving one hundred per cent support.

There would be a distinct north–south divide, with the London selectors supporting each other's players and the north using their muscle to get their players into the team; and, of course, the Midlands would have their little clique. Sometimes, a chairman would try to get his player out of the side because he wanted him for an important League match in the days when clubs had to play regardless of whether they had players on international duty. Smith, a retired shoe manufacturer from United, would say, 'I think it's time our lad had a rest from international football. Give some one else a chance.' The rest of the committee, knowing what he was up to, would vote to keep his player in. The meeting would drag on for two, sometimes three hours with each of the chairmen – retired butchers, greengrocers, builders, motor dealers, brewers and farmers – fighting his corner for a player from his own club. They would lobby each other before the meeting, promising support for a selector's choice in return for support for his own player.

Walter would sit listening to all this, sucking on his pipe and trying hard not to bite through the stem as the committee called for four or five changes to his selection. He would then with the patience of Job explain why you should not have two left-footed players together on the right side of the pitch, how player 'A' and player 'B' were too alike in style to fit together, and he would quietly have to point out that one of the men recommended by the selectors was recovering from a broken leg. By the time the meeting was over he would have persuaded them to virtually accept his original nominations with perhaps one or two changes forced on him by the selectors.

I fell about laughing when Sir Stanley told the story, but then the sheer stupidity of it all hit me and I wanted to cry for our football. Walter himself later told me:

Even this selection system was an improvement on what I first had to put up with. Each selector would arrive at our meetings with his personal list of who should play. We used to discuss and discuss until we were down to, say, two goalkeepers and then a straight vote would decide. Then on to the next position, and so on through the team. It was asking almost the impossible to get the right blend with this way of selecting a team. At least in the later years I was able to present my team and then let them try to argue me out of it. The trick of it was to stick to the men who were most important, and to make concessions to the committee where it didn't matter so much.

England had the players with the ability to win the World Cup when we first entered the tournament in 1950, but the Football Association made a complete hash of it. They organized a goodwill tour of Canada at the same time as the World Cup finals in Brazil, and Manchester United requested that none of their players should be considered because they had arranged a trip to the United States. Winterbottom, battling against this club-before-country attitude, almost had to get on his knees to have first choice for the World Cup. As it was he had to go to Brazil without our most famous player, Stanley Matthews, who was sent on the totally meaningless Canadian trip as a footballing ambassador. Special arrangements had to be made to fly him down to Rio for the World Cup, and he arrived after England had won their opening match 2–0 against Chile. Winterbottom wanted to play Matthews in the second game against the United States, and Sir Stanley Rous argued the case for him with the chairman of the selectors, a Grimsby fish merchant called Arthur Drewry, who had been appointed the sole selector for the World Cup. 'My policy is to never change a winning team', Drewry said dismissively. On one of the blackest days in English football history, England were beaten 1–0 by the United States with Stanley Matthews among the spectators.

An off-the-pitch story from that 1950 World Cup tournament captures the amateurish way in which we approached international football. Nobody had bothered to check what food the hotel would serve in Brazil, and the players complained that they could not eat it because it was too spicy. Winterbottom decided the only way round the problem was to go into the hotel kitchen and do the cooking himself! Talk about head cook and bottle washer.

In 1958, England's squad arrived in Sweden just two days before the start of the World Cup finals without having organized a training camp. Winterbottom had to chase around seeking facilities while his players kicked their heels in the hotel. It really was amateur night out, and things had not improved four years later when I had my first experience of World Cup football in the 1962 finals in Chile. With what I considered was close to madness, Winterbottom and the FA planning committee decided to stick the England squad in a tiny mountain mining-village called Coya 8,000 feet above sea level. The only way to reach it was by rail car or narrow mountain path. To have our meals we had to walk from our barrack-style quarters across a narrow, rickety wooden bridge with a 500-foot drop either side. It was great for building up an appetite. Bobby Moore and I shared a miner's shack that had a corrugated roof, and when it rained (which was often) it sounded as if the Grenadier Guards were marching above us. It was Walter who had recommended the training camp after a reconnoitring trip to Chile, and I said to him after my first view: 'Well done, Walter, you've really hit the jackpot. Even the dogs here run round with their tails between their legs.'

We were marooned in the back of beyond and often bored out of our minds, and we were unprofessional enough not to have a team doctor in the party. There were at least ten doddery, blazered FA officials accompanying us, retired butchers, bakers and candlestick-makers, but not a doctor among them. When our centre-half Peter Swan went down with a stomach virus he was given the wrong treatment, and very nearly died. Just before he was struck down, poor old Peter joined the rest of us in a village hall to watch a local folk-dancing troupe. A photographer snapped a picture of Peter clowning around with one of the girl dancers, and this made the next day's sports pages. As he lay in a Chilean hospital on what he thought was his death-bed, Peter received a letter from his wife – also in hospital after having a baby – saying very pointedly that he was obviously having a good time.

On another tour, I was leaving the stadium with Wolves defender Ron Flowers when one of the FA selectors came up and patted Ron on the back. 'You've had an outstanding tour, son', he said. 'You have a great future with England. Well done, Bobby.' And off he shuffled, leaving Ron – who had not played a game on tour – speechless and me rolled up with laughter. In fairness, Ron was blond like Bobby Moore but there the similarity ended.

I tell these stories only to illustrate the environment in which Walter Winterbottom had to work. He was surrounded by well-meaning buffoons. I first met Walter when I made my début for the England Under-23 team against Bulgaria at Stamford Bridge in 1957. I was seventeen and in my opening League season with Chelsea. My first impression was that he reminded me of my old school headmaster, and I never had reason to change that view during the five years that I played in his teams. He was a distinguished, quietly spoken man who talked as if he had swallowed a dictionary, and often sounded more like a university lecturer than a football coach. I remember him using phrases in his team talks such as 'peripheral vision' and it all went whizzing high over my head. If he could have conveyed the plans he had in his head to the pitch, he would have been rewarded with a World Cup triumph long before Alf Ramsey, but his message too often got lost in a web of words that left players like me wondering what the hell he was talking about.

Winterbottom's one major weakness in my view was that when talking tactics he seemed to think he was addressing the Oxford Union. I once listened to him explaining the way he he wanted us to play in a match and after ten minutes I put up my hand and said, 'Would you mind repeating that please, Walter.' The rest of the lads fell about laughing because they thought I was joking, but I honestly did not understand a word that he was talking about. About ten years earlier, Len Shackleton, the clown prince of football, listened to Walter giving one of his involved tactical talks, and he explained how he wanted Tommy Lawton and Shack to concentrate on moving through the middle and scoring after an interchange of wall passes. 'Excuse me', said Shack, 'which side of the net do you want me to put the ball?'

Winterbottom was under fire for his tactical talks before I came on the scene. At the close of his distinguished three-decade England career, Stanley Matthews went on record with this sweeping criticism:

> A will to win was sadly lacking in the England team ... I blame this on the pre-match talks on playing tactics that had been introduced for the first time by our team manager. You just cannot tell star players how they must play and what they must do on the field in an international match. You must let them play their natural game, which has paid big dividends in the past. I have noticed that in recent years these pre-match instructions have become more and more long-winded while the playing ability of the players on the field has dwindled. So I say scrap the talks and instruct the players to play their natural game.

Winterbottom took this savage swipe on his dimpled chin, and put up just a muted defence as he replied in that professorial way of his:

> In principle I can state quite firmly that it is grossly untrue that I have encouraged this trend of team instruction before an international match. In fact, I have repeatedly insisted on our players having every opportunity to play as a team before an important match to enable us to cut down on these instructions. Indeed, I can state quite categorically that players are always encouraged to play their own game.

In fairness to Winterbottom, I must say that he always used to stress to me that I should play my natural game ... but he would then confuse the issue by spending ten minutes telling me how to play my natural game! I respected and admired Walter, but he could talk the ears off an elephant.

On a personal level, he went out of his way to help me during my traumatic transfer to Italy in 1961 and I recall us then getting drenched together. I was trying to wriggle out of the move from Chelsea to AC

Milan, and Walter came to the Surrey house of my then agent, Bagenal Harvey, to give me some confidential advice. Jimmy Hill, who was the dynamic chairman of the players' union, was also there, and we had just sat down with Bagenal when a Fleet Street news reporter and photographer arrived in search of me. The quick-thinking Bagenal ushered Walter and me through a back window into the garden, and then invited the snoopers in. He explained that he and Jimmy Hill were the only two in the house – the truth – and showed them the manuscript of a book by Hill's Fulham team-mate, Johnny Haynes, who was another client of Bagenal's. He pretended that this was what they were discussing and he read them excerpts and asked for their opinions. Meantime, a downpour had started and Walter and I were getting soaked while we giggled like schoolboys in the garden.

We eventually climbed back into the house once the newsmen had left, and I listened to Walter and Jimmy handing me sound advice as to why I should not go to Italy. It's history that I was finally lured to Milan for an unhappy four-month spell before signing for Tottenham for what was then a record fee of £99,999. It was typical of Walter's caring nature that he should put himself out to help me, and I do not want to close my personal assessment of him without placing on record the fact that I considered him one of the nicest people I ever met on my football journey. He really was a gentleman and a scholar.

It was disgraceful that he was allowed to leave the world of football in 1962 after he had given so much to the game. He should have been made Secretary of the Football Association, but politicians at Lancaster Gate ganged up on him because of his close association with Sir Stanley Rous and their support went to FA treasurer Denis Follows. When it was clear that he was not going to get the job for which he had all the right qualifications, Winterbottom moved on to the Central Council of Physical Recreation where he was knighted for his services to sport. With his brainpower, this born administrator could have revolutionized the way the game was run. For the last time, he was frustrated by the tin-pot gods of the Football Association.

Winterbottom's Record

During his sixteen years in charge of the England team, Winterbottom's record was:

P	W	D	L	F	A
139	78	33	28	383	196

Home international matches only:

	P	W	D	L	F	A
v. Scotland	16	9	4	3	40	22
v. Wales	17	12	4	1	49	17
v. Northern Ireland	17	11	5	1	57	24

International matches played in England against overseas opposition:

P	W	D	L	F	A
33	23	7	3	115	47

International matches played outside England against overseas opposition:

P	W	D	L	F	A
56	23	13	20	122	86

On paper it is a creditable record, but on the pitch England lost the matches that really mattered. Winterbottom had four cracks at winning the World Cup, and never once got within shooting distance of the Final. This was his World Cup finals record, which is far from distinguished:

P	W	D	L	F	A
14	3	5	6	19	21

In the 1950 finals Winterbottom's England suffered a humiliating 1–0 defeat by the United States. The football writers failed to do their home-work, and reported that England had been beaten by a team that had come from Ellis Island, with only a couple of true Americans among them. But research has since proved this to be false information; all but three of the United States team were native Americans. They were boosted by immi-grants Joe Maca from Belgium, Ed McIllveney from Scotland and the goal scorer, Joe Gaetjens from Haiti.

Billy Wright, skippering the side from right-half, recalled when I discussed the match with him many years later during our days together in the same Central Television team:

> It was the biggest freak result I ever experienced throughout my playing
> career. I promise you that ninety-nine times out of a hundred we would
> have won the match. It was played on a cramped, narrow pitch that
> meant we were unable to make full use of our strength down the wings. I
> recall that the dressing-rooms were so dingy and rat-infested that Walter
> ordered us on to the coach, and we changed in a sports club a ten minute
> drive away. During the most frustrating game in which I ever played we
> must have had twenty shots to their one, when the ball deflected off the
> head of Gaetjens and into the net. I had never felt worse on a football

pitch than at the final whistle. Walter took it all in his stride, but inside I am sure he was hurting just as much as the rest of us. He was never one to show his feelings. In victory and defeat he adopted the same sporting, controlled attitude. A lot of people said he was long-winded, but I thought he was a beautiful speaker. I could listen to him all day. He was such a cultured, intelligent man and I always considered it a privilege to be in his company.

England were eliminated from the 1950 World Cup when in their next match – Stanley Matthews and all – they went down 1–0 to Spain. Winterbottom was savaged by the English press, but they failed to get him removed from his job. The bungling amateurs at the Football Association knew they could not lay the blame for England's exit solely on his shoulders.

A devastating thing happened to English football on the way to the 1954 finals in Switzerland. The Hungarians – the Magical Magyars – trounced England 6–3 at Wembley and 7–1 in Budapest, a result that the *Daily Mirror* dubbed 'Disaster on the Danube'. The defeat at Wembley was the first ever on home territory by an overseas team (not counting a 1949 setback against the Republic of Ireland at Goodison in 1949), and the seven-goal tanking in Budapest remains the heaviest defeat ever suffered by an England team.

'It was as if the Hungarians had stepped off another planet', said Billy Wright, who to this day is haunted by a classic goal scored by the one and only Ferenc Puskas in the first match at Wembley on November 25, 1953. 'Even now, thirty years on, people ask me about that goal', he told me.

> Puskas controlled the ball with the sole of his left boot on the right side of the penalty area, and as I made a challenge he pulled the ball back like a man loading a shotgun, and fired it into the net all in one sweet movement while I was tackling thin air. Geoffrey Green described it beautifully in *The Times*. He wrote that I went flying into the tackle like a fire engine going in the wrong direction for the blaze. To this day I have never seen football to match that played by Hungary. They were a phenomenal side.

It was the moment of truth. England could no longer claim to be the masters of world football. Winterbottom led the inquests into the defeats, and it was accepted that we had fallen behind the times with our tactics and our technique. We were still playing the old-fashioned WM formation, with two wide full-backs, a 'stopper' centre-half in the middle and two defensive wing half-backs feeding the ball to two ball-playing inside-forwards. Two wingers patrolled the touchlines and a centre-forward led the line right down the middle. It was called 'WM' because that is the stereotyped pattern the players formed on the pitch. The Hungarians played their number nine Hidegkuti as a deep-lying centre-forward and Blackpool centre-half Harry Johnston had no idea how to mark him.

Hidegkuti played hide-and-seek, and nipped in unseen for a hat-trick. Even the old men who ran our football were forced to pull their heads out of the sand, and leading club managers were called together for their opinions. Winterbottom took careful note of their views, and it all led to a gradual change in training methods, playing tactics and style of kit – out went the heavy boots, bulky shinpads, baggy shorts and shirts and the thick socks. Appearance money for international players was increased from £30 to £50 (the equivalent of more than two weeks' wages), and the FA selectors at last accepted that they had to start listening to professional opinion, although they were not willing to go so far as to give up the job of picking the team, despite pressure from the press.

The new approach did little to help England in the 1954 World Cup finals. England scrambled through to the quarter-finals with a draw against Belgium and a 2–0 victory over Switzerland, and were then beaten 4–2 by Uruguay. The Fleet Street knives were out again for Winterbottom, but he survived the attempted assassination and in 1955 came up with an imaginative plan that excited even his army of critics.

Winterbottom prepared a list of thirty players he felt he needed to mount a winning challenge for the 1958 World Cup. The selectors went along with him, and in the twenty-five months following the introduction of his ambitious plan England played sixteen matches without defeat.

Then came the horrific Manchester United disaster at Munich on February 6, 1958, a date burned in the hearts and minds of anybody who was involved in football at the time. Of the eight United players tragically killed in the air crash, three (Roger Byrne, Duncan Edwards and Tommy Taylor) were key men in the Winterbottom plan. To lose three players of their calibre – Duncan was the greatest all-rounder I ever saw – would have knocked any team sideways. England lost all their impetus during the build-up to the World Cup, and were walloped 5–0 in a warm-up match against Yugoslavia. It was a dispirited team that Winterbottom led to Sweden with just two days to go to the kick-off and without a proper training camp. The amateurs were back in command. In a World Cup dominated by the brilliant Brazilians and their seventeen-year-old boy wonder, Pelé, England – with three drawn games and a 1–0 defeat by Russia in a play-off match – failed to reach the last eight. Their only noteworthy performance was a goalless draw with Brazil, who had yet to launch Pelé. This was achieved thanks to the meticulous planning of future Tottenham manager Bill Nicholson, who was in Sweden as Winterbottom's right-hand man. He watched Brazil play and then worked out a man-to-man marking system that frustrated the Brazilians: with the right planning and preparation England could compete with the very best.

If nothing else, the Football Association could not be criticized for lacking loyalty to Winterbottom. Yet again he came under heavy fire from the assassins of Fleet Street, but with what was becoming Houdini-style skill he escaped the sack and got on with making preparations for the World Cup challenge in Chile in 1962.

This was when I was called into the international arena. I made my England début against Peru in Lima in 1959 during a disastrous South American tour. I managed to score our goal in a 4–1 defeat, and on the trip I got a taste of the appalling organization that had bugged our footballers for years. Our travel schedule would have worn out Captain Cook. We played Brazil, Peru, Mexico and the United States during a span of just fifteen days. We were beaten 2–0 by world champions Brazil, 4–1 by a Peruvian side packed with highly skilled individualists, and then 2–1 by Mexico in the high altitude of Mexico City. We took all our frustration out on the United States and hammered them 8–1 (after being held to a 1–1 draw at half-time), and the result was some sort of revenge for Winterbottom's humiliation against them in the 1950 World Cup. The result also provided sweet satisfaction for skipper Billy Wright, playing his 105th and final match for England. Three of the players in our eighteen-man squad – Roy Gratrix, Graham Shaw and Ron Baynham – travelled halfway round the world without getting a kick at a ball, and Wilf McGuinness got on for only forty-five minutes. It was my first close-up look at international football from the inside. I was not impressed. In Brazil, for instance, we trained under the full blast of a midday sun for a match that was kicking off at 4.00 p.m. – mad dogs and English footballers! We were worked really hard in the training sessions, which I felt was pretty pointless because we were all knackered after a full League season. I have to confess that I was never the most enthusiastic of trainers, but even the fanatics in our squad had to admit we were being over-cooked.

Winterbottom showed he could be tough if he felt it necessary when, in Rio, several of the players pestered him to let us go to the famous Copacabana beach for a swim. But he refused and stressed that we were in Rio for football duty not a holiday. Fair enough. You can imagine how angry we felt when airmail editions of the English newspapers arrived with stories that we were spending all our time lounging around on Copacabana. It was one of the rare occasions when I saw Winterbottom close to losing his temper. He did not mind reporters expressing strong opinions or putting down hard facts, but he objected strongly to fabricated stories. The one day Walter did allow us to go to Copacabana it poured with rain.

In Mexico we were booked into a downtown hotel that was seedy and smelly, and we were squashed three and four to each already cramped room. You must bear in mind that this was in the days before package tours when overseas travel was something of a novelty, and we were not given sufficient warning about the danger of sunbathing in the thin air. Several of the lads got painfully sunburned and within a matter of just a few hours Blackburn skipper Ronnie Clayton's back was a mass of blisters. A Mexican doctor was summoned when they burst and decided that the cure was to pour methylated spirits on to the blisters. I think poor old Ronnie's yells could be heard back at Ewood Park. After Ron Flowers had pointed out the minor fact that he was having to share his room with four Mexican strangers, Winterbottom arranged for us to move to a much better hotel where the press were staying, and they gave us terrible stick in their stories cabled home, describing us as 'spoilt brats' simply because we wanted the same creature comforts that they were enjoying.

The reporters came up with a beauty during the match against Mexico. They cabled back stories about the stadium being rocked by an earthquake while we were playing. Not a single player or team official felt a thing. I think the high altitude must have gone to the heads of the reporters.

As was to be learned in the Olympics of 1968 and the World Cups of 1970 and 1986, you need at least two weeks to acclimatize to the thin air of Mexico City. We were thrown in to action after just a few days, and it was all we could do to catch our breath on the way to a 2–1 defeat. The press made no allowance for this, and then hammered us for attending a bull-fight after the match at which we were guests of the Mexican FA. One of the bulls refused to fight, and all the England players were in hysterics at the sight of this brave bull ignoring all attempts to get it into a fighting mood. In the English newspapers it was reported that we were interested only in enjoying ourselves, and that we could not have cared less about the defeat in the football match earlier in the day.

I watched Winterbottom dealing with the press and wondered at his calm manner. He continued to co-operate with them regardless of the mud that they threw, and I quickly realized that he had a major flaw as a manager: *he was too nice.*

The FA officials on the tour had, however, taken careful note of the reporting (or, more accurately, misreporting), and Joe Mears – chairman of Chelsea and of the international selection committee, and one of the more enlightened FA officials – lodged an official complaint with the Press Council. I personally got on well with most of the football writers, but I was unable to understand how they could be so vicious and unfeeling with their criticism of Winterbottom in particular and the players in general. Nearly every one of them held the private view that Walter was a charming man they respected and admired, but in public they held him up to ridicule with their scorching criticisms.

Winterbottom deserved praise and recognition for all his pioneering work. But all he seemed to get was barrel-loads of abuse. Several of his Fleet Street critics did not allow facts to spoil a good story, and their put-the-boot-in-regardless style of reporting was a forerunner of what was to become commonplace in the 'tabloid' era. In the autumn of 1959 the

Football Association was forced to issue a statement officially denying stories in the media that Winterbottom was about to be sacked. It is indicative of the mood of the time that the denial was less easy to digest than the newspaper rumours.

The press called off their 'Winterbottom witch hunt' when England hit a winning streak during which we scored thirty-two goals and conceded eight in winning five matches in the 1960–61 season. The highlight was a 9–3 victory against Scotland at Wembley. I managed to bang in three goals, but the real star of an extraordinary performance against a Scottish side that included Dave Mackay, Billy McNeill, Denis Law and Ian St John was our skipper Johnny Haynes, who paralyzed the Scots with his pin-point passes. He got two goals himself, with Bobby Smith, Bobby Robson and Bryan Douglas also getting in on the scoring act. The victory was a vindication of a team policy that Winterbottom had adopted at the start of the season. He was determined to mould a settled side and got the selection committee to agree to keep an unchanged team provided, of course, that everybody played reasonably well. It was a plan Winterbottom had tried to introduce a year earlier, but the FA selectors slapped him down because England could 'only' draw with Scotland and Yugoslavia – results that persuaded them that they could not possibly allow the manager a free hand. A European tour party was due to be named, and Winterbottom emerged from a tense meeting to tell reporters with a shrug, 'I cannot give you a single name for the tour. The committee have decided to defer the naming of a squad until further discussion at a future meeting. I have nothing more to say.' It was a statement that proved he was still the puppet of the amateurs who were running (or ruining) our game.

But Winterbottom finally got his way, and the team he settled on at the start of the 1960–61 season was the best with which I played during my England career. Our strong team spirit was boosted by Winterbottom's faithful trainer Harold Shepherdson, a warm, friendly character who provided an ideal balance for the calculating, slightly aloof Winterbottom. Shep was following in the footsteps of Bill Ridding, Jimmy Trotter and the legendary Wilf Copping, a Norman Hunter-style hardman of football before becoming part of the establishment as England trainer.

For that success run of the early 1960s we had switched to this 4–2–4 formation, which had worked so successfully for the 1958 Brazilian world champions:

Ron Springett

Jimmy Armfield   Peter Swan   Ron Flowers   Mick McNeil

Bobby Robson   Johnny Haynes

Bryan Douglas   Bobby Smith   Jimmy Greaves   Bobby Charlton

If you could have grafted this attack on to a team containing the 1966 England defence, you would have had the greatest England international side of all time. Unfortunately this 1961 team came to the boil too early. We were past our peak by the time the 1962 World Cup came round, and we were eliminated by Brazil after struggling through to the quarter-finals. All of the Fleet Street critics came back out of the woodwork, and this time they showed no mercy. I was one of several players accused of wearing the England shirt like a white flag of surrender. Johnny Haynes was described as a selfish captain who thought only of himself. This was tame compared with the burning oil poured on Winterbottom.

Walter, a thoroughly decent man, gave an insight into the pressures he was facing when he revealed that his wife, Ann, was being greeted with stony silence in supermarkets and local shops and that his son, Alan, came crying home from school after being teased and taunted.

I believe that Winterbottom knew that his time was up even before the 1962 World Cup finals, and when he failed to get the FA secretary's job, which should have been his by right, he resigned. Waiting in the wings (an intended pun) to take his place was one Alf Ramsey.

Winterbottom's Players

These were the 160 players chosen by the Selection Committee and capped during Winterbottom's 139 matches as England team manager:

Alan A'Court (Liverpool: 6)
Tony Allen (Stoke: 3)
Ronnie Allen (West Bromwich: 5)
Stan Anderson (Sunderland: 2)
John Angus (Burnley: 1)
Jimmy Armfield (Blackpool: 32)
Ken Armstrong (Chelsea: 1)
Gordon Astall (Birmingham: 2)
John Aston (Manchester Utd: 17)
John Atyeo (Bristol City: 6)

Eddie Baily (Tottenham: 9)
Joe Baker (Hibernian: 5)
Tommy Banks (Bolton: 6)
Ray Barlow (West Bromwich: 1)
Malcolm Barrass (Bolton: 3)
Ron Baynham (Luton: 3)
Roy Bentley (Chelsea: 12)
John Berry (Manchester Utd: 4)

Frank Blunstone (Chelsea: 5)
Peter Brabrook (Chelsea: 3)
Geoff Bradford (Bristol R: 1)
Warren Bradley (Manchester Utd: 3)
Peter Broadbent (Wolverhampton: 7)
Ivor Broadis (Manchester City/
   Newcastle: 14)
Johnny Brooks (Tottenham: 3)
Ken Brown (West Ham: 1)
Johnny Byrne (C. Palace: 1)
Roger Byrne (Manchester Utd: 33)

Raich Carter (Derby: 7)
Bobby Charlton (Manchester Utd: 39)
Ray Charnley (Blackpool: 1)
Allenby Chilton (Manchester Utd: 2)
Eddie Clamp (Wolverhampton: 4)
Danny Clapton (Arsenal: 1)
Harry Clarke (Tottenham: 1)

Ronnie Clayton (Blackburn: 35)
Brian Clough (Middlesbrough: 2)
Henry Cockburn
  (Manchester Utd: 13)
Leslie Compton (Arsenal: 2)
John Connelly (Burnley: 9)
Ray Crawford (Ipswich: 2)
Chris Crowe (Wolverhampton: 1)
Norman Deeley (Wolverhampton: 2)
Jimmy Dickinson (Portsmouth: 48)
Ted Ditchburn (Tottenham: 6)
Bryan Douglas (Blackburn: 33)

Bill Eckersley (Blackburn: 17)
Duncan Edwards
  (Manchester Utd: 18)
Bill Ellerington (Southampton: 2)
Billy Elliott (Burnley: 5)

Johnny Fantham (Sheffield
  Wednesday: 1)
Tom Finney (Preston: 76)
Ron Flowers (Wolves: 39)
Bill Foulkes (Manchester Utd: 1)
Neil Franklin (Stoke: 27)
Jack Froggatt (Portsmouth: 13)

Tom Garrett (Blackpool: 3)
Colin Grainger (Sheffield Utd: 7)
Jimmy Greaves (Chelsea/
  Tottenham: 25)

Jimmy Hagan (Sheffield Utd: 1)
Jack Haines (West Bromwich: 1)
Jeff Hall (Birmingham City: 17)
Johnny Hancocks
  (Wolverhampton: 3)
George Hardwick (Middlesbrough:
  13)
Peter Harris (Portsmouth: 2)
Harold Hassall (Huddersfield: 5)
Johnny Haynes (Fulham: 56)
Mike Hellawell (Birmingham: 1)

Freddie Hill (Bolton: 2)
Alan Hinton (Wolverhampton; 1)
Gerry Hitchens (Aston Villa/
  Inter Milan: 7)
Alan Hodgkinson (Sheffield Utd: 5)
Doug Holden (Bolton: 5)
Eddie Holliday (Middlesbrough: 3)
Eddie Hopkinson (Bolton: 14)
Don Howe (West Bromwich: 23)
John Howe (Derby: 3)
Lawrie Hughes (Liverpool: 3)
Roger Hunt (Liverpool: 1)

Beford Jezzard (Fulham: 2)
Harry Johnston (Blackpool: 10)
Bill Jones (Liverpool: 2)

Derek Kevan (West Bromwich: 14)

Brian Labone (Everton: 2)
Jimmy Langley (Fulham: 3)
Bobby Langton (Blackburn: 11)
Tommy Lawton (Chelsea/
  Nottingham County: 15)
Jackie Lee (Leicester: 1)
Nat Lofthouse (Bolton: 33)
Eddie Lowe (Aston Villa: 3)

Colin McDonald (Burnley: 8)
Bill McGarry (Huddersfield: 4)
Wilf McGuinness
  (Manchester Utd: 2)
Mick McNeil (Middlesbrough: 9)
Wilf Mannion (Middesbrough: 26)
Reg Matthews (Coventry: 5)
Stanley Matthews (Blackpool: 36)
Jimmy Meadows
  (Manchester City: 1)
Les Medley (Tottenham, 1951–52: 6)
Gil Merrick (Birmingham: 23)
Vic Metcalfe (Huddersfield: 2)
Jackie Milburn (Newcastle: 13)
Brian Miller (Burnley: 1)

Arthur Milton (Arsenal: 1)
Bobby Moore (West Ham: 8)
John Morris (Derby: 3)
Stan Mortensen (Blackpool: 25)
Bert Mozley (Derby: 3)
Jimmy Mullen (Wolverhampton: 12)

John Nicholls (West Bromwich: 2)
Bill Nicholson (Tottenham: 1)
Maurice Norman (Tottenham: 6)
Mike O'Grady (Huddersfield: 1)
Syd Owen (Luton: 3)

Ray Parry (Bolton: 2)
Alan Peacock (Middlesbrough: 4)
Stan Pearson (Manchester Utd: 8)
David Pegg (Manchester Utd: 1)
Bill Perry (Blackpool: 3)
Len Phillips (Portsmouth: 3)
Brian Pilkington (Burnley: 1)
Ray Pointer (Burnley: 3)
Jesse Pye (Wolverhampton: 1)

Albert Quixall (Sheffield
   Wednesday: 5)

Alf Ramsey (Southampton/
   Tottenham: 32)
Stan Rickaby (West Bromwich: 1)
George Robb (Tottenham: 1)
Bobby Robson (West Bromwich: 20)
Jack Rowley (Manchester Utd: 6)

Laurie Scott (Arsenal: 17)
Jackie Sewell (Sheff. United: 6)
Len Shackleton (Sunderland: 5)
Graham Shaw (Sheffield Utd: 5)

Eddie Shimwell (Blackpool: 1)
Peter Silllett (Chelsea: 3)
Bill Slater (Wolverhampton: 12)
Lionel Smith (Arsenal: 6)
Bobby Smith (Tottenham: 7)
Trevor Smith (Birmingham: 2)
Ron Springett (Sheffield
   Wednesday: 28)
Ron Staniforth (Huddersfield: 8)
Bernard Streten (Luton: 1)
Peter Swan (Sheffield
   Wednesday: 19)
Frank Swift (Manchester City: 19)

Bobby Tambling (Chelsea: 1)
Ernie Taylor (Blackpool: 1)
Jim Taylor (Fulham: 2)
Phil Taylor (Liverpool: 3)
Tommy Taylor
   (Manchester Utd: 19)
Tommy Thompson (Aston
   Villa/Preston: 2)
Derek Ufton (Charlton: 1)

Dennis Viollet (Manchester Utd: 2)

Tim Ward (Derby: 2)
Willie Watson (Sunderland: 4)
John Wheeler (Bolton: 1)
Bert Williams (Wolverhampton: 24)
Arthur Willis (Tottenham: 1)
Dennis Wilshaw
   (Wolverhampton: 12)
Ray Wilson (Huddersfield: 17)
Ray Wood (Manchester Utd: 3)
Billy Wright (Wolverhampton: 105)

The fifteen most capped players during the Winterbottom reign were Billy Wright (105), Tom Finney (76), Johnny Haynes (56), Jimmy Dickinson (48), Bobby Charlton (39), Ron Flowers (39), Stanley Matthews (36), Ronnie Clayton (35), Roger Byrne (33), Bryan Douglas (33), Nat Lofthouse (33), Alf

Ramsey (32), Jimmy Armfield (32), Ron Springett (28), Neil Franklin (27). Franklin, one of the most stylish centre-halves ever to play for England, would have doubled his collection of caps but for dropping out to play in the outlawed Colombian league with Bogota. He was desperately missed by Winterbottom during the disastrous 1950 World Cup campaign.

Johnny Haynes was injured in a car smash just after Alf Ramsey had taken over as England manager, and was never recalled after battling back to full fitness. All his caps were awarded to him while Winterbottom was in charge.

The fact that thirty-four players won just a single cap is evidence of the way the selectors chopped and changed the team, allowing Winterbottom little opportunity for vital continuity. Brian Clough was among the twenty-one players discarded after winning two caps.

The biggest injustice was that Len Shackleton was awarded just five caps. Players not fit to tie his bootlaces have since won ten times that number. Shack was a genius, but too much of an individualist for the FA officials to stomach. They wanted players who would toe the line; all Shack wanted to do was give them the toe of his boot. He could almost make the ball sit up and talk, and thought nothing of squatting on the ball during a match or dancing with the referee. For Shack, football was fun. What a pity the asses who ran our game did not share his outlook. A story that Len told me years ago helps to capture the suffocating environment in which Winterbottom had to work:

> After scoring what I rated one of my finest ever goals to help England beat world champions Germany at Wembley in 1954, I was handed a third-class rail ticket for the overnight sleeper back to Sunderland. I said, 'Couldn't you raise enough money for a first-class ticket?' The FA official said that all the first-class tickets had been sold. When I got to Kings Cross I had no trouble transferring to first-class because there was plenty of space, and I was happy to pay the five pounds difference out of my own pocket. By the time I'd paid tax and expenses, I was left with just £20 out of my £50 match fee. The Wembley receipts for the match were over £50,000, but we footballers who had drawn the crowd and the money were considered third-class citizens by those blinkered fools who ran the Football Association.

This was the sort of miserly treatment that stopped Walter Winterbottom from being a more successful manager on the world stage. He was expected to run our football in the days when the £20-a-week players were treated like slaves – and the most shackled man of them all was Winterbottom himself. He was never given the freedom he needed (and deserved) to do the job properly.

His successor was determined not to suffer the same treatment.

CHAPTER TWO

Alf Ramsey

(1963–1974)

A WINNER, WARTS 'N' ALL

A lf Ramsey was not the first choice as successor to Walter Winterbottom as England manager. The man the Football Association wanted was Burnley coach and former captain Jimmy Adamson, who had been Winterbottom's assistant during the 1962 World Cup finals. Adamson saw at first hand the pressures piled on Winterbottom by the interference of the FA officials and the insensitive interrogations of the press. He was strong enough and wise enough to say 'thanks, but no thanks'.

Adamson did himself a favour by turning down the job. I am convinced he would have hated it because, in some ways like Winterbottom, he was simply *too nice*. No such accusation could ever be levelled at Alf Ramsey.

All eyes will be on what I have to say about Ramsey. It is widely believed that we are sworn enemies because he left me out of the England team for the match of a lifetime, the 1966 World Cup final. So a lot of people are going to be surprised when I go on record as saying that not only do I quite like Alf but that *I rate him, by some distance, the greatest manager England have ever had.*

But this apparent softness on my part will not stop me presenting Ramsey warts 'n' all in what I want to be an honest assessment of the men who have been the guardians of English football. I am not sure there was another manager in the country who could have chopped down to size the power-hungry officials at the Football Association. Right from the start he made it clear that he would take the manager's job only on his terms. During his days as a rather slow but extremely gifted England right-back (as good as any who have worn the number two shirt) he had seen the way Winterbottom was obstructed by amateurs. His first demand, met with some reluctance, was that the selection committee be abolished, with the selectors reduced to a mere, quite irrelevant Senior International Committee that carried gnat's weight in terms of picking the team. Ramsey was the sole selector, listening to recommendations and then largely ignoring them.

He treated many of the FA councillors with an abruptness bordering on contempt, and he made 'enemies within' on his way to creating a world-beating football team. I recall a short speech he made at the end of his first summer tour with the England team in 1964. He thanked we players for our efforts, he thanked the trainers Harold Shepherdson and Les Cocker for their support, he thanked the journalists for their courtesy and, finally, he thanked the travelling band of FA officials 'for their good sense in keeping out of our way'.

There was uneasy laughter at what was clearly not meant as a joke, but it sowed seeds of distrust and, in some cases, extreme dislike of the new man in charge. It took the old boys of the Football Association a long while, but they finally got the knife in when he suddenly failed to deliver in a botched 1974 World Cup campaign. The men he had trodden on in the previous eleven years could not wait to kick him out.

But Ramsey's reign had been mostly about winning, and while he upset many people on the periphery with his cold, often rude manner, he won the lasting loyalty of his players. You will find that all but a handful of the ninety-five players capped by Ramsey have warm things to say about a man who was at his most relaxed and natural when in a tracksuit, plotting tactics and talking football.

He returned loyalty for loyalty, and many of his critics considered that it was one of his weaknesses that he often ignored club form and stood by players whose week-in-week-out performances did not justify a place on the international stage. His determination to back his players at all costs was never clearer than during the 1966 World Cup when the knives were out for Manchester United's 'toothless tiger' Nobby Stiles. Nervous FA officials suggested he should drop Stiles following a particularly vicious tackle on French star Jacky Simon right in front of the Royal Box at Wembley in England's third – and my last – match of the tournament. Ramsey, with his intimidating cold-eye stare that was a trademark, replied: 'If Stiles goes, I go.' It was the end of the conversation. They both stayed, and England went on to capture the World Cup with Nobby playing a crucial role as a ball winner.

Apart from being the only England manager to lift the World Cup, Ramsey will be longest – and most unfairly – remembered as the man who removed wingers from football. He devised a 4–3–3 formation that played to the strengths of the players in his 1966 squad, and for the final three games of the tournament he sent out a team without a recognized winger. The fact that England won the World Cup with these tactics inspired an army of imitators, and over the next couple of years wingers disappeared almost without trace at club as well as international level. It had never been Ramsey's intention to kill off wingers. If a Matthews or a Finney had been around at the time, or if George Best had done us the favour of being born on the other side of the Irish Sea, there is no question that he would have selected them.

Ramsey introduced a 4-3-3 formation as a means to an end, little realizing that end would be the virtual eradication of specialist wingers. There is a nasty school of thought that Alf got rid of them in a silent act of revenge against all those wingers who had given him a chasing in his days as a full-back, but I'll give him the benefit of the doubt on that one! The demise of wingers was saddest of all for spectators because I am convinced that football became less exciting and entertaining to watch once the flying flank players had been eliminated. But don't blame Ramsey. Blame the imitators who copied him.

Ramsey,
THE MAN AND THE MANAGER

Born in my old hunting ground of Dagenham in Essex, just past the outskirts of East London, Ramsey was brought up on a smallholding where his father traded in hay and straw. He first started learning ball control in nearby fields when playing with his three brothers, Albert, Len and Cyril. Those fields were soon turned into sprawling housing estates for the overspill population from London's East End, and when I was growing up in Dagenham and then nearby Hainault, locals used to refer to the Ramseys as gypsy stock. Alf certainly has the strong, dark looks associated with gypsies, and one of his early nicknames in his playing days was 'Darkie' Ramsey. But nobody has ever found out for sure about the Ramsey roots because he has always seemed so secretive and sensitive about his background. Once, when being interviewed on the radio, he was asked: 'Are your parents still alive, Mr Ramsey?' 'Oh yes,' he replied. 'Where do they live?' 'In Dagenham, *I believe.*'

He was determined to keep his private life private, and when a journalist started to write an unofficial biography he asked, in vain, how he could stop its publication. The only 'dirt' the book could dig up was that he had apparently told a porky about his age before signing as a professional with Southampton in 1946, knocking off a couple of years from his birthdate of January 22, 1920. It was hardly a crime. Sportsmen can be as sensitive as actresses when it comes to admitting their age. The book also 'revealed' what all of us in the game knew – that Ramsey had taken elocution lessons to try to iron out his broad Cockney accent. (Perhaps I should have followed his example!)

Alf should have asked for his money back because in my opinion the accent he finished up with was so forced that he left himself open to ridicule. He often put aitches in the wrong places and sounded like Dick van Dyke's cardboard Cockney in *Mary Poppins*. But regardless of how he talked, he got through to the players because he could speak their language. Ramsey, for all his airs and graces, was a football man through and through. The war delayed his entry into the Football League until he was twenty-six, and he had a remarkably successful playing career considering how late he was in starting. He had been posted to the south coast while serving in the army with an anti-tank brigade, and he started guesting for Southampton as a centre-forward who later converted to right-back. When he joined the Saints as a full-time professional in the first season after the war his wages were £6 a week in the summer and £8 a week in the season.

Within two years Ramsey's studious rather than spectacular play had earned him an England cap. After he had made his international début in a 6-0 victory over Switzerland at Highbury he was surprised to be told that his first-team place at Southampton was under threat. He jumped at the chance to join Tottenham in a deal worth £21,000 after turning down an offer to sign for Sheffield Wednesday. Like me in my playing days, Alf thought anything north of Watford was foreign land.

I used to get a close-up view of Ramsey from the White Hart Lane terraces when he played a key role in the Tottenham 'push-and-run' team that won the Second and First Division championships in successive seasons in 1949–50 and 1950–51. In those days he was known to his teammates as 'The General' because he was always talking tactics. 'Alf was a real salt-and-pepper man', his team-mate and later Totteham coach Eddie Baily told me.

> The minute you sat down at a meal table he would have the cruet, the sauce bottle and the sugar bowl on the move as he outlined new tactical ideas. He was also worth listening to about greyhound racing. He knew the form of all the dogs, and used to be one of the lads when we used to go and cheer on the dogs that we had backed.

Through my schoolboy eyes, Ramsey looked a beautifully composed player. He always seemed to have so much time to play the ball, and his distribution from the back was never anything less than constructive. At Southampton and Tottenham he was renowned for putting in extra time sharpening his ball skills and passing tehnique, even when he was an established international. He was not the fastest thing on two feet (Tommy Docherty said that he had seen milk turn faster), but he had such good positional sense that he was usually able to jockey off the ball wingers who had him beaten for pace. His big-match temperament showed with the way he coolly put away vital penalties for both Tottenham and England. He never liked to be reminded that along with the many sound performances he gave in his thirty-two appearances for

England, he also played a reluctant part in the 1950 World Cup defeat by the United States and the 6–3 hammering by the Hungarians, which was his best-forgotten farewell to the international stage as a player. Neither did he enjoy references to the suicidal last-minute back-pass to the goal-keeper that cost Tottenham the match against Blackpool in the 1953 FA Cup semi-final. If Alf had not gambled on a pass that was intercepted there may never have been that famous 'Stanley Matthews' final against Bolton. All he would say afterwards was: 'It was the right thing to do at the time, and I would do the same again.' That gives an insight into his stubborn nature.

He used to go into a cocoon of concentration for every game, and this was never better illustrated than after a match he played for Tottenham. Not long after his marriage to a charming divorcée called Vicky, he came out of the dressing-room deep in thought and walked right past her until a team-mate shouted, 'Oi, Alf, you've forgotten your wife!'

It was only when I got to know Alf in later years that I realized the way he played on the pitch was the way he behaved off it. He was a perfectionist, ice cold, calculating, deliberate in everything he did, and bloody minded – the same qualities he showed as a determined defender who refused to concede an inch to any opponent. Another thing about Ramsey the player that lapped over into Ramsey the man was his immaculate appearance on the pitch. He never seemed to have a hair out of place even in the heat of battle, and that was how he was in his days as a manager, always smartly groomed and highly polished. The joke among we players was that Alf used to go to bed in a well-pressed suit. He very rarely wore casual clothes, and would even come down to breakfast wearing a shirt and tie.

He liked to give the appearance of the English gentleman, something that I believe rubbed off on him from his close relationship with John Cobbold, who was the chairman of Ipswich Town when Ramsey started his manage-rial career there in 1955. Cobbold was a wonderfully eccentric, warm and likeable Old Etonian, who introduced Alf to a lifestyle that was certainly a long, long way from the Dagenham environment in which both Alf and I spent our youth. I could provide a hundred stories to show that Cobbold – or 'Mister John' – was, to put it mildly, quite a character, who might have stepped out of the pages of a P. G. Wodehouse book. Just a couple of tales will help paint the picture. When Ipswich were slipping down the table after a run of defeats, a reporter asked him how he was handling the crisis. 'Crisis? What crisis?' said Cobbold, aghast at the suggestion. 'A crisis at Ipswich, dear boy, is when the white wine served in the boardroom is not sufficiently chilled.' Once when Mister John was returning from a skiing holiday, he got off the train at Ipswich station and presented his skis to an astonished train driver. 'Well, you tip a taxi driver ... why not a train driver', explained the whimsical Cobbold, who was a millionaire Suffolk brewer and a nephew of the Governor of the Bank of England. I tell these stories about the late, much-loved John Cobbold because tales about him are always worth repeating, and because he was such a strong influence on Ramsey. Coming into such close contact with Cobbold and his delightfully aristocratic English family was, for Alf, a new and radical experience that must have made an enormous impact on a man born and brought up on a smallholding in Dagenham.

It was Cobbold who was a calming influence on Ramsey when, in his first season at Ipswich, he was reported to be less than happy with what he considered to be the shadow cast over him by his long-serving predecessor as manager, Dally Duncan, who had switched to the secretary's job. Little did Ramsey know it, but he was getting ideal experience in how to handle the interference that was to come his way when he became England manager.

What Ramsey achieved as manager at Ipswich was on a par with what he was to do with England. He took a backwoods Third Division South team and steered them into the Second Division in 1956–57, and then in successive seasons in 1960–61 and 1961–62 captured the Second and First Divison championships, a repeat of the double he enjoyed as a player with Tottenham. The remarkable thing was that he did it all on a shoestring budget. The most he ever paid for a player was £12,500, and he conquered the giant money-no-object clubs in the League by brilliant tactical planning and excellent team organization. One of his great strengths was that he had total recall of just about every match and every key player he ever saw, and so he was able to give expert assessments of all the opposing players during pre-match team talks. It was a gift he took with him into the international arena.

It was at Ipswich that he began to experiment on the theme of the 4–3–3 formation that was to bring him lasting fame in the World Cup. He used a cagey old Scot called Jimmy Leadbetter as a withdrawn winger, playing him in midfield from where he took defences apart with a procession of precise passes. Two of the most powerful attacking partners in post-war League football, Ray Crawford and Ted Phillips, were the twin strikers and Roy 'Little Rocket' Stephenson ran like an express train down the right wing. They brought Ipswich the titles that pointed the Football Association in the direction of Ramsey after Jimmy Adamson had told them he was not interested in taking over from Winterbottom.

Ramsey was great at winning trophies, but never learned how to relax and enjoy his triumphs. The day they clinched the Second Division championship, he ducked out of the champagne celebrations to watch Ipswich juniors play. When he was asked to join the party, he said: 'I'm working.'

John Cobbold told me that late on the night Ipswich won the League title, he found Ramsey sitting all alone in the deserted stand, staring at the empty pitch. Alf, who had given his favourite tipple of gin and tonic a good hiding, took off his jacket and then handed it to the chairman. 'Alfred then climbed over the wall and started to run round the outside of the pitch', said Cobbold. 'He ran a lap of honour with me as the only spectator. It was a bloody marvellous, intimate moment. People say Alfred is cold. What tosh! He is a very private man, but has enormous warmth.'

Alf even held his emotions in check on the touchline, where many managers and coaches scream themselves almost to the brink of a nervous breakdown. This is illustrated by the moment in the 1966 World Cup Final when the referee dithered over whether Geoff Hurst's extra-time shot had crossed the German goal-line after hitting the bar. Everybody on the England bench jumped to their feet with the excitement of it all – everybody that is apart from Ramsey. He remained sitting on the end of the bench with the result that it tilted and he was dumped on his backside. When England clinched victory with Hurst's third goal, Alf remained impassively on the bench while all about him were leaping about. 'I would have got to my feet, but the Doctor was thumping me on the shoulder', Ramsey explained. 'The Doctor' was Doc Alan Bass, one of the few people – along with loyal trainer Harold Shepherdson – who Ramsey confided in. He was one of Ramsey's first appointments when he took over as England manager because he realized the vital importance of having a team doctor. Doc Bass, a larger-than-life character and a medical specialist who had the complete faith of the players, became a vital cog in the Ramsey machine, as did his successor Dr Neil Phillips, a Welshman whom the players made an honorary Englishman.

Ramsey was never out-going enough to win the full support of the League managers he had left behind, and when I caught this reserved man in a rare moment with his defences down he confessed that his was 'one of the loneliest jobs in the world'. He missed the day-to-day involvement of club management, and the only man with managerial experience that he used to turn to for advice was Arthur Rowe, his old boss at Tottenham who had been the tactical genius behind the 'push-and-run' Spurs. Ramsey's distance from the League managers was evident in the way he continually had players pulled out of his squads at the last minute as the thorny club-or-country dilemma became a controverial issue. Close to the end of his reign he made an astonishing broadside against 'the cheating clubs and managers' who had denied him use of players for crucial matches.

Ramsey did not suffer fools gladly, or even at all. He was famed and feared for his one-line put downs of anybody who got on the wrong side of him. It has gone down in the Ramsey legend how an FA official approached him during a summer tour and commented brightly, 'We're doing well, Alf.' Ramsey gave him what became known as 'The Stare'.

'We?' Alf replied contemptuously. 'Don't you mean the players? *You're* just here for the cocktail parties.' The only way the FA officials could get a little upmanship on Ramsey was to stick him in the smallest office at Lancaster Gate – 'Welcome to my cubby hole', he used to say to visitors. But Alf considered the training ground his real office where he liked to gather his players and pass on tactical ideas in a down-to-earth style that was free of the technical jargon that used to make Walter Winterbottom so difficult to understand. He always wore a tracksuit, and was anxious to get into the action even though he was giving more than twenty years to most of the players.

Alf had a deep in-built dislike and distrust of foreigners, and there were times when he included Scots in this category. Once when we landed in Glasgow for a match at Hampden, a Scot said at the arrivals lounge, 'Welcome to Scotland Mr Ramsey.' 'You must be bloody joking', said Alf.

Another time, a South American journalist came up to Ramsey with an outstretched hand and said with a wide, friendly smile: 'Mr Ramsey, you remember me …'.'Yes', said Alf. 'You're a pest.'

Then there was the time at the end of a tour when a respected Fleet Street sportswriter went up to him at Heathrow and said, 'I'll be off now, Alf. I just want to thank you on behalf of myself and my colleagues for your co-operation on the tour.' 'Are you taking the piss?' said Alf, unused to (and never seeking) compliments.

There is no question that his biggest weakness was in what had become the all-important field of press and public relations. He was continually on a collision course with the media, who either liked him or loathed him, and his uneasy and vinegary handling of press conferences with foreign journalists used to have observers cringing with embarrassment. Three of the most distinguished football writers of the 1960s, Brian James *(Daily Mail)*, Clive Toye *(Daily Express)* and Ken Jones *(Daily Mirror)*, were among the minority who supported him through thick and thin. On the day after England won the World Cup – a Sunday – they went to see Ramsey, who was with the players at a TV studio. 'Can you spare us a few minutes?' they asked. 'Gentlemen, this is my day off', he said curtly.

Among the hundreds of crushing sports page criticisms of Ramsey, I came across this spiteful gem – or perhaps I should say germ – from a Fleet Street cynic, 'He is so cold and aloof that before retiring to bed at night, I am sure he shakes Lady Ramsey by the hand.' That would have cut deep with Sir Alf and Lady Ramsey because they are a loving and devoted couple, and they must have had indigestion when they read it over the breakfast table.

The only time that Ramsey lost his renowned restraint with a football reporter was in Spain in 1965 when a Lancastrian gentleman of the press continually and loudly criticized his England team in the hotel where the players and journalists were housed together. This tirade went on into the early hours of the morning as Alf attempted to celebrate an England victory over Spain that was notable for the fact that he had introduced his 4–3–3 formation for the first time, a revolutionary system that was to win England the World Cup just a year later.

Finally, Ramsey snapped and lost his famous cool. He was in the process of removing his jacket ready for battle when he suddenly regained his dignity and bearing, and turned what onlookers thought was going to be a punch into a handshake.

Ramsey could make himself very difficult to like, yet for all his faults – warts 'n' all – there was so much passion in the man for football and for his players that those who came into close contact with him now think back on his reign with fondness. He was not without a sense of humour, and I remember many gin-and-tonic sessions when he would drop the 'Old Stoneface' mask behind which he used to hide and give as good as he got in the wise-cracking stakes. But generally speaking he was aloof, and he consciously kept that divide that separates the captain from the crew. Nobody could ever take things for granted with him. Our great goalkeeper Gordon Banks once said to him as he was about to set off for home after a winning international, "Bye Alf. See you next time.' 'Will you?' said Ramsey without a flicker of a smile.

Alf saw through me in five minutes flat. He was a shrewd judge of people and quickly had me weighed up as a carefree, non-conformist character whose thinking on football was completely the opposite of his cautious, methodical, well-organized approach to the game. He knew me for what I was from the moment of our very first conversation outside the boundaries of football.

It took place just before one of Ramsey's early games in charge of the England team against Czechoslovakia in Bratislava. Alf was giving us the after-match agenda. 'The coach will be ready to leave forty-five minutes after the game and we shall go back to the hotel *together*', he said with that unblinking stare of his that gave listeners the feeling they were being hypnotized. There was an uneasy shuffling of feet, and I could sense that my drinking pals in the England squad were waiting for me to act as their spokesman.

'A few of us were wondering, Alf', I said, 'whether we could nip out for a couple of drinks before going back to the hotel?' I quote Ramsey's reply verbatim because, as I was to discover over the years, he only swore when he wanted to make himself perfectly understood. 'If you want a fucking beer you can come back to the hotel and have it.'

He had made himself perfectly understood! It wasn't said in a nasty way and there was a hint of a twinkle in those cold blue eyes of his as they fastened on to me from beneath rich, thick eyebrows. Alf was just letting me know that he was in charge, and from that moment on he had me marked down in what was almost a photographic memory as a ringleader of the drinking squad.

Bobby Moore, my long-time pal, room-mate and drinking partner, sadly no longer with us, was Ramsey's faithful captain for ninety matches, yet even he would never claim to have got truly close to Alf. And there was a time during the build-up to the 1966 World Cup finals when I honestly thought Ramsey was going to leave Bobby on the sidelines.

Our liking for a good bevvy got Mooro and I into several scrapes together long before the infamous Blackpool Affair when we were at West Ham in the autumn of our careers (see the Ron Greenwood chapter for the grisly background details). It reached the point where it was strongly believed that Alf was going to relieve Bobby of the England captaincy, and only a procession of regal performances by one of the greatest defenders of all time kept him in command.

The first time we upset Ramsey was on the eve of England's departure for a match against Portugal in Lisbon in May, 1964. Mooro and I called for volunteers for an evening stroll into London's West End from the Lancaster Gate Hotel where we were staying. With thirsty 'elbow men' like Mooro, Johnny 'Budgie' Byrne and me leading the outing, it was odds on the stroll becoming a stagger before the night was through. In tow along with Budgie, we had Gordon Banks, Bobby Charlton, George Eastham and Ray Wilson. We stopped off at a favourite drinking oasis called The Beachcomber, and it was fairly late – close to midnight – when we got back to the hotel. Each of us realized that our absence-without-leave had been noticed when we found our passports lying on our beds.

This was Ramsey's stunning but subtle way of letting us know that he was, to put it mildly, not pleased. He left it until the eve of the match four days later before mentioning our little escapade. After our final training session, he said: 'You can all go and get changed now apart from the seven players who I believe would like to stay and see me.'

Sheepishly, we gathered around Ramsey while the rest of the squad went back to the dressing-room with quizzical looks over their shoulders. Alf was short, sharp and to the point:

> You are all lucky to be here. If there had been enough players in the squad, I would have left you behind in London. All I hope is that you have learned your lesson, and that you will never – never – do anything as stupid again. I will not tolerate a repeat performance from any of you. I hope that is understood. Thank you gentlemen. You may now get changed.

Ramsey named all seven of us in the England team, and we repaid him by beating Portugal 4–3 in an epic match. Two of the 'absentees' – Budgie

Byrne and Bobby Charlton – scored the goals, Budgie completing the sweetest of hat-tricks with a cheekily chipped goal in the last minute. Alf joined us for quite a few gins and tonics that night.

Less than two weeks later Mooro and I were in Ramsey's bad books again. This time it was not booze but boogie that got us into trouble – or, more accurately, the jazz singing of the one and only Ella Fitzgerald. Throughout his career Bobby was a chronic insomniac, and he used to find any excuse not to go to bed for a night of tossing and turning. The pair of us decided to put bedtime back by slipping out of our New York hotel on the eve of the match against the United States to catch the 'First Lady' in concert. Neither Bobby nor I were playing against the States (who were hammered 10–0) and we saw no harm in taking a night off. Alf didn't say very much, but his cold manner at breakfast the next morning was a sure sign that he was displeased and he chalked up a mental note that perhaps Bobby Moore was not the right man to lead England into the coming World Cup campaign. All these memories of my mate Mooro came flooding back at the news of his tragic death from cancer in the winter of 1993. It is not sentiment but fact that prompts me to describe him as the greatest England defender that ever breathed. Bobby and I were as close as brothers during our playing careers, and I considered it a privilege to be on the same pitch as him. We were brought up just a mile apart on the east side of London, Bobby in Barking and me in Hainault. A generation earlier Alf Ramsey had been taking his first footballing kicks in the same manor.

It was clear that Alf had decided to keep a close eye on Mooro and me after the New York escapade.

Our next stop was Rio de Janeiro for a match against Brazil. We stayed nine days for an international tournament and we worked and played hard both on and off the pitch. In fact we thought we were being worked too hard in training, and it was Mooro who was our spokesman when we made a slight protest to Ramsey. That was another black mark against Bobby.

Budgie Byrne, always the life and soul of any party, was full of funny tricks, such as pushing me into the deep end of the hotel swimming pool while I was wearing my new England suit. Budgie then had to dive in to pull me out. It was a frightening experience that convinced me I should learn to swim.

Ironically, the next day Budgie, a strong swimmer, nearly drowned off the Copacabana beach from which Walter Winterbottom had banned us five years earlier. Budgie got trapped in rough water, and goalkeeper Tony Waiters – a Blackpool lifeguard – had to use all his strength and skill to save him.

The football tournament got our full concentration and effort. We were holding Brazil to a 1–1 draw with just twenty minutes to go when Pelé hit one of his purple patches and lifted them to a flattering 5–1 victory. This really choked us because for an hour we had been more than a match for the world champions. Ramsey knew how we felt and, with four days before the next match, he let us off the leash for the night.

At dawn the next morning a team of seven dishevelled-looking England footballers were beaten about 10–0 in an impromptu match against a side of a dozen Copacabanan beach boys whose skills were out of this world. Thankfully the result never got into the record books. Ramsey was as amused as everybody else when we returned to the hotel with exaggerated tales of our adventure, and at last there was a thawing of the ice barrier he had put up against some of we – what he would have considered – less dedicated players. We knew how to unwind, something that Alf had never learned to do.

We flew up to São Paulo from Rio to watch the second match of the mini-World Cup between Brazil and Argentina, and I can honestly say that to this day I have never witnessed scenes like it. Because there were no seats left in the stand, the entire England party – including Ramsey, trainers Harold Shepherdson and Les Cocker, the players, journalists and officials – were assigned to touchline benches that were just two yards from the pitch and eight or so yards from the fenced-in capacity crowd. It was far too close for comfort.

As soon as we sat down the spectators spotted us and set up a deafening chant of '*Cinco-Uma!*' – Portuguese for five-one – and a derisive reminder of our defeat in Rio. Budgie Byrne could not resist the bait and, deaf to 'sit down and shut up' shouts from Ramsey, he stood up on the bench and started conducting the fans like the man in the white suit before a Wembley cup final. The Brazilians loved it, and they started chanting in time to Budgie's waving arms. His choir switched their attention to cheering the Brazilian team when they came out on to the pitch and they lit up the night sky by firing dozens of three-stage firework rockets high above the stadium. Then we had fireworks of a different kind on the pitch.

Right from the first whistle Argentinian defender Messiano made it clear that his one intention was to stop Pelé from playing. He kicked him, tripped him, spat at him, wrestled him to the floor and pulled his shirt or shorts any time he seemed likely to get past him. Finally, after about thirty minutes of this almost criminal assault, Pelé completely lost his temper. He took a running jump at Messiano and butted him full in the face. The Argentinian was carried off with a broken nose and, incredibly, the Swiss referee let Pelé play on.

The calculated, cynical fouling by the Argentinians – a method of play carefully noted for future reference by Ramsey – knocked all the rhythm and style out of the Brazilians, and the stadium became as quiet as a morgue when two minutes from the end the player substituting for the injured Messiano scored his second goal of the match to make it 3–0 to Argentina.

Budgie Byrne unwisely chose this moment to do an insane thing. He stood on the bench again to face the fans and, holding up three fingers, invited them to join in a chant of 'three–zero ...'. It was the worst joke Budgie ever made. Suddenly stones and fireworks rained down from the terraces as the fans turned their disappointment on us. They would have much preferred to have reached the hated Argentinians, but we were easier targets. As a rotten apple hit him in the back, the usually impassive Ramsey took one glance at the avalanche of missiles coming our way and gave the shortest tactical talk of his life, 'Run for it, lads!'

Luckily the final whistle had just blown and we made a mad dash for the centre-circle. It was then Budgie's quick wits that finally got us off the pitch in one piece. As the fans began to scream blue murder, despite the intimidating presence of dozens of armed police, Budgie shouted the wise instruction, 'Grab yourself a Brazilian player.'

He then seized goalkeeper Gylmar lovingly by the arm and walked with him off the pitch, knowing full well that no fans would try to harm one of their idols. We all followed Budgie's lead and went off arm-in-arm with bewildered Brazilian players. You may consider that we were over-reacting, but uppermost in the minds of everybody in that stadium was the fact that just ten days earlier 301 people had been killed in a riot at the national stadium in Peru where Argentina had been the opponents. I am sure that the way Argentina played against Brazil that night – brutally and coldly vicious – stayed imprinted on Ramsey's mind and was one of the reasons he made his sensational 'animals' outburst against them during the 1966 World Cup. His rare loss of composure came following the quarter-final in which England beat the ten men of Argentina 1–0 after captain Antonio Rattin – an exceptionally gifted but excitable player – had been ordered off for arrogantly trying to undermine the referee, querying every decision and gesturing his contempt.

When Ramsey said at a press conference that 'the Agentinians are animals', few people outside the England squad knew that he was refer-ring as much to their off-the-pitch behaviour as to their violent play. I was nursing an injury from the previous match against France, and I was one of the first back into the dressing-room after the victory over Argentina. I was walking round congratulating the lads when suddenly there was a crashing noise at the door. The Argentinian players were outside kicking, spitting and one even urinating as they staged an ugly protest over their defeat. They were convinced they were victims of some European plot, and it was this crude display as much as their petty fouling on the pitch that triggered Ramsey's 'animals' comment. I thought Alf should have been disciplined for what he said – by the RSPCA, for insulting animals.

Talking of animals reminds me of one of my favourite Ramsey anecdotes. In the summer of 1972 he took the England Under-23 squad to Russia, and after several unnecessary delays at the airport a bad-tempered Alf led his young players into a Kiev hotel just after midnight, only to find there were not sufficient rooms available.

Sir Alf spent a harrowing two hours trying to make an interpreter stress the urgency for his footballers to be in bed. Having at last won the battle for the beds against a hotel manager giving the distinct impression of being deliberately obstructive, an exhausted Ramsey told the interpreter: 'Please order tea with milk to be taken to the players in their rooms.'

'Milk? Vas is milk?' asked the puzzled interpreter, who had been having problems understanding Alf's clipped, posh-Cockney accent.

'You know,' said Alf. 'It comes from a cow.'

'Cow? Vas is a cow?' asked the Russian, now completely perplexed. He had found Alf's breaking point. 'A cow is brown', he slowly explained with smouldering anger. 'It has four legs, horns, a tail and bloody tits hanging from its belly.'

'Bloody tits?' asked the interpreter in total despair. 'Vas is bloody tits?'

Even Ramsey had to laugh. The players got their tea – without milk.

There was another animal-linked episode during an England trip to Canada for the Expo '67 international tournament. The pitch on which the first match was to be played had been used the day before by a circus. When Alf saw it he called the organizer over and said, 'Either get that pitch cleared up or we are going straight home.'

'What's wrong with it?' said the organizer to whom soccer was a foreign sport.

'I am not', said Alf in his poshest voice, 'going to ask England's finest footballers to play on elephant shit.'

As John Cobbold always insisted, Ramsey did have a lot of warmth but it was buried deep. He even at times appeared quite friendly when dealing with the senior citizens on the FA Council, and there were many of them who felt he was badly treated by the power-men at Lancaster Gate. I recall once seeing one of the octogenarians, who used to accompany us on tours in their England blazers, fall asleep at Ramsey's elbow during an after-match banquet following an England game abroad. He had succumbed to the local wine.

Sir Alf handled it beautifully. He went on talking to his other neighbours at the table as if nothing had happened, then – with the old boy in danger of drowning in the *soup de jour* – excused himself to spend a pfennig, and gently manoeuvred the councillor out of the banqueting hall and up to his bedroom.

Another story about Alf that always makes me smile concerns his love of westerns. No matter where we were, if there was a western showing he used to organize a trip to the cinema and would make sure we all went with him. Once in East Germany he got the hotel concièrge to find out what films were showing. Sure enough, there was a western on at a local international cinema, and Alf was assured that it had subtitles – which meant the original soundtrack would be used. So off we all trooped to the pictures. Sure enough, the film had German subtitles; the only problem was that it was a spaghetti western, and we were seeing the European version with everybody rabbiting away in Italian. We were not too popular in the cinema when, after about five minutes, we all got up and – laughing like schoolchildren – pushed our way out into the aisle and returned to the hotel.

This conjures another priceless memory of a visit we paid to Pinewood studios during the 1966 World Cup to see Sean Connery shooting scenes for the James Bond film *You Only Live Twice*. Ramsey was called on to make a short speech at the end of our visit. 'I'd just like to thank Seen Connery for giving up his time', Alf said, not understanding why we players were fighting to suppress a mixture of laughter and embarrassment. I said to Mooro, 'That's the funniest thing I've ever shawn or heard.'

This is a chapter about the man and the manager Ramsey, not me, but I need to briefly put myself centre stage as I discuss my exit from the 1966 World Cup. It provided the most heartbreaking moment of my football career, but it emphasizes that he was a manager who was not frightened to make a decision.

I got a nasty gash on my shin in the third match against France, and it needed six stitches. The injury put me out of the reckoning for the quarter-final against Argentina. Geoff Hurst took my place and scored the winning goal that lifted England into the semi-final against Portugal. By the time England had qualified for the final against West Germany I was just about back to fitness, and the press had a field day advising Ramsey whether or not to pick me. Along with Bobby Charlton, I was England's leading goal scorer; Geoff Hurst had been an international player for less than a year. When I read that a football writer who purported to be one of my best friends was urging Ramsey to select Hurst ahead of me, I guessed my chances of playing were slim. Let's be honest, it was not an easy decision for Alf. He knew that if he left me out and England lost, his 'enemies' in the press would tear him apart.

The Saturday of the Final came and still I did not know for sure whether I was in or out. But I sensed that Alf was being a little distant, and guessed he had made up his mind not to play me. Sure enough he came to me at around midday and said simply, 'I've decided on an unchanged team. I know you'll understand.' He put his faith at the feet of Hurst, and Geoff came up with an historic hat-trick. Ramsey three, Greaves nil. End of argument.

It would be an understatement to say that I was disappointed. Shortly after taking over the job Ramsey had put a load on his own back by making an out-of-character statement that England would win the World Cup, a prediction that was continually stuffed down his throat whenever the team stuttered in the build-up to the finals. I had been equally convinced that England would win, and I had always envisaged that I would be part of the greatest day in the history of our game.

Ramsey was seen at his best after West Germany had forced extra-time in the Final with a last-minute equalizer. The England players were, understandably, feeling sorry for themselves, but he showed Churchillian powers of motivation as he told them: 'You've won the World Cup once. You had them beaten. Now go and do it again.'

Alf's reward was a knighthood, which somehow served to make him more aloof and untouchable, even though he tried to be chummy by telling the players, 'Please still call me Alf.' His success did little to win him the support and affection of some reporters who considered him uncooperative, rude and arrogant. He gave a rare insight into the pressure he was under when he complained that he was being 'crucified' for not selecting me when I started hitting my old goal form with Tottenham in the 1968–69 season. Ramsey revealed, much to my surprise, that I had asked not to be considered for England. What I had actually said was that I did not want to be called up for his squads if I was not going to get a game. One of us was the victim of a misunderstanding.

It was not only the press who had been putting the pressure on him. He had also been deeply wounded by the attitude of some of his players. Nobody can question that Ramsey had enormous pride in England and English football. Money was never his big motivator, and he liked his players to share the feeling that to pull on the white shirt was reward enough. When England were playing West Germany in an international match in Hanover in 1968, representatives of the major German sportswear firms, Adidas and Puma, descended on the England camp and offered massive cash incentives for the players to wear their boots.

Several of the players took the bait, and went into the match wearing new boots. Any pro will tell you that you should never try out new boots for the first time in a match – and for it to be done in an international is just crazy. Alf did not try to hide his distress and his disgust that they had jeopardized England's chances for profit, and after a 1–0 defeat he said that the players had let him – and England – down.

Ramsey had been to the top of football's Mount Everest, and the only way was down. In the years that followed the 1966 triumph he was more and more sharply criticized for the negativity of his tactics, and his seeming preference for sweat before skill, the hard worker ahead of the artist. He struggled in particular to come to grips with the substitution rule, introduced in 1965 after he had left club football, and he was suddenly looking like a man behind his times.

At his peak, Ramsey had few peers as a manager, but comparative failure in the 1970 World Cup followed by a disastrous showing in the 1972 European Nations Cup had his enemies in the Football Association sharpening their knives. They got the chance they were seeking to remove him when England were eliminated by Poland in a qualifying match for the 1974 World Cup finals.

It looked at first as if Ramsey had survived the calls for his head, but he was finally brought down by a man whose pedigree was closer to that of John Cobbold than the Dagenham background that Ramsey was always reticent to acknowledge. Professor Sir Harold Thompson, CBE, MA, DSC, FRS, an academic and scientist whose entry in *Who's Who* filled fifty-nine lines, was the powerful vice-chairman of the Football Association. He was one of the world's leading experts in molecular spectroscopy, and a man more opposite to Ramsey it would be difficult to imagine. It was the sixty-seven-year-old Professor who led the campaign that eventually brought an end to the Ramsey reign. They had been daggers drawn from the moment during a 1973 England tour when Thompson walked into the players' breakfast room smoking a cigar, and was told icily by Ramsey to put it out.

The players did not take kindly to the Corinthian Thompson – an Oxford Soccer Blue in the 1920s – calling them by their surnames, and I am sure Alf's blood used to boil when the Professor gave him the same autocratic treatment. It was the intellectual Thompson's powerful arguments against Ramsey's style of management that did most to persuade the Football Association to terminate his contract shortly after he had requested an increase in his paltry salary of £7,200 – about a third of what the top First Division managers were earning at the time.

The late Peter Lorenzo was the sportswriter who had always been closest to Ramsey, and he and Norman Giller were the first journalists to talk to him after his dismissal.

I went with Peter to Alf's home in Ipswich', Norman recalled. 'I thought I knew Alf well until that night. Few – if any journalists – had been welcome into the Ramsey house during his time as England manager. To see him relaxed in his carpet slippers in a home environment, and with his charming wife, Vicky, fussing lovingly over him gave him the human face he had hidden from so many people over the past eleven years. It was May Day, 1974, and Alf seemed more concerned about what a late frost was doing to his garden plants than the loss of his job. I had always got on well with Alf and found him approachable provided you did not waste his time with stupid questions. When Peter and I heard his side of things, it made us realize he had worked miracles overcoming the obstacles put in his way by the petty officialdom of the Football Association. I'll always remember his parting shot as he saw Peter and I to the door at the end of a three-hour visit. 'The sad thing', he said, 'is that the bloody amateurs are back in command.'

There was further criticism from some of his old Fleet Street adversaries when he sold the story of his sacking to a Sunday newspaper. They accused him of hypocrisy, but I can reveal that Alf was talked into doing an exclusive deal by Lorenzo and Giller. Peter told him, 'You owe it to yourself to get a decent payment. You're out of work now, and you've got bills to pay.'

The Football Association had been stingy with Ramsey throughout his contract with them, and even when he won the World Cup his bonus was a derisory £5,000. His pay-off following his dismissal was just £8,000 (Alf described it as a 'tissue handshake'), plus a pension of £1,200 a year. This for a man whose successful England teams – they lost only seventeen matches under his guidance – had brought millions into FA coffers. In the same week that Alf was being kicked out, Alan Ball – the 'baby' of the 1966 World Cup winning team – suffered a broken leg playing for Arsenal against Queen's Park Rangers. Ramsey, the man so many people considered cold and unfeeling, pushed his personal problems to one side and sat down and wrote Ballie a warm 'get-well-soon' letter.

He briefly returned to club football as manager of Birmingham City following a spell as a director, but a further sign that he was losing touch with the modern game came with his well-publicized clash with the young St Andrew's hero Trevor Francis, who did not take kindly to being fined £1,000 for speaking to the press. He seemed no longer able to communicate with players, and that had always been his strongest asset. In 1980 he spent a year as technical advisor to the Greek club Panathinaikos, but as far as English football was concerned Sir Alf Ramsey was suddenly yesterday's man. The *Daily Mirror* brought him in from the cold in the 1990s by giving him a platform for outspoken views that were every bit as blistering as some of the criticisms aimed at him during his days as England supremo. The gamekeeper had turned poacher.

Ramsey's Record

During his eleven years in charge of the England team, Ramsey's record was:

P	W	D	L	F	A
113	69	27	17	224	99

Home international matches only:

	P	W	D	L	F	A
v. Scotland	12	6	3	3	24	14
v. Wales	12	8	4	0	25	5
v. Northern Ireland	10	9	0	1	27	11

International matches played in England against overseas opposition:

P	W	D	L	F	A
34	20	11	3	64	24

International matches played outside England against overseas opposition:

P	W	D	L	F	A
45	27	8	10	85	43

Ramsey's record in the World Cup campaigns of 1966, 1970 and also 1974, which were the only finals for which England had to try qualify (they failed):

P	W	D	L	F	A
13	7	3	3	17	11

His overall record is remarkable considering that he kicked off with two defeats – 5–2 against France and 2–1 against a Jim Baxter-inspired Scotland. On the way out to Paris for that opening match against the French, Alf's case was lost at the airport. I am sure that at the end of the match as the fifth goal flew into the net past unhappy goalkeeper Ron Springett, Alf must have wondered if he had made a mistake leaving the peace of sleepy Suffolk.

Johnny Haynes, recovered from the injuries received in a car smash, came out to Paris with a party of fans to watch the first match of the Ramsey regime. They were on our 'plane on the flight home, and I don't know whether Haynes or Ramsey was the more embarrassed when the supporters started chanting things like 'Haynes for England' and 'You can't leave Haynes out now, Alf.'

Like me, Johnny had been privately convinced that England would win the World Cup in 1966 and, like me, he thought he would be part of it all. But I think Alf considered that Johnny had been too influential a member of the Winterbottom squads, and – mistakenly in my view – he did not give him a single cap.

England managers are judged by their achievements in the World Cup, and after he had hit the heady heights in 1966 Ramsey came down to earth with a nasty bump in the 1970 finals in Mexico.

I went to Mexico, but – not like ten others from the 1966 squad – as a player. I arrived in a battered Ford Escort with my co-driver Tony Fall, finishing in a proud sixth place at the end of the London–Mexico City car rally. The first thing I was told as I got out of the car after crossing the finishing line was that England skipper Bobby Moore had been arrested for stealing a bracelet in Bogota. I knew Bobby better than anybody, and realized that it was a trumped-up charge. He could not take a liberty, let alone a piece of jewellery. I tracked Bobby down to a British embassy official's home where he had been staying after his release from prison on a charge that was later quite properly dropped. Over a beer or three he told me that he had felt abandoned when Ramsey left him behind in Bogota. I agreed. Had I been in charge of the England team, there is no way on earth that I would have left a single player behind in such a hostile country when it was obvious that the charges being made against him were just a pack of lies. But Ramsey held the view that there was nothing he could achieve by hanging around in Bogota with the rest of the players kicking their heels, and so they moved on to Mexico, leaving FA officials to sort out the problems facing his captain. Mooro buried his anger over the way he had been left to face his accusers, and he produced a succession of magnificent performances to help England through to the World Cup quarter-finals. They looked certainties for the semi-finals as they powered to a 2–0 lead over their 1966 rivals West Germany. Then Alf, who was usually the last person in the world to take anything for granted, decided he could afford to rest Bobby Charlton for the semi-final. Within a minute of the Germans pulling back to 2–1 he took off Bobby in his record 106th (and last) England appearance. 'To see the back of Bobby Charlton was a great psychological boost for us', said Franz Beckenbauer. Colin Bell, sent on in place of Charlton, and then Norman Hunter instead of Martin Peters, could not get into the rhythm of the match, and Ramsey looked on in horror and disbelief as the Germans battled to a 3–2 victory after extra time.

Ramsey was desperately unlucky to have lost goalkeeper Gordon Banks with a mystery stomach upset that to this day Gordon is convinced was caused by somebody slipping him a dodgy drink. Peter Bonetti was called into the team at the last minute, and was having his first experience of playing in Mexico's thin air. Poor Peter, a totally reliable and brilliant goalkeeper with Chelsea for so many years, was not conditioned for the match at such short notice. He had a nightmare, and was saddled with the blame for two of the goals.

From then on, Ramsey's enemies at the Football Association started gathering like vultures. The Mexico World Cup had been a disaster from a PR point of view. The Mexican media had been antagonized by Ramsey's cold manner towards them, and they got their own back with a procession of wicked lies, exaggerations and innuendoes in their newspapers. The fact that Alf had insisted on importing special food from London, and that

England had also brought their own coach and driver gave the writers the excuse to accuse them of being rude, distrustful, unfriendly and anti-social. There were fabricated stories of orgies in local brothels, and marauding Mexicans, clearly believing the rubbish that was being reported, used to drive round the England hotel at the dead of night trying to keep them awake by honking their horns. Every time England went on to the pitch during the World Cup they were jeered and whistled at as if they were the deadly enemy. The English press – and Ramsey's critics in the Football Association – blamed Alf's appalling PR performances for the hostile reception.

More than three years later Ramsey's uncertainty about how and when to use substitutes was exposed again, this time against Poland at Wembley in a World Cup qualifying match that England had to win if they were to make it through to the finals in West Germany. There was farce as well as fear on the touchline bench as England struggled to get the ball into the net against a Polish side that was put under non-stop pressure.

The old master Bobby Moore, who had lost his place to Norman Hunter, was sitting alongside Alf and watched in stunned silence as Norman for once in his life missed a tackle and let the Poles in for a goal. An Allan Clarke penalty pulled England level, but a draw was no good to England, who managed to create and miss a dozen chances against the Poles. Mooro told me:

> For the first time that I had known him Alf looked close to panic. You could see that he knew his job was on the line, and his bottle had gone. I kept urging him to make a substitution, but he convinced himself that the men out on the pitch could do it for him. Finally, with just five minutes to go, I managed to persuade him to try Kevin Hector down the left side.
>
> When Alf ordered, 'Kevin, get stripped', Kevin Keegan heeded the command instead of Kevin Hector. Ray Clemence helped Keegan take off his tracksuit and was so keen to get his Liverpool team-mate into the action that his eager hands pulled Kevin's shorts down to his knees. While Keegan was suffering from embarrassing over-exposure he became further embarrassed when Alf had to make it clear that he meant the other Kevin. By the time Hector got on there were just one hundred seconds left – the shortest England début on record. And in that short time he had the best chance of the match, and headed inches the wrong side of a post.

It would have changed the course of English football history if Hector's header had gone into the net. England would have gone on to the World Cup finals, which would have killed off the growing campaign to get rid of Ramsey.

The axe fell six months after the elimination from the World Cup, and Ramsey departed with dignity and – considering his diabolical treatment – made only muted criticism of the FA officials who had finally got their own back for him cutting them down to size.

Ramsey's greatest achievement apart from winning the World Cup was that he brought to heel the amateurs who had mismanaged English football for so many years. He feared that they were about to regain control, yet the man they turned to as his successor was the arch professional Don Revie. It's a funny old game.

But first of all there was a short and sweet interlude supervised by care-taker manager, 'Uncle' Joe Mercer.

Ramsey's Players

These were the ninety-five players capped by Ramsey during his 113 matches as England team manager:

Jimmy Armfield (Blackpool: 11)
Jeff Astle (West Bromwich: 5)

Mike Bailey (Charlton: 2)
Joe Baker (Arsenal: 3)
Alan Ball (Blackpool/
    Everton/Arsenal: 66)
Gordon Banks (Leicester/Stoke: 73)
Colin Bell (Manchester City: 32)
Jeff Blockley (Arsenal: 1)
Peter Bonetti (Chelsea: 7)
Barry Bridges (Chelsea: 4)
Trevor Brooking (West Ham: 1)
Tony Brown (West Bromwich: 1)
Gerry Byrne (Liverpool: 2)
Johnny Byrne (West Ham: 10)

Ian Callaghan (Liverpool: 2)
Mike Channon (Manchester City: 12)
Jack Charlton (Leeds: 35)
Bobby Charlton
    (Manchester Utd: 67)
Martin Chivers (Tottenham: 24)
Allan Clarke (Leeds: 16)
Ray Clemence (Liverpool: 2)
Ralph Coates (Burnley/
    Tottenham: 4)
George Cohen (Fulham: 37)

John Connelly (Burnley,
    Manchester Utd: 11)
Terry Cooper (Leeds: 19)
Tony Currie (Sheffield Utd: 6)

Martin Dobson (Burnley: 1)
Bryan Douglas (Blackburn: 3)

George Eastham (Arsenal: 19)

Ron Flowers (Wolverhampton: 10)

Jimmy Greaves (Tottenham: 32)

Colin Harvey (Everton: 1)
Kevin Hector (Derby: 2)
Ron Henry (Tottenham: 1)
Alan Hinton (Nottingham Forest: 2)
John Hollins (Chelsea: 1)
Emlyn Hughes (Liverpool: 29)
Roger Hunt (Liverpool: 33)
Norman Hunter (Leeds: 25)
Geoff Hurst (West Ham: 49)

Mick Jones (Sheffield Utd/Leeds: 3)

Tony Kay (Everton: 1)
Kevin Keegan (Liverpool: 2)

Brian Kidd (Manchester Utd: 2)
Cyril Knowles (Tottenham: 4)

Brian Labone (Everton: 24)
Frank Lampard (West Ham: 1)
Chris Lawler (Liverpool: 4)
Francis Lee (Manchester City: 27)
Larry Lloyd (Liverpool: 3)

Roy McFarland (Derby: 22)
Bob McNab (Arsenal: 4)
Malcolm Macdonald (Newcastle: 5)
Paul Madeley (Leeds: 16)
Rodney Marsh (QPR/
  Manchester City: 9)
Mick Mills (Ipswich: 1)
Gordon Milne (Liverpool: 14)
Bobby Moore (West Ham: 100)
Alan Mullery (Tottenham: 35)

Keith Newton (Blackburn/
  Everton: 27)
David Nish (Derby: 3)
Maurice Norman (Tottenham: 17)

Mike O'Grady (Leeds: 2)
Peter Osgood (Chelsea: 4)

Terry Paine (Southampton: 19)
Phil Parkes (QPR: 1)
Alan Peacock (Leeds: 2)
Mike Pejic (Stoke: 1)
Martin Peters (West Ham/
  Tottenham: 66)
Fred Pickering (Everton: 3)

John Radford (Arsenal: 2)
Paul Reaney (Leeds: 3)
John Richards (Wolverhampton: 1)
Joe Royle (Everton: 2)

David Sadler (Manchester Utd: 4)
Ken Shellito (Chelsea: 1)
Peter Shilton (Leicester: 16)
Tommy Smith (Liverpool: 1)
Ron Springett (Sheffield
  Wednesday: 5)
Nobby Stiles (Manchester United: 28)
Peter Storey (Arsenal: 19)
Mike Summerbee
  (Manchester City: 8)

Bobby Tambling (Chelsea: 2)
Derek Temple (Everton: 1)
Peter Thompson (Liverpool: 16)
Bobby Thomson
  (Wolverhampton: 8)
Colin Todd (Derby: 2)
Terry Venables (Chelsea: 2)

Tony Waiters (Blackpool: 5)
Dave Watson (Sunderland: 1)
Gordon West (Everton, 1969: 3)
Frank Wignall (Nottingham
  Forest 1965: 2)
Ray Wilson (Huddersfield/
  Everton: 46)
Tommy Wright (Everton: 11)

Gerry Young (Sheffield
  Wednesday: 1)

The fifteen most capped players during the Ramsey reign were Bobby
Moore (100), Gordon Banks (73), Bobby Charlton (67), Alan Ball (66),
Martin Peters (66), Geoff Hurst (49), Ray Wilson (46), George Cohen (37),
Alan Mullery (35), Jack Charlton (35), Roger Hunt (33), Jimmy Greaves
(32), Colin Bell (32), Emlyn Hughes (29), Nobby Stiles (28).

What surprised me was to find that Emlyn Hughes won more caps with
Ramsey than Nobby Stiles, who seemed part of the fixtures and fittings

with Alf's team. Bobby Charlton was the only player to have made the top
fifteen in both the Winterbottom and the Ramsey most-capped lists.

Despite his occasionally brittle moments with Ramsey, Bobby Moore
was rewarded with 100 caps – 90 of them coming as captain, which
equalled the record set by Billy Wright on his way to 105 caps with Walter
Winterbottom.

The England record under Wright's leadership was:

P	W	D	L	F	A
90	49	21	20	234	135

The England record under Moore's leadership was:

P	W	D	L	F	A
90	57	20	13	171	75

These statistics reveal the way the game changed after Ramsey had taken
over from Winterbottom. Wright's incredible sequence of seventy successive
matches as skipper gives him the edge over Moore, whose longest run
without a break was twenty-seven games.

The Winterbottom teams captained by Wright averaged more than two
goals a game, but gave them away like a registered charity during an era
when the emphasis was on attack. Ramsey's England under the leadership
of Moore were much more miserly in defence, but not nearly as productive
in front of goal. Speaking as somebody who bridged the two eras as a
player, I can vouch for the fact that it was considerably easier to score
goals in the 1950s before the game became hooked on the drug of defensive
football in the 1960s.

The finger of blame for the shift towards negative tactics is often pointed
in the direction of Alf Ramsey, but he can always claim that he merely
played to the strengths of the best players around at the time.

Nobody can ever take away from him the fact that he gave English football its finest hour. I just wish that for his sake he had enjoyed it more.
Joe Mercer, his temporary successor, knew what enjoyment was all about.

CHAPTER THREE

Joe Mercer

(1974)

A COMIC
INTERLUDE

Joe Mercer, of the banana grin, bandy legs and heart bigger than his head, was like everybody's favourite uncle, and he brought a little light relief to the troubled England football stage when he briefly took over as caretaker manager following the messy exit of Sir Alf Ramsey.

The blood of Ramsey was still on the carpet at the Lancaster Gate headquarters of the Football Association when it was announced in May 1974 that 'Uncle Joe' was taking over on a temporary basis. Aged fifty-nine and general manager of Coventry City, Mercer stressed that he did not want to be considered for the permanent job. 'I shall just hold the reins for a few weeks', he told the media. 'There will be no pressure on any players while I'm in charge. I shall just tell them to play their natural game and go out and enjoy themselves.'

It was a statement that neatly captured Mercer's philosophy throughout his distinguished career as a club player, England international and club manager. He once tried to sign me for Manchester City when I was coming to the close of my career with Tottenham, and I now regret not having had the experience of playing for a man who was one of the most loved and respected characters in sport.

If they had tried, the Football Association could not have found a manager more contrasting in outlook and personality to Ramsey. Where Alf was guarded, unsmiling and defensive in his tactical approach to football, Joe was outgoing, always smiling and liked his teams to play with a flourish and a swagger. Where Alf treated the press like his worst enemies (which in some cases they were), Joe saw reporters as friends who could help him get his message across. Like almost any man walking this earth, Joe had his faults. He could at times seem casual to the point of carelessness and his tactical talks were described to me by one player as being 'woolly'. But his warm personality helped him across most bridges, and for the fort-holding job England wanted after the departure of Ramsey they could not have chosen a better man.

Mercer's seven-match spell with England was a happy and at times almost comical interlude. It was scarred by just one nightmare moment when 'Uncle Joe' had to urgently adopt the role of peacemaker following an ugly incident involving Liverpool's rising star Kevin Keegan. Mercer led the England party to Yugoslavia for the final match of a summer tour before handing over to Don Revie, and soon after the squad arrived at Belgrade Airport Keegan was pounced on by airport guards, arrested and beaten up. All Kevin had been guilty of was a little skylarking with a couple of the other players, but the treatment he got in a cell-like room was the sort an international drugs smuggler or gangster might have expected.

Journalist Bob Harris, now sports editor of the *Sunday Mirror,* witnessed Keegan's arrest, which had happened out of sight of Mercer and the England officials, who were still queueing at passport control. By the time Harris alerted the manager, Keegan had been frog-marched into the 'torture room' and was forced to kneel in front of the guards. Like most of the other members of the squad, he had arrived at the airport in casual clothes, and the sadistic guards laying into him with fists and truncheons had no idea they were assaulting one of England's finest young footballers.

Once it became clear that they had taken liberties with somebody who was quite a celebrity, the guards began to panic and invented charges that would possibly explain and excuse their brutality. They accused him of sexually assaulting an air-hostess on the flight from Bulgaria to Belgrade, assaulting an airport security guard, disturbing the peace and obstruction. In fact, all Keegan had done was to fall about laughing at the antics of Liverpool team-mate Alec Lindsay, who was fooling around on the luggage conveyor belt. It was childish, but hardly criminal.

Mercer, FA secretary Ted Croker and chairman Sir Andrew Stephen demanded Keegan's immediate release, but the airport security chief said that the charges were far too serious and that he would have to stay in custody. The England players held a quick meeting, and announced that in protest they wanted to return straight home without playing the scheduled international match against Yugoslavia. Then diplomat Mercer took over. He, along with Croker and Stephen, spent an hour arguing the case for Keegan, and they did it so powerfully that all charges were dropped and there were mutterings about 'misunderstandings' and 'mistaken identity'.

Keegan was lucky to have Croker and Stephen backing up Mercer. They were two of the more in-tune and sensible FA officials. I could name some FA councillors who would have merely made matters worse for Kevin by their attitude. One thing I know for sure is that the incident would not have happened under Ramsey's strict code of behaviour. We always had to dress properly when going to or from airports. 'You are representing your country', Alf used to say. 'I insist that you behave properly at all times while you are with the England party, and that you look the part of England foot-ballers.' If Keegan had been wearing his England blazer, it is unlikely that the security guards would have reacted in such thuggish manner.

The late Bernard Joy, once a distinguished footballer with Arsenal and the last amateur capped by England, was at the airport in his role as soccer correspondent for the London *Evening Standard*. The incident happened in the morning, too late for the daily newspapers and out of sight of his evening newspaper rivals. Bernard told me later:

> I saw it as the scoop of the year. I dashed to a telephone kiosk and after the usual heart-aching delays caused by international operators I was put through to my London office. 'It's Bernard Joy here in Belgrade', I said to the switch-board. Just then Joe came walking by and I shouted down the line, 'Hold on for one moment.' I scribbled down a quick statement from Joe who gave me the latest situation. When I returned to the telephone, the London oper-ator said brightly, 'Hello, Mr Joy. Are you having a pleasant time out there?' 'I've got no time for small-talk', I said. 'I've got an exclusive story to file. Put me through to the copytakers immediately.' 'But Mr Joy', came the reply, 'it's a Sunday. There are no copytakers in today.' I had been so excited by it all that I had lost sight of the fact that it was a non-publication day! It was the greatest exclusive I never had.

There was a last laugh for Keegan. He scored a late equalizer to force a 2–2 draw against the Yugoslavs for a happy finale to the pleasant Mercer interlude. Under 'Uncle Joe', England had played seven matches, won three, drawn three and lost just one. His skipper, Emlyn Hughes, spoke for a lot of the players when he said: 'It was a pity for England that his appointment was not a permanent one.'

Mercer,
THE MAN AND THE MANAGER

Born in Ellesmere Port in 1915, Mercer followed in the footsteps of his father and grandfather – both former professional footballers. Two things about Joe were just unforgettable: his wide, crooked grin and his unmis-takable bow-legged walk. 'You've got a pair of legs that wouldn't last a postman his morning round,' he was told by his wise-cracking Everton club-mate 'Dixie' Dean when he arrived at Goodison Park for the first time at the age of sixteen in 1931. 'Like a spiral staircase' was another of Dean's descriptions of the extraordinary Mercer limbs. Odd in shape they may have been, but Joe's legs served him well throughout a twenty-one-year playing career that bridged the Second World War and during which he became a football idol both in Liverpool and London.

Mercer came to the attention of Everton when playing for Cheshire schoolboys alongside his great chum Stan Cullis, later the master of Molineux. He made his League début for Everton in 1933 and, in return for a wage of £5 a week, gave them tremendous service. He stood just over 5 ft 10 in. and weighed around eleven stone, but he seemed to grow six inches the moment he stepped on to a football field where he tackled like a clap of thunder and was always inspiring the players around him with his dynamic energy and enthusiasm.

Mercer collected a League championship medal with Everton in 1938–39 and had established himself at left-half in the England team before the Second World War interrupted his progress. During wartime service he appeared twenty-two times for England, playing alongside his old schoolboy pal Stan Cullis and skippering the side in seven matches. His career seemed almost at an end when League football resumed in 1946–47. He was thirty-two and suffering from a recurring knee injury that required a cartilage operation. Everton lost faith in him and Mercer was contemplating retirement when, as much to his surprise as anybody else's, Arsenal agreed to pay £7,000 for him in November, 1946. It looked a crazy gamble by Arsenal manager Tom Whittaker, who made Mercer skipper of a team struggling one from bottom in the First Division.

Everybody – with the important exception of Mercer – thought Whittaker was asking too much of Joe on those bent old legs of his. But it proved to be a master-stroke. Mercer's fighting spirit galvanized Arsenal and they climbed clear of the threat of relegation, and the following season captured the League championship with Mercer playing a vital role as a solid defensive wing-half, in contrast to the swashbuckling, attacking style that had been a feature of his game at Everton. Under his driving leadership, Arsenal won the FA Cup in 1950, were runners-up in 1952 and won the League title again in 1952–53. Elected Footballer of the Year in 1950, Joe's astonishing career ended when he broke one of his famous legs in a collision with a team-mate during a League match against Liverpool at Highbury in April, 1954. Mercer was thirty-eight and he knew as he was being carried off on a stretcher that it was the end of his playing days. As he approached the players' tunnel, Joe – despite his pain – lifted an arm in a final salute to the fans, who roared in a mixture of affection and respect for one of the great lions of the game.

Just as Mercer was considering quitting football to go full time into his father-in-law's Hoylake grocery business, he was talked into taking the job of manager at struggling Sheffield United in 1955, but too late to save them from relegation. What attracted Joe to Bramall Lane were the honest words of their chairman, Senior Aitken. 'He called me from the bacon counter at the grocery business to offer me the job', said Joe. 'I remember his exact words, and they are worth recording for the attention of any other club chairmen and directors who reckon they can run a football team – "I know nowt about the game and the fourteen directors on the board know even less. We'll leave you alone to get on with the job as you see fit."'

Three years later, again halfway through a season, he was called on to try to do another salvage operation, this time for Aston Villa who were bottom of the table when he was appointed manager on Christmas Eve 1958. He failed to keep them up but steered them to promotion the following year and in 1959–60 he became the first manager to lift the new League Cup. What happened then was enough to destroy Mercer's faith in football – or, rather, in the people who ran it. For all his broad smiles and bubbling humour, Joe was a born worrier and in 1964 he drove himself so hard in the service of Villa that he collapsed from nervous exhaustion and suffered a mild stroke. He was just getting himself back to full health when Villa sacked him. It's a cruel old game.

It was in a mood of total disillusionment that Mercer turned his back on football 'for good'. In 1965 after a year of self-exile, Mercer was invited to take over as manager of Manchester City. Against medical advice and the pleadings of his wife, Norah, he agreed to take the job and started the most glorious chapter in his football life.

Mercer was wise enough to appreciate that the job was too big to do on his own. He summoned the help of the man he was to label the best coach in the world – Malcolm Allison, an irresistible character who had served his managerial apprenticeship with Bath City and Plymouth Argyle after tuberculosis had cost him a lung and finished his playing career with West Ham. Malcolm – known throughout the game as 'Big Mal' – was an old drinking buddy of mine, and I wondered how Joe would cope with his extrovert personality. It was a case of Lime Street meets Carnaby Street.

As it turned out, the Mercer–Allison partnership developed into one of the most effective in the history of English football. They were a perfect balance for each other, and over a span of five years the wise old manager and the colourful, inventive young coach inspired City to challenge the traditional supremacy of their neighbours and deadly rivals at Old Trafford. In their first season in harness, City were promoted as Second Division champions. Two seasons later they carried off the League title, and in 1969 they captured the FA Cup followed by the double of the European Cup Winners' Cup and the League Cup in 1969–70. Their team of thoroughbreds, with Colin Bell, Mike Summerbee and Francis Lee as the main motivators, played with a flair and a flamboyance that mirrored the personalities of Mercer and Allison.

Big Mal continued to lead an extravagant, last-playboy-of-the-western-world lifestyle at the height of the City success, and some of his escapades made old Joe wince. Once flagged down by a traffic patrol car that had overtaken him when he was speeding on the M62, Joe wound down his window and said: 'All right officer, what's Mal been up to now?' Allison had a lot of critics in the game, but I doubt if there have been more than two or three better English coaches during my lifetime, and certainly none more imaginative and creative.

Both Mercer and Allison became regular faces on television, Joe as an old charmer with the BBC team and Big Mal as a flamboyant character on the ITV parade of football panellists. Like Jack Charlton today, Joe struggled to get his tongue around the names of some of the foreign players and he used to have viewers in stitches with some of his pronunciations. Pelé will be surprised to know that when Joe was voicing his opinion for the Beeb he became known to the nation as 'that feller Peely'.

I moved from Tottenham to West Ham in preference to Manchester City in March 1970, and in my début match for the Hammers I scored two League goals on a soaking pudding of a pitch at Maine Road. Joe's banana smile was in good working order as he told me after the game, 'A great start, son, but for the wrong team!'

Inevitably, Allison wanted to flex his muscles as manager, and in 1971 Mercer – battling with fragile health – became general manager before eventually moving on to Coventry City in a similar role alongside Gordon Milne in 1972. Then came the call from England, and 'Uncle Joe' – as during his playing days – proudly served his country on what was a final lap of honour for those distinctive bandy legs of his.

Mercer's Record

During his eventful five weeks in charge of the England team, Mercer's record was:

P	W	D	L	F	A
7	3	3	1	9	7

Mercer inherited a squad that had been selected by Ramsey before his sudden departure. In his final game against Portugal – knowing his position was under close scrutiny – Sir Alf had awarded début caps to Trevor Brooking, Martin Dobson, Mike Pejic, Stan Bowles and Phil Parkes. When Joe first met the players for a training session he broke the ice with his opening statement that was greeted with a gale of laughter. 'I didn't want this bloody job in the first place', he said. Then he added, 'For the next few weeks we're all going to have a laugh and a joke. It's not life or death. It's a game, and we're all going to enjoy it. The only thing I'll insist on is that you represent your country with pride. Give me pride, give me a smile and play your own natural game. Let's have some fun.'

Mike Pejic, a serious-looking left-back from Stoke, lost his place in

Mercer's team for the oddest reason I have ever heard. Dear old Joe confided to me when we talked about his England adventure some years after his retirement, 'He never effing well smiled. I couldn't have that. He might have made the other players miserable.'

Mercer sent out a team that mixed youth with experience in his first match against Wales at Ninian Park, and he was rewarded with a 2–0 victory. Seven days later Mercer's England beat Northern Ireland 1–0 at Wembley. The Home Championship rested on the match at Hampden Park, and the Scottish attack of Lorimer, Johnstone, Jordan and Dalglish was too powerful for the England defence. Scotland won 2–0 to share the Championship with England. The Mercer squad was a happy one with the exception of Stan Bowles, who was so upset at being dropped for the match against Scotland that he walked out. 'A moody lad, Stan', said Joe. 'If he could pass a betting shop like he passes a ball his life would be much happier.'

An improved performance against a gifted Argentinian team at Wembley earned a 2–2 draw, but Mercer briefly dropped his smile when he criticized his skipper Emlyn Hughes for getting involved in a half-time skirmish with the Argentinians. 'I expect Emlyn as skipper to set the right sort of example', he said. 'If he loses his temper how can he expect his team-mates to keep cool? I want a smile on the face of English football, not a snarl.'

On a three-match tour, England had creditable draws against East Germany and Yugoslavia and a 1–0 victory over Bulgaria. 'All three teams had qualified for the World Cup finals, so we had to be more than satisfied with our efforts', said Mercer as he prepared to hand over the reins to Don Revie. 'I've enjoyed every minute of my time with the England lads. We had some good laughs along the way. That was as important as the winning.'

They don't make them like 'Uncle Joe' any more, and a bright light went out on the soccer stage when he passed on to the great football pitch in the sky in 1990.

Mercer's Players

These were the twenty players capped by Mercer during his seven matches as England team manager:

Colin Bell (Manchester City: 7)   Martin Dobson (Burnley: 3)
Stan Bowles (QPR: 2)
Trevor Brooking (West Ham: 4)   Emlyn Hughes (Liverpool: 7)
                                        Norman Hunter (Leeds: 2)
Mike Channon (Southampton: 7)
Ray Clemence (Liverpool: 3)   Kevin Keegan (Liverpool: 6)

Alec Lindsay (Liverpool: 4)   Martin Peters (Tottenham: 1)

Roy McFarland (Derby: 2)   Peter Shilton (Leicester: 1)
Malcolm Macdonald (Newcastle: 2)   Colin Todd (Derby: 7)
                                               Dave Watson (Sunderland: 5)
David Nish (Derby: 2)   Keith Weller (Leicester: 4)
Mike Pejic (Stoke: 3)   Frank Worthington (Leicester: 6)

Four players appeared in all seven of Mercer's matches: Colin Bell, Mike Channon, Emlyn Hughes and Colin Todd.

In his short spell in the England hot seat, 'Uncle Joe' had managed to put the smile back on the face of football. Don Revie was soon to wipe it off.

CHAPTER FOUR

Don Revie

(1974–1977)

THE ULTIMATE PROFESSIONAL

D on Revie will, sadly, always be remembered as the man who
deserted England and then had the dirty linen of football washed
in the courts, yet he could so easily have gone down in the record
books as the greatest of all the managers. As club boss at Leeds United he
became one of the great untouchables, but his conduct when he switched
to the England team manager's job turned him into one of the undesirables.

A more abiding memory for those closest to Revie is of the great dignity
and courage he showed in his last years as he faced up to approaching
death from motor neurone disease. He finally succumbed on May 26, 1989,
and the tributes that poured in from his former players at Leeds were testi-
mony to the fact that he was a man who during his lifetime had won a lot
of respect and affection.

But as I am giving an honest assessment of the men who have managed
the England football team, I have to say that Revie made a complete cock-
up of the job and ultimately left himself open to accusations of ducking
his responsibilities. He had never ever been a quitter, but he walked out
on England in a disgraceful manner.

The way he defected after just thirty matches was like something out of a
Carry On Spying comedy film, although it was hardly comical when seen
through the eyes of the FA officials who had appointed Revie as manager with
great hopes that he could do for England what he had done for his all-
conquering Leeds United team. In the summer of 1977 the England squad that
Revie had selected was on a South American tour, thinking that he was going
to join them after watching Finland play Italy as part of his World Cup
preparations. Instead – as exclusively revealed in the *Daily Mail* by his close
confidant, Jeff Powell – Revie disguised himself in a bulky coat and dark
glasses and visited Dubai to discuss terms for the highly paid post of national
team coach to the United Arab Emirates. When he finally caught up with the
England team in Buenos Aires he kept his plans secret, and following a
sequence of uninspired and heavily criticized performances he told the FA

officials that he was willing to resign if his contract was paid up and a tax-free bonus of £5,000 added. The Football Association did not bite, and called his bluff by telling him that they had every confidence in him.

A month later the same FA officials had indigestion over their breakfast tables when they read in the *Mail* that Revie was heading for the desert and a £60,000-a-year tax-free job with the United Arab Emirates. He told Jeff Powell:

> I sat down with my wife, Elsie, one night and we agreed that the England job was no longer worth the aggravation. It was bringing too much heartache to those nearest to us. Nearly everyone in the country seems to want me out. So I am giving them what they want. I know people will accuse me of running away, and it does sicken me that I cannot finish the job by taking England to the World Cup Finals in Argentina next year. But the situation has become impossible.

It was sensational stuff, and over the next few weeks it was open house on Revie with newspapers that had not got a sniff of the story firing from all angles as they tried to make up lost ground on the *Mail*. Revie was variously described as a traitor, a cheat, a greedy, money-grabbing mercenary, and even a crook. Allegations were made – and strenuously denied – that he had fixed matches while managing Leeds United. The Football Association deliberately added to the poison darts being aimed at Revie when they let it be known how he had tried to get released from his contract, with compensation, four weeks before his resignation.

The world of football in which we live is little more than a village, and the whispering factory worked overtime pushing out rumours and innuendo about Revie. It was made public that, behind his back, the press knew him as 'Don Readies' because of his habit of seeking hush-hush, cash-in-the-hand payments for interviews. It was also reported that he was known as 'The Godfather' because of the way he liked to rule his team. Revie was rubbished at every turn, and his reputation crushed into the ground. No amount of money he was receiving from the Arabs could compensate for the disparagement and ridicule he was having to suffer at home. 'Don the Deserter' was a new nickname that stuck.

His former England skipper Alan Ball – who had never forgiven him for dropping him unceremoniously – came in with a two-footed tackle when he alleged that Revie had made cash payments to him during an illegal approach to try to persuade him to join Leeds from Blackpool back in the mid-1960s. It was a revelation that brought Ballie a £3,000 fine from the Football Association. When Ball went to Everton instead of Leeds, it was reported that Revie cried. He was a man of enormous passion and sensitivity, and he was also in tears after Italy beat England 2–0 in a crucial World Cup qualifying match in Rome in 1976. Less than a year later he was crying all the way to the bank as he deserted to the Arabs.

Sir Harold Thompson, the man who had brought down Ramsey, now had Revie in his sights. Thompson, elevated to FA chairman, got on even worse with Revie than he had with Ramsey, and he made no secret of the fact that he was going to make 'the deserter' pay for his unacceptable behaviour. The Football Association accused him of deceit, charged him with bringing the game into disrepute, and suspended him indefinitely.

Enraged by the verdict, Revie returned home a year later to face a commission headed by his bitter adversary, Sir Harold. It was later announced that the ban had been hardened to ten years.

Revie had taken most of the media criticism on his extra-large chin, but he was determined to fight the Football Association, and he sued for damages and asked that his ten-year ban be ruled illegal. Gilbert Gray, the QC representing Revie in the High Court in December 1979, charged that Sir Harold Thompson had shown continued hostility towards his client, and therefore was not a fit person to sit in judgement over him. 'Sir Harold was effectively prosecutor, witness, judge and jury', said Mr Gray.

Managers Jock Stein and Lawrie McMenemy and broadcaster Jimmy Hill were among the football big guns giving evidence for Revie, who told the court that his contract with the United Arab Emirates was the best in the history of football.

Revie won his case against the Football Association, who were ordered to lift the ten-year ban. Justice Cantley said in his summing up that although Sir Harold Thompson was 'an honourable man', he should not have chaired the committee that banned Revie, because it could be considered that there was a bias against the former England manager. Revie heard the judge describe him as 'deceitful, greedy and selfish'. It was a hollow victory.

The lifting of the ban meant Revie was able to receive an income from Leeds under the terms of a nine-year consultancy contract to start in 1980 and negotiated in 1972 when he was the king of Elland Road. But The Don was never again to play an active role in the English game in which he had made a considerable impact both as a player and manager. Throughout his career, he was motivated by a mixture of a will to win and a desire to make money. Revie was the ultimate professional.

Revie,
THE MAN AND THE MANAGER

Born in Middlesbrough in 1927, Revie grew up in tough circumstances that went some way to explain his naked ambition to become a rich man. His mother died when he was twelve, and his father, a joiner, was often out of work and not knowing where the next penny was coming from. He started out on his professional football career with Leicester City in the first season after the Second World War, recovering from a badly broken leg to become one of the League's most skilful and creative forwards. After playing a prominent part in shooting Leicester into the 1949 FA Cup Final, he missed the match at Wembley because of an horrendous nose injury when he lost so much blood that at one stage there was a fear for his life. He was so weakened that he could not even travel to watch the match, which was won 3–1 by Wolves.

When he moved on to Hull City the following season for a near-record £20,000 he had with him his wife, Elsie, who was a niece of the Leicester City manager Johnny Duncan. For the rest of his life, Elsie – a former school-teacher – was the most important person in Revie's world, and she was his greatest motivator as his career developed and widened into management.

He was a have-boots-will-travel professional in the days when most players saw their careers through with just one club. His most successful period as a player came with Manchester City, his next stop after Hull in 1951 at a fee of £25,000. Greatly influenced by the magical Hungarian international team that put thirteen goals past England goalkeeper Gil Merrick in two matches in the 1953–54 season, Revie perfected a deep-lying centre-forward style round which Manchester City created tactics that became known as 'the Revie Plan'.

A big, broad-shouldered and impressive looking man both on and off the pitch, he was known in the League dressing-rooms as 'Mister Handsome'. In 1955 he was voted Footballer of the Year after winning the first of his six England caps and steering City to the FA Cup Final against Newcastle United. City were beaten, but Revie was back at Wembley with them the following year and celebrated a victory over Birmingham City.

Following two seasons with Sunderland, Revie moved on to Leeds for the start of an association that turned him into a legendary figure at Elland Road where you will never hear a bad word said about him. When he arrived at Leeds in December 1958, the club was on the slide. They tumbled into the Second Division and seemed destined for the Third until Revie's appointment as player-manager.

It was during this period that Revie proved himself a club manager with few peers. First of all he sorted out a team-mate with whom he had a succession of blazing rows. 'If you would be a little less stubborn, adopt the right attitude and play the way I know you can, you will become England's centre-half', he told him. The player was Jack Charlton, who became everything that Revie said he could and more.

Revie then turned a home-sick, wild-tempered young Scot called Billy

Bremner into one of the world's most dynamic midfield players, and encouraged the development of youth players like Norman Hunter, Paul Reaney, Peter Lorimer and Eddie Gray. Working closely with his trusted lieutenants Maurice Lindley, Syd Owen and Les Cocker, he built a team that mixed method with muscle. First of all he had Bobby Collins and then Johnny Giles as the midfield orchestrators of a side that won few friends but influenced plenty of results with their at times ferocious football that made them feared, even hated, outside Leeds. I have the bruises on my memory to remind me that to try to find a way through the iron-clad Leeds defence was like plotting a way through a minefield. If Norman Hunter didn't bite yer legs, then Jack Charlton would. If you managed to avoid them both, there was Johnny Giles or Billy Bremner looking to give you a sneaky nip; even goalkeeper Gary Sprake could frighten the life out of you by showing you his studs.

Following promotion from the Second Division in 1964, Leeds finished 2, 2, 4, 4 in their first four frustrating seasons back in the First Division, lost the 1965 FA Cup Final in extra time to Liverpool, were beaten in two FA Cup semi-finals, and also in the 1966 Fairs Cup semi-final and in the final the following year. It was a League Cup final victory over Arsenal in 1968 that proved the breakthrough point, and by the time the 1970s dawned Leeds – League champions for the first time in 1969 – rivalled Liverpool and Manchester United as the number one club in the country. They had finally lost their 'second best' reputation.

In Leeds, Revie was revered, but elsewhere he was reviled because of the ruthless way in which his team appeared to follow his win-at-all-costs orders. In the summer of 1973, the Football Association disciplinary committee censured Leeds and threatened them with a suspended £3,000 fine for 'persistent misconduct on the field of play'. Most people in the game thought they had got off lightly, and the typically outspoken Brian Clough had the courage to say what many others were thinking. 'Leeds', he said, 'should have been instantly relegated after being branded as one of the dirtiest clubs in Britain.' Two months earlier, Revie had been offered a considerable salary increase to take over as manager at Everton. It was at a time of wage restraint and the Government were about to decide whether this move was legal when Revie announced that he was staying at Elland Road.

A football tactician who was always happiest in a tracksuit out on the training ground, Revie hated the 'Dirty Leeds' label that was hung on his team, and with a combination of clever public relations and some spectacular play on the pitch they at last began to win praise for football that was at times breathtaking. I remember them taking our Tottenham team apart at Elland Road with an opening half-hour of football that was as good as anything I had ever seen from a British club side. I might even had applauded them had I not been too busy chasing their shadows.

Revie's only relaxation away from football was either with Elsie and their son and daughter, or on the golf course where he was a fierce competitor playing off a single-figure handicap. He was desperately intense about football, and every time I saw him he seemed like a man who had the world on his rounded shoulders. Like Alf Ramsey, he did not seem to have found the secret of relaxing and enjoying the game. It was too much a matter of life or death with him, and it showed in the competitive way that Leeds played. The only thing that meant more to him than football was his family, and he did his best to protect them from the overlapping pressures of his job. He was distraught when he found his son, Duncan, then eleven, sobbing on the pavement outside Villa Park after Chelsea had beaten Leeds in the 1967 FA Cup semi-final. Revie later said:

> That was the day I realized that I had to take special measures to ease the burden that my job was putting on Duncan. He had deliberately missed the coach back to Leeds because he did not want to face the taunts of the supporters. He felt defeat even worse than me, if that's possible. My job in football was making his life a misery, and I took the decision to send him as a boarder to Repton school, so that he would be away from Leeds and the daily pressures of having to face foul-tongued supporters. It broke my heart because we are such a close family, but I knew it would be best for Duncan in the long term.

For a man who thought logically about almost everything, Revie was strangely eaten up with supersitions. He wore a 'lucky' blue suit, always followed the same routine on every single match day and once enlisted the aid of a gypsy to remove an old Romany curse from the Leeds ground. All his good luck charms did not help him in 1969–70 when Leeds challenged for three major trophies and lost them all in the space of two weeks – second in the League to Alan Ball's Everton, runners-up in the FA Cup to Chelsea and beaten European Cup semi-finalists.

A year later Leeds were again runners-up in the League, this time to Arsenal, and all they had left to play for was the European Fairs Cup. They had to travel to Turin for the first leg of the final against Juventus, and Revie decided to turn it into a family outing, arranging for the wives and girlfriends of the players to follow them to Italy. But his happy-families plan backfired on him when a rain storm forced the match to be postponed for forty-eight hours. He announced to the players that he was taking them off to a secret training-camp away from distractions, and for the first time his authority was challenged. The players argued that they would rather stay in Turin with their wives and girlfriends.

Revie was fuming, and he told the players that they could spend the rest of the summer with their families and if they were not prepared to leave them for just forty-eight hours, then the match and the club could not be very important to them. 'If that's what you want then I want nothing more to do with you', he said in a mixture of rage and disappointment. 'I might as well go home.'

With that, he walked out of the room leaving the players shocked into silence. Barely two minutes passed before club captain Billy Bremner caught up with him and said, 'You're right, Boss. The match must come first. We've decided to do what you want.'

Revie said later:

> I meant every word. And the players knew it. I was not bluffing. I was ready to catch the first available plane home. I was desperately hurt that the players were no longer acting like professionals. They were tearing down everything that mattered about Leeds. But, like the true professionals that they are, they saw sense and eventually did the right thing.

Leeds held Juventus to a 2–2 draw, and in the return leg an Allan Clarke goal earned them the Fairs Cup. Revie said that from then on his relationship with the players was stronger than ever.

He was the logical choice as successor to Alf Ramsey after Leeds had clinched their second League championship in 1973–74, and he kicked off the job like a man who really meant business. Revie quickly organized a meeting of the eighty-one players he had short-listed as candidates for places in the England squad. There would have been eighty-two, but Nottingham Forest winger John Robertson had to politely decline Revie's invitation on the reasonable grounds that he was a Scot! Revie gave his chosen few a rousing Churchillian call to arms, and promised that the first thing he was going to do was make sure that they were properly paid for playing for England; he stressed the importance of a professional outlook. The players were soon to discover that 'professionalism' was his favourite word.

He put action where his mouth was by getting the match fee raised from what in my time was a flat £60 to an incentive scale of £300 for a win, £200 for a draw and £100 as a guarantee. Old pros like myself wondered, perhaps enviously, about the principle of making money the motive for playing for your country. In my day, it was the honour of pulling on an England shirt that mattered above all else. But my day was long ago.

There was another shabby sign of the new professional era into which Revie was kicking English football when he clinched a deal with a shirt company that led to England running out to play with the word 'Admiral' emblazoned across their tracksuits, and wearing shirts that looked like red-white-and-blue pyjama tops rather than the traditional (and much loved) white shirt. This was, in my opinion, commercialism gone mad, and I know my view was shared by many FA councillors who were already beginning to worry about the man they feared was becoming a monster.

Revie pleaded for the England supporters to adopt 'Land of Hope and Glory' as their official song, and they responded lustily when England launched the Revie era with a 3–0 victory over Czechoslovakia at Wembley on October 30, 1974. It was a bright start after a worrying first hour against the Czechs, and the England players celebrated by singing the old Glasgow Celtic theme song that Revie had adapted for sing-alongs in the dressing-room, 'It's a grand old team to play for, it's a grand old team to see ...'

Just twenty-one days later Revie found out what a fickle lot fans can be when his England team were booed off the Wembley pitch after struggling to a goalless draw against Portugal. Denied the daily contact with players, Revie was already finding it almost impossible to build the the same rapport and fierce mutual loyalty that had been so important to him at Leeds. He employed as his right-hand man Leeds trainer Les Cocker, who was experienced in international football as an assistant in the Ramsey backroom team. But the pair of them struggled to get what they described as the 'Leeds spirit' into the England players, many of whom disliked the type of cameraderie that was almost forced on them. Revie and Cocker expected the England squad to take part in bingo sessions, carpet bowls and putting competitions because Revie considered that it helped knit them into what he called 'the England family'. To be honest, it was the sort of false togetherness that I would have hated had it been thrust on me during my time with England. In my experience, players like to be considered adult enough to be allowed to do their own thing. How many independent young men in their twenties and thirties would be content playing bingo and carpet bowls?

Most of Revie's players were not keen, either, on the dossiers that he expected them to read before every game. He would meticulously outline the style, strengths and weaknesses of every member of the opposing team, and each player would be given written instructions how to play against them. The result was that players would worry too much about the opponents and fail to play their natural game. In no time at all the England team was being dubbed 'Revie's Robots'.

Revie was going to extremes to do his job, and all his conscientious effort deserved better reward. But the fact is that it all back-fired on him because the players were hit with so much detail that many of them became frozen with fear before a ball had been kicked.

Mike Channon, who had launched Revie's England reign with a spec-tacular goal against Czechoslovakia, told me when we discussed Don's style of management:

> I don't think it ever dawned on Don that those dossiers used to frighten the life out of some players. They used to read them before going to bed and then struggle to sleep because they were trying to memorize all that was written down. Don was great at motivating us in team-talks, and he could make any player feel ten feet tall. When he first became manager he was so positive that

we all began to think we could really achieve big things, just like in 'sixty-six. The night we beat world champions Germany at Wembley in 1975 gave the whole country a buzz, and then we followed that up with a 5–0 thrashing of Cyprus with Malcolm Macdonald getting all five goals. Revie had got it just right. We had an attacking front six of Colin Bell, Alan Ball, Alan Hudson, Kevin Keegan, Macdonald and myself. I reckon it was as good a combination as we'd had since the 1970 World Cup. For the life of me, I'll never understand why Don broke up that team.

Revie, so positive with his decisions as manager at Leeds, seemed paralysed by indecision in the England chair. He was full of contradictions, and upset a procession of players by first telling them they were the men he was banking on and then dropping them without explanation. Emlyn Hughes, his skipper in his first two matches, was stunned and hurt to find himself suddenly ditched, and it was two years before he was recalled from the international wilderness. Peter Shilton felt that he was being messed about so much that he asked not to be considered for any more England squads. Revie later talked him into changing his mind, and, of course, Shilts went on to become the world's most-capped footballer. Kevin Keegan walked out on the squad after being axed without reason, but was later persuaded to return to play a key role in Revie teams that were chopped and changed so many times that supporters could not recognize many of the players wearing the England shirt.

Such was Revie's panic when criticism of his selections reached a crescendo that he once sent out an England team containing no fewer than five specialist central defenders, three of them playing out of position. It was almost as if he was picking the team by reaching into a hat and drawing out numbers.

Just as it looked as if Revie had found a world-class attack, he confused and confounded everybody by turning his back on his new skipper Alan Ball and gifted forwards Alan Hudson and Malcolm Macdonald. Ballie, the last survivor of the 1966 World Cup team, was never able to forgive him, and at every opportunity went on record with blistering criticism of Revie's selections. He went as far as calling them 'a bunch of donkeys' because of the blind way they followed Revie's instructions.

Everybody was mystified as to why Revie had dropped Ball, Hudson and Macdonald, when it was obvious they had so much to give the England team. He was also clearly not a fan of Tony Currie and Charlie George. All of them had something in common apart from their talent as footballers – all were individualists, strong characters who did not fit into the regimented way Revie wanted to run his teams. It later surfaced that Revie had put a black mark against Ball and several of the players when they broke a late-night curfew. For such a professional man, Revie was very puritanical, and sounded almost evangelical when he told the players:

'I believe it will help you if you pray every night before you go to sleep and ask God to make you become better players.' The thought of Ballie and Norman Hunter kneeling in prayer at the bedside is too much of a test for my imagination! (When Norman 'Bites Yer Legs' made his début for England against Spain, Ballie put his hands together in the dressing-room before the match and said, 'For what they are about to receive.')

Many people inside the game thought that one of Revie's major mistakes was in getting too close to a small, select group of football writers, Jeff Powell, of the *Daily Mail,* and Frank Clough, of the *Sun,* chief among them. It triggered resentment among the reporters who did not have his ear, and there were soon pro-Revie and anti-Revie camps in Fleet Street. Mike Channon told me: 'If ever we wanted to know what Don was thinking about the team, all we had to do was read the *Mail* or the *Sun.*'

The lowest point for Revie must have been successive defeats at Wembley in 1977, first by Wales and then by Scotland. Even with powerful friends in Fleet Street, he was suddenly like a man facing a firing squad. It was the first victory for Wales in England for forty-two years, and the first time England had lost consecutive matches at Wembley. This was when Revie started to look <u>for</u> pastures new. He revealed in court that he sensed the Football Association were getting ready 'to do a Ramsey' on him, and he said that he considered it wise to look for a way out before they kicked him out. I have already made it clear that I have no time for the Football Association way of doing things, but on this occasion they were the ones kicked in the teeth.

The main plank of Revie's managerial success had always been loyalty, but suddenly he became 'Don the Disloyal' as he crept off to Dubai for a bag of gold that no doubt made him rich beyond the wildest dreams of his hungry days as a child. But no amount of money could have compensated him for the scorn that was poured on him by the press and the public.

Revie's Record

During his three years in charge of the England team, Revie's record was:

P	W	D	L	F	A
30	15	8	7	52	16

Home international matches only:

	P	W	D	L	F	A
v. Scotland	3	1	0	2	7	5
v. Wales	4	2	1	1	5	4
v. Northern Ireland	3	2	1	0	6	1

International matches played in England against overseas opposition:

P	W	D	L	F	A
8	5	2	1	18	4

International matches played outside England against overseas opposition:

P	W	D	L	F	A
12	5	4	3	16	12

Incredibly, it was Revie's thirtieth – and final – match against Uruguay before he selected an unchanged team. His first side was not functioning properly in his opening game against Czechoslovakia on October 30, 1974, until he proved he had a better understanding of the substitute system than Alf Ramsey. He sent on Trevor Brooking and David Thomas in a double substitution on the hour that produced three goals in nine minutes. The Wembley terraces erupted with choruses of 'Land of Hope and Glory' and for that night Revie was the king of English football. But the crown quickly slipped, and England were jeered off the same pitch three weeks later after they flopped in a goalless stalemate against Portugal's man-to-man marking and sweeper system.

Both matches were European championship qualifiers, and it is possible to gauge how badly things went for Revie after this satisfactory start by the fact that it was Czechoslovakia who qualified for the final stages ahead of an England team that had thumped them 3–0. Just to rub it in, the Czechs went on to win the European title. It could easily have been England's championship if only Revie had tried to stick to a settled side, but he made so many team changes that it was difficult to know whether he or his players were the more confused.

England had one of their most rewarding victories under Revie in his third match when they beat world champions West Germany 2–1 at Wembley on March 12, 1975. It was the first defeat for the Germans since they won the World Cup in 1974, but it was not lost on neutral observers that they fielded an experimental side as they searched for a team to defend the championship in Argentina in 1978.

In their fourth match under Revie England hammered Cyprus 5–0, with all five goals coming from Malcolm Macdonald – four headers and one left-footed shot. One more goal would have given Malcolm an all-time England individual goal-scoring record. His reward was to be dropped from the squad after two more 90-minute appearances, another as a substitute and a fourth when he was pulled off.

The outstanding feature of the victories over West Germany and Cyprus was the creative work in midfield of Alan Hudson. He looked the answer to Revie's prayers as a world-class schemer who could dictate the pace and pattern of a match. But he kicked out Hudson along with skipper Alan Ball, and it was reported that this followed a complaint to the Football Association about their 'exuberant' behaviour while enjoying a day at the races at Royal Ascot. I am sure that for years afterwards Revie must have kicked himself that he did not make a greater effort to keep Hudson and Ball in his squad. Alf Ramsey had plenty of high-spirited characters in his teams – and I'll own up to being a ringleader! – and he knew just how much rope to allow us. With a more tolerant approach, I am sure that Revie could have coaxed many match-winning performances out of Hudson and Ball.

It was seven matches before England conceded a goal under Revie, but professional onlookers could not believe some of the selections he was making. There seemed to be no continuity, and players were not being given the chance to feel their way into the team. No sooner were they called into the side than they were out while Revie tried a new formation. A 5–1 victory over Scotland – including two goals from the inspiring Gerry Francis – lifted England to the Home Championship, but it was difficult to get really excited because of the poverty of the Scottish performance. It would have been impossible to predict that the Scots would qualify for the 1978 World Cup finals, leaving England kicking their heels at home.

In fairness to Revie, he might have got closer to a settled side had injuries not robbed him of key players Colin Bell, Roy McFarland and Gerry Francis, who had performed with pride and passion as England skipper until a recurring back problem pushed him on to the sidelines. What Revie's critics could not understand is why he continually asked players to operate in positions and styles different to that in which they specialized with their clubs. For the most crucial game of Revie's reign – a World Cup qualifier against Italy in Rome on November 17, 1976 – he picked the oddest team imaginable. He watched the Italians play no fewer than eight times as he prepared for the match, and I think he succeeded only in baffling and bewildering himself by doing too much homework on them. The side he selected was so badly balanced that it was obvious even before a ball was kicked that they had little or no chance of winning or even holding the Italians to a draw. His back four of Dave Clement, Roy McFarland, Emlyn Hughes and Mick Mills had never before played together as a unit, and in midfield he selected two ball-winners in Trevor Cherry and Brian Greenhoff, who were both happier in the back line. It threw a lot of responsibility on to schemer Trevor Brooking, who was still serving his apprenticeship on the international stage. At the front Revie played Kevin Keegan, Mike Channon and Stan Bowles, who were too alike in style and kept getting in each other's way. England were shut right out of the game as an attacking force by Italy's man-to-man marking, and there was nobody in the side who could break open their safe-door defence by running down the wings.

England were outclassed and lucky to escape with just a 2–0 defeat. Italian skipper Giacinto Facchetti said what a lot of English professionals were thinking: 'This is the worst England side I have ever seen. They were disorganized, confused, had only modest ability and, most surprising of all for a team from England, they seemed to have little heart for the battle.'

With the World Cup finals in Argentina suddenly looking a bridge too far, I believe that this must have been about the time that Revie started to consider a future as far away as possible from the Football Association, where he was beginning to come up against the sort of obstacles that had frustrated each of his predecessors. The clubs were getting in a mutinous mood over the way they were having to postpone the Saturday First Division programme before mid-week internationals, and outspoken League secretary Alan Hardaker said: 'These postponements are hurting to the point where I can see the League collapsing. It is costing the clubs thousands of pounds in lost revenue and for what? How can anybody argue that the postponements are making any diference at all to the performances of the England team?'

Suddenly Revie could see enemies every way he turned. Even his friend-liest supporters among the press were turning the torch of criticism on his selections, and when England were run ragged by a magnificent Holland team on the way to a 2–0 defeat at Wembley in their next match he had to face the fact that he was light years away from finding a team that could compete with the best in the world. His side against the Dutch was an even stranger combination than the one thrown to the Italian lions in Rome. He included six recognized back-four players, and while they were obstructing each other chasing the shadows of Johan Cruyff and Johan Neeskens, Jan Peters slipped through England's unhinged defence for two superb goals.

Just about the lowest moment for Revie must have come after Scotland beat England 2–1 to win the Home Championship on June 4, 1977. Scottish fans invaded the Wembley pitch and tore down the goals and took the woodwork home as trophies along with great patches of the hallowed Wembley turf that they dug up like gleeful gravediggers. They had turned Wembley into a burial ground for Revie's dreams.

Little did anybody – possibly even including Revie – realize that this would be the last match in which he would manage a team in England. By the time the summer tour of South America was over he had made up his mind to desert to the Arabs.

Revie's Players

These were the fifty-two players selected by Revie during his twenty-nine full international matches as England team manager (a thirtieth match against Team America was not classified as an official international):

Alan Ball (Arsenal, 1974–75: 6)
Colin Bell (Manchester City,
   1974–75: 9)
Kevin Beattie (Ipswich, 1975–77: 8)
Stan Bowles (QPR, 1977: 2)
Phil Boyer (Norwich, 1976: 1)
Trevor Brooking (West Ham,
   1974–77: 13)

Mike Channon (Southampton,
   1974–77: 26)
Trevor Cherry (Leeds, 1976–77: 12)
Allan Clarke (Leeds, 1974–76: 3)
Ray Clemence (Liverpool,
   1974–77: 25)
Dave Clement (QPR, 1976–77: 5)
Terry Cooper (Leeds, 1974: 1)
Joe Corrigan (Manchester City,
   1976: 1)
Tony Currie (Sheffield Utd, 1975: 1)

Martin Dobson (Everton, 1974: 1)
Mike Doyle (Manchester City,
   1976–77: 5)

Gerry Francis (QPR, 1974–76: 12)
Trevor Francis (Birmingham, 1977: 7)

Charlie George (Derby, 1977: 1)
John Gidman (Aston Villa, 1977: 1)

Gordon Hill
   (Manchester Utd, 1976–77: 4)
Alan Hudson (Stoke, 1975: 2)
Emlyn Hughes (Liverpool,
   1974–77: 11)
Norman Hunter (Leeds, 1974: 1)

David Johnson (Ipswich, 1975: 3)

Kevin Keegan (Liverpool,
   1974–77: 24)

Ray Kennedy (Liverpool,
   1976–77: 9)

Brian Little (Aston Villa, 1975: 1)

Roy McFarland (Derby, 1975–76: 4)
Malcolm Macdonald (Newcastle,
   1974–75: 7)
Paul Madeley (Leeds, 1974–77: 8)
Paul Mariner (Ipswich, 1977: 2)
Mick Mills (Ipswich, 1976–77: 12)

Phil Neal (Liverpool, 1976–77: 7)

Stuart Pearson (Manchester Utd,
   1976–77: 12)

Jimmy Rimmer (Arsenal, 1976: 1)
Joe Royle (Manchester City,
   1976–77: 4)

Peter Shilton (Stoke, 1975–77: 3)

Brian Talbot (Ipswich, 1977: 6)
Peter Taylor (Crystal Palace,
   1976: 4)
Dave Thomas (QPR, 1974–76: 8)
Colin Todd (Derby, 1974–77: 18)
Phil Thompson (Liverpool,
   1976–77: 8)
Tony Towers (Sunderland, 1976: 1)
Denis Tueart (Manchester City,
   1975–77: 6)

Colin Viljoen (Ipswich, 1975: 2)

Dave Watson (Sunderland/
   Manchester City, 1974–77: 18)
Steve Whitworth (Leicester, 1975: 7)
Ray Wilkins (Chelsea, 1976–77: 7)
Frank Worthington
   (Leicester, 1974: 2)

The most capped players during Revie's reign were Mike Channon (26), Ray Clemence (25), Kevin Keegan (24), Dave Watson (18), Trevor Brooking (13), Trevor Cherry (12), Gerry Francis (12), Brian Greenhoff (12), Mick Mills (12), Stuart Pearson (12), Emlyn Hughes (11), Colin Bell (9) and Ray Kennedy (9).

An indication of how confusing it all became – for the players as well as the spectators – is that Mike Channon only twice had the same attacking partners in successive matches on his way to twenty-six caps under Revie.

Away from football, Revie was a kind and caring man who was always looking to quietly help charitable organizations and individuals down on their luck. But inside the game, he was a miserly figure who refused to give a thing away. Defeat to him was like a disease, and this is why he instilled win-at-all-costs methods into his teams. There was no better organized and positive manager in club football, but when he stepped up on to the international stage he managed to lose himself in a maze of his own making.

When he ran out on the job, the Football Association searched for a successor who could restore their faith in their fellow man.

And now for somebody completely different: Ron Greenwood.

CHAPTER FIVE

Ron Greenwood

(1977–1982)

RIGHT MAN, WRONG TIME

Ron Greenwood was enjoying the sea breezes of Brighton in semi-retirement when he was summoned to put his finger in the dyke as England's caretaker manager following the sudden desertion of Don Revie. It was like inviting a village vicar to take over from a foot-in-the-door salesman.

We used to call Greenwood 'Reverend Ron' because of his gentlemanly conduct and his tendency almost to preach to footballers when giving tactical talks that could have come out of the gospel according to Walter Winterbottom, the man he admired above all others. I thought Ron was the right man for the England job but at the wrong time. He was approaching fifty-six when called on, and to the players he was selecting he was not far off a grandfatherly figure.

There is no question that the people's choice as successor to Revie would have been Brian Clough, who was one of six candidates for the permanent job of England manager inteviewed by the FA selection committee in December 1977. His rivals were Bobby Robson of Ipswich, Dave Sexton of Manchester United, Jack Charlton of Sheffield Wednesday, Lawrie McMenemy of Southampton, and Greenwood, who had been in charge for three matches in a caretaker capacity. The fact that the third of these games produced a 2–0 victory over Italy in a World Cup qualifying match made a great impression on the FA officials under the leadership of our old friend, Professor Sir Harold Thompson, who at sixty-eight chaired a committee with an average age of sixty-two.

Clough was convinced he had got the job after what he described as 'a magnificent interview.' But the committee plumped for the veteran Greenwood, and insulted Cloughie by putting him and his partner Peter Taylor in charge of the youth team. Many people inside the game saw this as a clumsy way of trying to silence the outspoken Clough. As the old Arab saying has it: 'Invite the infidel into the tent so that he pees out rather than leave him on the outside peeing in.' Cloughie and Taylor made their excuses and left after several clashes with the blazered brigade from the Football

Association. The breaking point came during a youth tournament in the Canary Isles when an FA official ordered the young England players to board a coach to go to a match, only for Clough and Taylor to then shepherd them back into the hotel. 'It was baking hot and I did not want the players sitting in a stifling coach', Cloughie told me. 'Peter and I sat in the hotel with the lads, joking with them and getting them relaxed. The old boys sat in the coach, and I made it clear that we would only go when *we* were ready. It was all so unprofessional.' If Cloughie had got the top job, he would have swept the hangers-on and the busybodies out of his way at a rate of knots, and this I feel sure is what the Football Association feared.

In my opinion Clough should have been given the job ahead of Greenwood. He was the right age, was the best motivator and had a better track record. I believe that the FA officials were frightened of him. They had already been burned by Revie, and they sensed they would have found Cloughie far too hot to handle. He would have given our game the shake-up that it needed, and that would have meant a lot of dead wood being cleared out. I am convinced a lot of FA councillors were concerned that they would be on his hit list.

The Football Association played safe and appointed Greenwood who got on with the job of building an England squad with first the 1980 European championships and then the 1982 World Cup finals in mind. The team he inherited from Revie had already missed the boat to Argentina for the 1978 World Cup despite the spirited performance against Italy.

I have personal reasons why Greenwood is not my favourite person in football, but I will not allow this to cloud my judgement of him. My honest assessment is that he was an exceptional coach of players with tactical awareness, and was a good but not outstanding manager. He lacked the will-to-win of a Revie, the steel of a Ramsey, the charisma of a Mercer, and the dynamism of a Clough, but he had a deep sincerity about him that appealed to many players who swore loyalty to him. The one area in which he was the tops was that nobody could match his knowledge of international football. The England job suited him better than club football, but it had come at least ten years later than was ideal. When he was appointed, the time was exactly right for Clough. Ron is a nice man – a very, very nice man – but nice men rarely come first. Cloughie can be 'orrible, but he refuses to accept second best.

Greenwood was so enmeshed in the theory of the game that I always got the impression he would have been happy to have supervised his football in an empty stadium without the intrusion of a crowd or the media. Football to Ron was almost like a game of chess, and he could see depths and subtleties in every match that escaped the notice of all but committed theorists and tacticians.

Our paths crossed at the start and finish of my playing career. He was manager of the England Under-23s when I was a youngster at Chelsea firing my first shots in international football. In those days Ron was very much a disciple of Walter Winterbottom, and he was looked on as one of the brightest coaches in the game. Some eleven years later I made the mistake of signing for Greenwood when he was having an uncomfortable time as manager of West Ham United after a long run of comparative success. I had always promised myself that the moment I stopped enjoying my football I would quickly hang up my boots, and from the start of my only full season with West Ham in 1970–71 I was thoroughly miserable about West Ham's game and my contribution to it. There was a lack of confidence and cohesion in the side, and Greenwood was in danger of losing the rapport that a manager needs with his players.

I will hold up my hands and admit that I did little for West Ham's cause in a season when the threat of relegation was hanging over the club. My appetite for the game had been blunted by nine hard but happy years at Tottenham, and there was nothing happening at Upton Park to reawaken my love for the game. I needed a manager who could relight the fuse for me, but Greenwood was not that man. I suppose Cloughie was one of the few people who could have motivated me, but I had chosen to join West Ham rather than Derby County. Greenwood had taken me as the makeweight in a deal that transported Martin Peters to Tottenham. He wanted me because he remembered the way I banged in goals at my peak and also because it made the loss of Peters look better in the eyes of the Upton Park fans. They were starting to give Greenwood a rough ride after the glory years in which he brought the FA Cup and the European Cup Winners' Cup to West Ham and had produced and polished the great England trio of the 'sixties, Bobby Moore, Geoff Hurst and Martin Peters.

I am now going to dig up the infamous Blackpool Affair, for the only reason that it gave me first-hand – and painful – experience of how Greenwood the manager handled (I would say mishandled) an incident that was blown out of all proportion by the media. These are the true facts: on New Year's Night, 1971, my long-time pal Bobby Moore and I were preparing to go to bed after a couple of lagers each in the restaurant of the Imperial Hotel where West Ham were staying on the eve of a third-round FA Cup tie at Blackpool. As we were walking through the hotel lobby we got into conversation with a BBC television production team who were in town to cover our match. They were waiting for a taxi to take them to ex-boxer Brian London's 007 nightclub. 'There's no chance of the game being played tomorrow', one of them said. 'The pitch is iced over. It will be a miracle if it's fit to play. I think we're all wasting our time up here. What a way to start the New Year.'

Then we were interrupted by the hotel doorman calling to the television crew: 'Your two taxis have arrived.'

'But we only wanted one', said a BBC man. Completely on impulse, I said: 'Don't worry. We'll take the other one.'

Little did I know it but I had set a time-bomb ticking. It would be another seventy-two hours or so before it went off. Mooro, that well-known insomniac, was only too willing to join me and we jauntily walked towards the hotel door, collecting the thirsty Brian Dear and the casually interested Clyde Best on the way. 'We're just nipping down to Brian London's place for a quick nightcap', we told them. Dear came along for the drink; Best came along for the ride.

Two hours later – at about 1.45 a.m. – we were back at the Imperial ordering coffee and sandwiches. It was as stupid, as unprofessional, and as innocent as that. I was the only one who really got stuck into the lagers at the club– these were the early days of what was to become a well-publicized problem for me. But I was totally in control of myself, and there was no way in a million years that I would have relaxed to this extent if I had thought there was a chance of the game being played.

Later that morning, after we had slept through until about ten, we went to the Blackpool ground where a skating rink of a pitch had somehow been passed fit for play. Torvill and Dean might have felt at home on it. We then committed the real 'crime'. We lost to Blackpool. We lost not because of that late-night drink . . . not because of the state of the pitch . . . but simply because we were not good enough. The team lacked any pattern or fighting spirit.

On the Monday a West Ham supporter telephoned the club and a newspaper saying that he had seen us rolling drunk in Brian London's nightclub on the eve of the match. He may have seen us, but we were certainly not drunk. There is one sportswriter I will never forgive for writing a story full of innuendo and demanding that the club 'name and punish the guilty to protect the innocent'.

This was when Ron Greenwood, in my opinion, showed that he was not the manager he was cracked up to be. He should have handled it as an internal matter, but I got the feeling we were being thrown to the wolves. West Ham fined us, dropped us and did it in the full glare of publicity. Greenwood later admitted that he had asked the directors to sack us, but they were too wise to go that far. The story was plastered all over the front pages as if we had been guilty of the crime of the century. We deserved to have disciplinary action taken against us, but it could so easily have been done privately. I was particularly nauseated by the treatment handed out to Bobby Moore after all that he had done for the club. What a way to treat a hero. The only 'favour' they did him was witholding the announcement of our suspensions until the following Thursday. Like me, Ron Greenwood was in on the secret that Bobby was to be 'booked' by Eamonn Andrews on *This Is Your Life* on the Wednesday evening.

It was this stupid Blackpool Affair that persuaded me that I should retire at the end of the season, and even more than twenty years on I am still convinced that Greenwood could have saved a lot of heartache by using more discreet methods of management. So now that I have explained why he is not my favourite manager, I will attempt to give a balanced view of his achievements in club and international football. Despite any biased views that I might have, he can justifiably claim to have had an outstanding career and was always an exceptional advertisement for the game he served so well, both with his behaviour and his knowledge.

Greenwood,
THE MAN AND THE MANAGER

Born in Burnley in 1921, Greenwood spent his early days in a terraced house in the village of Worsthorne close to the outskirts of the Lancashire mill town. In those hungry 'twenties, the Greenwood children wore clogs with iron bars underneath; shoes were only for Sunday-best wear. The Depression hit the Greenwood family hard and they moved to Alperton in Middlesex where his father became a signwriter at Wembley Stadium. Leaving school at fourteen, Ron followed his father as an apprentice sign-writer at Wembley where thirty years later he would have the greatest triumphs of his managerial career. But all the signs were grim for Greenwood at the end of the 'thirties. He had just joined Chelsea after being spotted playing in a local club side when war was declared. His best football-playing years were lost to the Second World War.

Following wartime service in the RAF, during which he played club football with Belfast Celtic and Hull City, he returned to Chelsea who immediately sold him to Bradford Park Avenue for £3,500, while retaining his registration. He was a strong, constructive wing-half at Bradford, but later switched to centre-half. Brentford brought Greenwood back to London where he linked up with a young, jut-jawed player called Jimmy Hill, who was then a forceful wing-half. The half-back line of Harper–Greenwood–Hill was rated one of the best in the League.

The Greenwood–Hill partnership was broken in 1952, with Hill moving to Fulham and Greenwood back to Chelsea where he collected a League championship medal as a member of Ted Drake's title-winning squad of 1954–55 (playing in twenty-one matches with the championship team). He then teamed up with Jimmy Hill again, this time at Fulham. Both were keen coaches and they attended FA courses where they were deeply influenced by the thoughts and theories of England manager Walter Winterbottom. Hill recalled:

Ron was a thinking centre-half who was always constructive. He was a strong, decisive tackler and an inspiring captain. Even in those days he gave tremendous thought to the game, and had great vision. Like the rest of us, he was enormously impressed by the Hungarian performances against England in 1953–54 and he set out to widen his knowledge of the game beyond the boundaries of British football.

With a thirst for knowledge that had not been nearly satisfied, Ron embarked on a course of self-education and people who were to meet him later in life were convinced he was a university graduate. The closest he got was as a coach to the Oxford University team. He also coached Walthamstow Avenue and Eastbourne United, before being appointed assistant manager to George Swindin at Arsenal in 1957. Walter Winterbottom rated him the best young coach in the country, and put him in charge of the England Under-23s and the youth team where he first met a lad called Bobby Moore. 'I had an enormous respect for Ron in those days', Mooro told me. 'He was a walking encyclopaedia on football, not just the domestic game but the world game. He really got through to me, and when I heard he was coming to West Ham in place of Ted Fenton I guessed some great times were ahead for the club.'

I remember those early days when Greenwood was working with Winterbottom and the Under-23 squad. He used to say things like: 'Space is only space so long as you don't run into it.' *Uh, yes, Ron.* 'Space needn't just happen. It can be created.' *Uh, yes, Ron.* 'Good football stems from good habits, from the mastery of the logical principles of the game to such a degree that you do things by instinct.' *Uh, yes, Ron.* 'Football is an attitude of mind.' *Uh, yes, Ron.* It was like listening to an echo of Walter Winterbottom, and at team talks I used to see players with glazed looks in their eyes. I'm talking for the non-tactical breed who liked to play football off the cuff; in fairness to Greenwood there were many footballers who considered him something of a guru.

When he took over as West Ham manager in 1961, Greenwood inherited a playing staff overflowing with talent and he had the skill, knowledge and expertise to mould it into a winning unit. Geoff Hurst said: 'When Ron arrived at Upton Park I was struggling to establish myself as a regular wing-half. He saw my potential as a striker and taught me how the game should be played. There is no finer coach.'

Norman Giller was sports editor of the local newspaper in the early days of Greenwood's reign at Upton Park, and he says he learnt more about the game listening to Greenwood during weekly two-hour meetings than from anybody else he has ever met in football. Norman also used to attend Greenwood's famous after-match talk-ins when Ron would hold court in his Upton Park office while pouring sherry and analyzing the game. He says that he had never met anybody to match Ron for being able to assess and dissect a game, but as Norman was among the football writers who went into print encouraging Alf Ramsey not to select me for the 1966 World Cup final I do not have too much respect for his opinions! I know that Ron got through to many people when talking about the sport that he loves so passionately, but speaking as a player who had to carry out his orders, I have to say that for many footballers he made a simple game seem complicated.

He found willing listeners and learners when he arrived at Upton Park, and reward came in the 1964 FA Cup Final. West Ham came from behind to beat Preston 3–2 at Wembley, a late goal from Ron 'Ticker' Boyce securing what neutral obervers considered a fortunate victory over their Second Division opponents. While his players were sleeping off after-match celebration hangovers, Greenwood was in church with his wife, Lucy, giving his own private thanks for the success. Listen to John Bond, who was the veteran right-back in the Cup-winning team: 'I was proud to be a member of that West Ham side because it put skill and style above all else. It was all down to Ron. He instilled in us all confidence and self-respect. Ron stood for everything that is good about the game.'

Greenwood used to keep his emotions on a tight rein, but 'Budgie' Byrne once caught him in a rare moment with his defences down. He recalled:

> We were on the train home from Sheffield after we had beaten Manchester United in the FA Cup semi-final and the restaurant car was really rocking. Players and supporters were dancing on tables and the champagne was flowing like water. Suddenly, in the middle of all this and out of sight of all but a handful of us, Ron started crying. His eyes filled with tears as if we had just been relegated and he'd been sacked. Mooro and I went to him quietly and asked, 'What's wrong, Ron?' He pointed to the far end of the carriage where our supporters were dancing with the players. 'We've got this far without all these hangers-on', he said. 'We don't need these people.' It was the only time I ever saw Ron so emotional.

A year later West Ham captured the European Cup Winners' Cup by beating Munich 1860 in a classic contest at Wembley. It was rated one of the showpiece matches of the decade with West Ham really putting on the style. Greenwood said: 'If anybody wants to know what my thinking on football is all about then I would like to be judged on this game. It was close to perfection.'

The mid-1960s were glorious days for West Ham in general and for Greenwood in particular, and it reflected on him when England won the World Cup in 1966 with West Hammers Moore, Hurst and Peters playing a prominent part in the triumph. Greenwood's expertise and tactical understanding was acknowledged worldwide, and he was chosen for the prestige job of panellist on the FIFA technical study committee for the 1966 and 1970 World Cup tournaments.

But it was at the bread-and-butter level of League football where

Greenwood found himself struggling, and it was a widespread view among clubs that the Hammers were 'a soft touch' for any team willing to chase, hustle and play with steel. In many ways it is to Greenwood's great credit that he refused to get involved in the muscle-before-method style of football that scarred the game in the late 'sixties, but there were less principled people in the League who saw it as a failure to be competitive.

Greenwood became so disillusioned that in September 1970 he told Mooro and I that he was considering resigning. Mind you, the circumstances in which he made his confession were strange to say the least. We were in the upstairs bar of a Jumbo on the way to New York at the time. West Ham were to play Santos – including Pelé – in an exhibition match in New York. It was laughable really after the exhibition we had made of ourselves at Newcastle two days earlier when we were demolished 4–1. Anyway, Mooro and I plus a business pal of his, Freddie Harrison, were getting stuck into the golden liquid at the bar when Greenwood joined us from downstairs and requested a Coke. It was none of my doing but I must admit to having a supressed juvenile giggle when I noticed Freddie lacing the Coke with Bacardi. Ron was famous in football for being strictly an after-match sherry man, nothing stronger. During the next hour he must have had another five or six Cokes, all of them doctored by the mischievous Harrison, with Mooro and I egging him on with nudges and winks. It was a diabolical thing to do and I shouldn't think Ron ever forgave Mooro and I for it, although we were only onlookers.

Ron finally realized what was going on, and to his credit he laughed it off. The alcohol made his tongue much looser than he would have liked and he confessed that he was thinking of resigning. I felt choked in a way because here was a man who had always done his honest, level best for West Ham and had made them a club renowned throughout Europe for the quality of their football. But he had recently lost his way and I had done absolutely nothing to help him get back on the right path. Ron was a kind, caring and Christian man in the truest sense, and he did not deserve the old-pro cynicism that I brought into his life. Anyway, after our immature prank with the drinks he returned to his seat where he went into a heavy, alcohol-sedated sleep. Peter Eustace, a spirited Yorkshireman who was hardly Ron's number one fan, had the rest of the West Ham party in fits of laughter as he leant over the snoring figure of Greenwood, miming as if he was telling him exactly what he thought of him. I think Ron would have had a fit if he had woken up.

It is almost as if flying brought out resigning tendencies in Greenwood. On the flight home with the England team in the summer of 1981 he told the team that he had resigned. He was sickened by the criticism being aimed at him by the media. The players showed how highly they rated him by persuading him to change his mind, and then they saw to it that the

Football Association did not announce his intention to resign when they landed. It demonstrates how Greenwood was able to win the loyalty of players less cynical than me.

He could certainly never be accused of wearing blinkers when it came to football tactics, and he was always looking to the great international teams and top continental clubs for ideas. I doubt if there has ever been another manager to touch him for knowledge of the game abroad, and throughout his career he was always innovative and continually searching for ways to make improvements. I recall the time he tried to fit the West Ham players with lightweight radio receivers so that he could give them individual instructions during a training match. It was a good idea in theory, but lousy in practice.

Most of the players, me included, found it off-putting to have someone rabbiting in our ear when we were trying to concentrate on the game. We were quick to vote 'Radio Greenwood' a miss, but Ron was keen to give it a proper go because representatives of the radio manufacturers were there to judge how it worked. During the half-time break in our training match several of us were voicing strong opinions that the idea was a flop. Ron was insisting that we persevere when there was a crackling sound on our receivers and they suddenly went dead. Behind us the two radio company reps were holding their heads in anguish. They pointed almost disbelievingly in the direction of Wally the groundsman. He had been cutting the grass on his sit-on mower and had sliced right through the radio wires that ran round the perimeter of the pitch. Radio Greenwood was off the air. We voted Wally 'Groundsman of the Year'.

After a run of mediocre performances by his West Ham team – and not helped by my brief stay at Upton Park – he 'moved upstairs' in 1974 to the passive role of general manager, with John Lyall taking over the running of the team. I believe that one of the main reasons that Greenwood began to lose his grip after those triumphs of the mid-1960s is that he no longer had the total confidence of his skipper Bobby Moore. They were never as close as many people believe, and when I roomed with Mooro during the 1966 World Cup he was quite vicious in his criticism of West Ham because of what he considered was their low wage structure. In fact he was on the verge of a transfer until his magnificent leadership of the World Cup winning team persuaded West Ham that they should meet his terms or risk a crowd riot at Upton Park. What only a handful of us knew was that Mooro would almost certainly have joined me at Tottenham if West Ham had agreed to let him go. I was surprised to find how much ice there was between Greenwood and Moore, and it reached iceberg proportions when Bobby and I were publicly executed over the Blackpool Affair. But all this petty nonsense melted away to nothing when dear old Bobby surrendered to cancer in the winter of 1993, and Ron – always the gentleman – could not have been warmer with his tribute to his old club skipper who served him so well. Time heals old wounds, and I know that Bobby would have been the first to acknowledge that for all his differences with Greenwood he was, at his peak, a marvellous manager; just as Bobby was a marvellous player.

John Lyall remains a Greenwood disciple and after West Ham won the FA Cup in 1975 (against Fulham and Bobby Moore!) and again in 1980 he said:

> When I took over I was determined that West Ham would continue to play the Ron Greenwood way. I owe everything to Ron and rate him one of the best coaches there has ever been in British football. I will always adhere to the principles that he ingrained in me – that football is a game of skill before strength, and all about doing the simple things well.

Greenwood was winding down his career while living peacefully on the south coast when he got the call to help out his country. He had always thought of football in international terms, and considered many people in the English league too insular and parochial in their outlook. For him, managing England was a dream come true. What a pity from his point of view that the call did not come ten years earlier when his work as a track-suit coach was rated highly by all the top tacticians in the game.

Greenwood's Record

During his four and a half years in charge of the England team, Greenwood's record was:

P	W	D	L	F	A
55	33	12	10	93	40

Home international matches only:

	P	W	D	L	F	A
v. Scotland	5	4	0	1	7	2
v. Wales	5	2	2	1	5	5
v. Northern Ireland	6	5	1	0	17	2

International matches played in England against overseas opposition:

P	W	D	L	F	A
16	11	3	2	26	7

International matches played outside England against overseas opposition:

P	W	D	L	F	A
23	11	6	6	38	24

To say that Ron Greenwood and his England team took a roller-coaster ride to the World Cup finals in Spain in 1982 would be an understatement. He surrounded himself with an impressive back-up team including Bill Taylor and his old West Ham stalwart Geoff Hurst as coaches. Bobby Robson and Don Howe were put in charge of the revived 'B' team (Greenwood had won a 'B' international cap when with Chelsea), Dave Sexton and Terry Venables took control of the Under-21 squad with Howard Wilkinson as assistant coach, and, controversially, Brian Clough and Peter Taylor were given responsibility for the youth team that already had a manager in Ken Burton.

On the way to Spain, Greenwood used fifty players but not quite in such a bewildering way as his predecessor Don Revie. He took the calculated gamble of playing to an attacking 4–2–4 formation, with Steve Coppell and Peter Barnes as withdrawn wingers. It paid off in his third and final match as caretaker manager when England hustled Italy to a 2–0 defeat in a World Cup qualifier. All hope of reaching the finals had disappeared with dismal performances in the earlier qualifying games, but this victory at least restored England's pride and it virtually clinched the permanent job for Greenwood.

Even in defeat in the next match against West Germany in Munich, it looked as if Greenwood was on the right lines. The world champions snatched a 2–1 victory with a disputed late winner after trailing to an England team in which Ray Wilkins, Trevor Brooking and Kevin Keegan were outstanding. A 1–1 draw with Brazil was followed with a 1–0 defeat of the Scots that sent 'Ally Macleod's Army' marching off to the World Cup finals in Argentina with something less than a bounce in their stride. Greenwood ended his first season as England supremo with a crushing 4–1 victory over the Hungarians. It was all heartening stuff and there was as yet no hint of the shockwaves that would be felt on the way to Spain.

By trial and error, Greenwood's team gradually took shape. He relied on an orthodox back four, with Dave Watson the kingpin at the heart of the defence. Behind them he could not make up his mind between Ray Clemence and Peter Shilton for the goalkeeping role, and he elected to play them almost on a rota system which I saw as a worrying show of indecision. In midfield he had Ray Wilkins playing a slightly negative role, and Trevor Brooking in a more positive, forward position from where he could link with Kevin Keegan. It was Keegan's buzzing energy that made the England team tick, and he was particularly effective when operating with Bob Latchford as the spearhead. What astonished me was Greenwood's reluctance to use Glenn Hoddle on a regular basis. He was the best passer of the ball in the League, and was a real class player on a par with any other schemer in Europe. His critics claimed that he was a luxury player, who could only perform when the team was on top and that he was unable to tackle. He was the sort of player Greenwood would have loved to have developed in his peak years at West Ham, but as he settled for a more defensive 4–4–2 formation, he continually overlooked Hoddle.

Overcoming the tragic death of coach Bill Taylor, Greenwood met his first target when he guided England to the 1980 European championship finals in Italy, but his team had lost their early impetus and made an early exit after dismal displays against Belgium and Italy. The tabloid press started to snipe at Greenwood, and calls for his head reached a crescendo when England suffered a defeat on a par with the humiliation against the United States in the 1950 World Cup finals. Norway, a team that had never previously conceded less than four goals against England, beat them 2–1 on a 'night of disaster' (as the *Sun* put it) in Oslo on September 9, 1981. It was in a World Cup qualifying match, and the defeat seemed certain to stop England reaching the finals.

England's World Cup campaign had kicked off on September 10, 1980, with a predictable 4–0 victory over the Norwegians at Wembley. This was followed by a 2–1 defeat by Romania in Bucharest, an unimpressive 2–1 home win against Switzerland and then a depressing goalless draw in the return match with the Romanians.

The fear that England were not going to qualify for the finals first surfaced on May 30, 1981 when they were beaten 2–1 by Switzerland in Basle. It was the first victory by the Swiss over England in eleven meetings since 1947. Just three days earlier Liverpool had won the European Cup in Paris, the fifth successive year that an English club had won the premier prize in club football. Everybody was asking the same question: how could a country so dominant in club football perform so poorly on the international stage? Greenwood had tried to come to terms with this early in his reign when he selected seven Liverpool players, but they were unable to knit their club patterns into the England framework.

A week after the setback in Switzerland, unpredictable England produced their finest performance under Greenwood with a surprisingly brilliant 3–1 victory over Hungary in Budapest, where in 1954 Winterbottom's England had hit rock bottom with a 7–1 defeat. Trevor Brooking scored two excellent goals, and Kevin Keegan produced a world class display.

Then came the spirit-shattering débâcle in Norway, and it looked odds-on England missing the finals. 'Whatever happens now is in other people's hands', Greenwood said at what was the lowest point in his long, distinguished football career.

It's the unpredictability of football that helps make it such a compelling game. A month after England's nose-dive in Oslo, Switzerland went to Bucharest and unexpectedly beat the group favourites Romania 2–1. Suddenly England had only to get a point from their final game against Hungary at Wembley to clinch a place in the finals, and they scrambled through thanks to a Paul Mariner goal against one of the most ineffective Hungarian teams I had ever seen.

England's record at the end of 1981 was the poorest of any major European country – just two wins in nine games – but the saving grace for Greenwood is that he had got his team into the World Cup finals. Along the way he had used fifty players, yet he had unearthed only three exciting new talents in Bryan Robson, Kenny Sansom and, almost begrudgingly, Glenn Hoddle.

England started to put some decent results together in the build-up to the finals in 1982 and won five and drew one of six consecutive games while conceding only two goals. Following what seemed some headless-chicken selections, Greenwood at last appeared to have a definite idea what his best side was. The Manchester United trio of Ray Wilkins, Steve Coppell and Bryan Robson brought understanding and cohesion to the midfield, where Graham Rix proved himself a useful deputy for the injury-hit Brooking. Peter Shilton had won the duel for the goalkeeper's jersey, and Terry Butcher had taken over from Dave Watson as the rock in the middle of the defence with Phil Thompson alongside him. Flanking them were an excellent pair of full-backs in Mick Mills and Kenny Sansom. Paul Mariner had emerged as the liveliest of the many candidates for the chief striker's role, with Trevor Francis in support. Kevin Keegan joined Brooking on the injury list, so the two players who had been the most productive for Greenwood went to Spain less than fully fit. Mick Mills took over as skipper, and the influence of Bobby Robson's fine Ipswich team was as important as that provided by Manchester United's key players. A year earlier England had been reduced to almost a laughing stock, but they had pulled themselves together and went into the finals in a mood of quiet confidence.

There was a lot of undisguised resentment that England were considered worthy of being one of the seeded countries following their pathetic performances in the qualifying matches, and they were drawn to play all their games in anglophile Bilbao. Many cynics believed this was a cop-out by the organizers, who wanted to make sure the hooligans among England's supporters were confined to territory where they could be controlled. Yet another bungle by the Football Association was the adoption of 'Bulldog Bobby' as the team's mascot. It captured all too accurately the brutal approach of a mindless minority of England's fans, and the foreign press were not slow to point out the similarities.

But the England players climbed above all the carping and criticism to give Greenwood a dream start to his World Cup challenge. After just twenty-nine seconds of their opening match against France, Robson forced the ball into the net from close range following a throw-in by Coppell that had been headed on by Butcher. It was the fastest goal in the history of the World Cup, and it was just the confidence boost that England needed.

They beat France 3–1, and Greenwood was so impressed (and relieved) that for the next game against Czechoslovakia he kept the same team together for the first time in thirty-three matches. Brooking and Keegan were still fighting for fitness, and they were on the sidelines to see England win 2–0 with two goals in three minutes midway through the second half, the first from Francis and then an own goal. It was England's ninth consecutive match without a defeat – eight of them won – and hopes in the camp were now sky high.

Greenwood was forced to make changes for the third game against Kuwait because of slight injuries to Robson and Sansom. Glen Hoddle and Phil Neal were the replacements, with Steve Foster taking over from Terry Butcher in the middle of the defence to save the Ipswich centre-half from the risk of a second yellow card. Francis scored the only goal of an easily forgettable match, and so England had stretched their winning unbeaten run to ten games and joined Brazil as the only other team in the tournament to qualify for the second stage of the finals with maximum points.

Kevin Keegan had flown from Bilbao to a specialist in Hamburg for treatment to his recurring back injury, but he was still not fit for the vital second-stage game against West Germany. Robson and Sansom were both fully recovered, and so Greenwood reverted to the 4–4–2 formation that had served him so well against France and Czechoslovakia.

The Germans had been struggling to get into any sort of rhythm in the tournament, and they played a totally negative game. I agreed with Pelé's assessment of West Germany: 'They are fielding Karl-Heinz Rummenigge and ten robots.'

It was Rummenigge who went closest to breaking the deadlock in a generally dull goalless draw with a 25-yard shot four minutes from the end that shook the England crossbar. When you think of the classics that England and West Germany have been involved in, this match was a disappointing anti-climax. I thought England played reasonably well considering that the Germans clearly had a draw in their minds from the moment they stepped on to the pitch. Bryan Robson was England's most inspiring player, and his nineteenth-minute header deserved the reward of a goal which was denied him by a fine save from Schumacher.

England had to beat the host nation Spain by two clear goals to overtake West Germany and earn a place in the semi-finals. Judging both teams on their performances in the finals to date it was a target well within their sights, but England became gripped by tension in front of goal and failed to function at anything approaching their best. With twenty-seven minutes of a goalless stalemate left, Greenwood took a gamble by sending on the fit-again partners Keegan and Brooking, who had been expected to play such a major role in England's World Cup campaign. Keegan had hardly broken sweat when the best chance of the match fell to him, and England's spirits dropped when he headed wide with a gaping net facing him. He was honest enough afterwards to admit, 'No excuses. I should have buried it.'

The game finished without any goals, and England went out of the World Cup an unbeaten and unhappy team. Greenwood deserved a better farewell. The day before the match against West Germany Bobby Robson had been named as his successor.

Greenwood departed with the satisfaction of having led England to within shooting distance of the World Cup semi-finals. The misery of that nightmare defeat in Norway had been erased.

Greenwood's Players

These were the fifty players selected by Greenwood during his fifty-five international matches as England team manager:

Viv Anderson (Nottingham Forest: 10)

Dave Armstrong (Middlesbrough, 1)

Peter Barnes (Manchester City/West Bromwich/Leeds: 22)

Kevin Beattie (Ipswich: 1)

Gary Birtles (Nottingham Forest: 3)

Trevor Brooking (West Ham: 34)

Terry Butcher (Ipswich: 8)

Mike Channon (Manchester City: 1)

Trevor Cherry (Leeds: 15)

Ray Clemence (Liverpool: 29)

Steve Coppell (Manchester Utd: 40)

Joe Corrigan (Manchester City: 7)

Laurie Cunningham (West Bromwich/Real Madrid: 6)

Tony Currie (Leeds: 10)

Alan Devonshire (West Ham: 4)

Trevor Francis (Birmingham/Nottingham Forest/Manchester City: 28)

Eric Gates (Ipswich: 2)

Paul Goddard (West Ham: 1)

Brian Greenhoff (Manchester Utd/Leeds: 6)

Gordon Hill (Manchester Utd: 2)

Glenn Hoddle (Tottenham: 13)

Emlyn Hughes (Liverpool/Wolverhampton: 15)

David Johnson (Liverpool: 5)

Kevin Keegan (Hamburg/Southampton: 31)

Ray Kennedy (Liverpool: 8)

Frank Lampard (West Ham: 1)

Bob Latchford (Everton: 12)

Terry McDermott (Liverpool: 25)

Paul Mariner (Ipswich: 24)

Alvin Martin (West Ham: 4)

Mick Mills (Ipswich: 29)

Tony Morley (Aston Villa: 4)

Phil Neal (Liverpool: 32)

Russell Osman (Ipswich: 6)

Stuart Pearson (Manchester Utd: 3)

Steve Perryman (Tottenham: 1)

Phil Thompson (Liverpool: 32)

Kevin Reeves (Norwich/
   Manchester City: 2)
Cyrille Regis (West Bromwich: 3)
Graham Rix (Arsenal: 13)
Bryan Robson (West
   Bromwich/Manchester Utd: 23)

Kenny Sansom (Crystal Palace,
   Arsenal: 27)
Peter Shilton (Nottingham
   Forest: 19)
Brian Talbot (Arsenal: 1)

Dave Watson (Manchester
   City/Werder Bremen,
   Southampton, Stoke: 40)
Trevor Whymark (Ipswich: 1)
Ray Wilkins (Chelsea/
   Manchester Utd: 45)
Peter Withe (Aston Villa: 6)
Tony Woodcock (Nottingham
   Forest/Cologne: 24)

The most capped players during Greenwood's reign, including appearances as substitutes, were Ray Wilkins (45), Steve Coppell (40), Dave Watson (40), Trevor Brooking (34), Phil Neal (32), Phil Thompson (32), Kevin Keegan (31), Ray Clemence (29), Mick Mills (29), Kenny Sansom (29), Trevor Francis (28), Terry McDermott (25), Paul Mariner (24), Tony Woodcock (24), Bryan Robson (23).

Apart from the devastatingly bad patch in the middle, Greenwood's career as England manager was one of which he could justifiably be proud. He was always a champion of decency, sportsmanship and positive, attractive football. After the disgrace of Revie's departure he brought dignity back to the number one job. If his chance had come ten years earlier, he might have proved himself the greatest England manager of them all. He gave Bobby Robson a tough act to follow.

CHAPTER SIX

Bobby Robson
(1982–1990)

NOT SUCH
A PLONKER

Bobby Robson rode more storms than a round-the-world yachtsman on his way to finally winning respect as one of England's finest managers. When his eventful voyage ended with a semi-final place in the 1990 World Cup, the England football team was in its best shape for more than twenty years but there had been several times when he had looked certain to hit the rocks.

The use of nautical metaphors is deliberate. Robson once told me how he had sailed to the United States with Fulham when he was a young player, and he said that the Atlantic had been so rough that everybody on board had been sea-sick. Everybody except Robson. He showed the same equilibrium when the tabloid press set out to sink him.

First of all he survived a vicious head-hunting attack by the tabloid press in general and, in particular, the *Sun*, who made no secret that Brian Clough was the man they had wanted to see in the England manager's chair. They issued readers with 'Robson Out – Clough In' badges, held phone-in polls in a bid to prove that he was about as popular as rabies, and made sweeping criticisms of his selections and his playing tactics. He had to wake up to headlines like PLONKER!, and IN THE NAME OF GOD GO! Then, after a 1–1 draw with Saudi Arabia in Riyadh, the head-line screamed IN THE NAME OF ALLAH GO!

The campaign gradually ran out of steam as England started to put together some impressive results under Robson's enthusiastic leadership, and he was comfortably on his way into the 1990 World Cup finals when a crisis of his own making brought new calls for his dismissal. His private and public lives became entangled when not one, but two redheads went into print with lurid details of extra-marital affairs they claimed to have had with the England manager. Many people considered that Robson had made his job untenable because the role of England manager demands a whiter-than-white image if he is to command the full respect and discipline of his players. For once, the Football Association showed common sense and, by their standards, a remarkably understanding attitude. Bert Millichip, the seventy-five-year-old FA chairman, and Dick Wragg, the seventy-eight-year-old chairman of the international committee, both came out in support of Robson, and he survived another pounding from the press. The grandads who run our game accepted that what Robson did in private was his business and nobody else's. I have been fierce with my criticism of the Football Association in previous pages, but for this charitable decision they deserved applause. Millichip and Robson had known each other for years. Bert – later knighted for his services to football – was the solicitor who did the conveyancing for Robson and his wife, Elsie, when they bought their first house while he was a player with West Bromwich Albion in 1958. Millichip later became chairman of West Brom, the club that parted with their manager Vic Buckingham after he had been cited in a divorce action in 1959. Not long after, Bobby and I became England team-mates and good buddies, and I remember that the 'Vic Buckingham scandal' was still the gossip of the village world of football. Bobby's hanky-panky thirty years later became the talk of the nation.

I had selfish reasons for wanting Robson to be as successful as possible in his role as England manager. After we had played together in the 9–0 defeat of Luxemburg in 1960 he and I drank a glass or three in celebration. Our conversation got on to the subject of money, and he insisted in that persistent Geordie way of his that I would earn more out of the game than he would. I made him put it in writing, and I still have the piece of paper on which he pledged to swap bank balances with me if he earned more out of football than I did. The time is about right for me to swap my overdraft with his bank balance! You will gather from this anecdote that I am fond of Robson, but I will not let our old friendship get in the way of the facts about what was his occasionally confused time as England manager.

My concern when he was given the job was that he was not decisive enough, and my choice at the time would have been Brian Clough. I described Robson as the type who would dither over whether to choose brown or red sauce, but he quickly shot me down with his first major decision as England manager. He decided not to consider Kevin Keegan for his squad. This was certainly not the action of a ditherer because Keegan had twice been voted European Footballer of the Year and was a key man in the England teams of Joe Mercer, Don Revie and Ron Greenwood.

Robson, not for the first or last time, was dragged into a controversy when Keegan made it public that he was disgusted that he had to learn that his sixty-three-cap England career was over by reading about it in the newspapers. I did not blame Robson, who had his hands full with his new job. The fault lay with the FA, who should have detailed somebody to let Keegan know quietly what was about to happen before the media made a meal of it. I was surprised that Keegan expected any different treatment to all his predecessors who had been proud to wear the shirt of England, and I would have thought that he had learned over the years that the FA does not have a heart. By their standards, Keegan did not deserve the courtesy of a telephone call to tell him that his England days were numbered. I had seen it happen time and again. Bobby Charlton, Bobby Moore and Ray Wilson come easily to mind as world-class players who did not receive a telephone call or a letter when their time had come to be put out to pasture.

I recall a fine England player of the 1950s getting the axe without warning on the eve of the 1962 World Cup finals to make way for a young- ster called Bobby Moore. Nobody thanked him for his past services. His name was Bobby Robson, and so he knew just how Keegan must have been feeling after the way he himself had been treated.

When Robson returned home to Geordieland to watch Newcastle play a few weeks after he had dropped Keegan, he told me that he was abused, threatened and spat at. It was the sort of treatment he would get used to as England manager.

Robson,
THE MAN AND THE MANAGER

Born in a coal-miner's terraced cottage in the small County Durham village of Sacriston in 1933, Robson was six months old when his family moved to a similar National Coal Board-owned cottage in nearby Langley Park, where he grew up in a large, close-knit mining community. Bobby used to tell me with a mixture of pride and pity how his father had missed only one shift during more than fifty years working down the pits. Robson, one of five brothers, was determined not to follow his dad down the mines and he saw football as his escape route.

He looked trapped in the mining traditions when he left school at fifteen and became an apprentice electrician at the local colliery, but all his thoughts and dreams were about the world of football. Even at Langley Park Infants School, when instructed to write an essay entitled 'What I would like to be when I grow up', he had written about how he would one day be a professional footballer. His father was continually having to repair his shoes after kick-about street matches, and he became the star player for Langley Park Juniors. His dream was to play for Newcastle United alongside boyhood heroes Len Shackleton, Jackie Milburn and Albert Stubbins. But it was Southampton who came calling after Middlesbrough had shown only lukewarm interest in him. He had a one-month trial down on the south coast with Southampton, but never even got to meet their manager David Jack before being sent home without the hint of an offer. In those days, professional clubs could not sign a player until he was seventeen, and when Robson returned to Langley Park shortly after his birthday in 1950 he found a queue of clubs jostling for his signature, including Newcastle, Middlesbrough, Lincoln City, York City, Blackpool, Huddersfield and far-away Fulham. His first impulse was to join Newcastle, but it was pointed out to him that few local players made it into the first team because the club had a policy of buying stars from other clubs.

On the advice of Bill Rochford, an old pro who was winding down his career with Colchester, he accepted the Fulham offer. 'They are a friendly club and their manager Bill Dodgin and general manager Frank Osborne will care about you both on and off the pitch', Rochford told him.

His parents would only agree to him moving to London on the understanding that he continued his apprenticeship as an electrician. He combined his football with working on the Festival of Britain development with a Victoria-based electrical company, but he was soon lighting up the Craven Cottage stage with his skill and style. Robson formed a magnificent inside-forward trio with Bedford Jezzard and the pass master Johnny Haynes during what he looks back on fondly as among his happiest days in the game. Football was fun at Fulham where chairman Tommy Trinder was by no means the only comedian. You could count on a laugh when playing against Fulham, although the humour was not always intended. I remember one League match when their goalkeeper, Tony Macedo, kept bouncing the ball around the penalty area as if he was playing for the Harlem Globetrotters, then he would mime as if to throw the ball to an opponent before kicking it to a team-mate. He meant to pretend to throw the ball to me but it slipped out of his hand and went straight to my feet. Skipper Johnny Haynes called Macedo something more than a 'silly basket' as I whacked the ball back past him into the net. Then there was the famous incident when Haynes sent a perfect pass to his wing partner and best mate, Tosh Chamberlain, who failed to control the ball. 'You stupid f——— c——,' shouted Haynes, who had no patience with any player who did not match his perfectionist standards (which meant he had no patience with virtually any other player at Fulham!). As the referee booked Haynes for swearing, Tosh, one of the game's great characters, came to his defence. 'But ref', he pleaded, 'he can call me a stupid c———. I'm on his side... and I *am* a stupid f——— c—-!'

These were happy, carefree days for Robson, but it was also a frustrating time because with all the talent Fulham had at Craven Cottage they should have picked up a few prizes instead of always being among the also-rans. The Haynes–Jezzard–Robson partnership was finally broken in 1956 when hard-up Fulham sold Robson to West Bromwich Albion for

£25,000. Equally at home in midfield or as a front-line goal scorer, he became a key man for Albion in another trio, this time with the gifted Ronnie Allen and the bulldozing Derek Kevan as his partners. (We used to tell big Kev to his face that he was built like a tank but turned slower!) They collected seventy-seven goals between them in the 1958–59 season, Robson's twenty-eight goal contribution coming from a position as an attacking midfield player. In the previous season he had scored two goals for England in his début against France, the first of twenty caps, all but one of which were won in harness with his old Fulham partner Haynes. The pair of them had something in common in that they had each got out of giving up two years to National Service because of ear problems diagnosed by the Fulham club doctor. 'Pardon?' I hear you say. The then Fulham chairman Tommy Trinder, one of the most popular of all postwar comedians, said: 'They're never deaf when I ask them if they want a rise.'

Robson's first five appearances for England were as an out-and-out goal hunter in the number eight shirt that I was to inherit, but after two years in the wilderness he was recalled in 1960 as a vital cog alongside Haynes in midfield when England switched to a 4–2–4 formation. He was unlucky to lose his place on the eve of the 1962 World Cup to Bobby Moore, who was just setting out on his great international career. Mooro was a much better defender, but not nearly as effective an attacking player. If you could have got a mix of the two Bobbys, you would have had one of the most dominating players of all time (something on the lines of Duncan Edwards!).

While at West Brom, Robson and his team-mate Don Howe used to travel south to join his old Fulham colleagues Ron Greenwood and Jimmy Hill at coaching sessions set up by England manager Walter Winterbottom. He was laying the foundation to a career as a manager-coach that was to get off to a disastrous start.

Following a dispute with West Brom over his salary after the lifting of the maximum wage in 1961, he handed the captaincy over to Don Howe and returned to Fulham in 1962 for a fee of £20,000 and a weekly wage of £45 – £15 more than he had been offered by West Brom. Robson had two young sons, Paul and Andrew, to support, and a third, Mark, on the way. That extra fifteen quid a week was needed.

He had not long been back at Fulham when they appointed his old West Brom boss Vic Buckingham as manager. Vic was a highly intelligent, flamboyant and eccentric character, who dressed like a matinée idol and always had a silk handkerchief flowering from his breast pocket. Bobby used to have me doubled up with laughter at his Vic Buckingham stories. The players used to bet on how long his Friday team talk would last, and it was rarely less than an hour and the record was over two hours. One

Walter Winterbottom

A crouching Walter Winterbottom discusses tactics with, left to right, skipper Billy Wright, left-back Roger Byrne and trainer Harold Shepherdson before England's match against France at Wembley in November, 1957. Tragically, it was to be Byrne's last international appearance before his death three months later in the Munich air disaster.

(*Top*) Walter Winterbottom putting the case for the defence as he talks to defenders, left to right, Ron Flowers, Ron Springett, Tony Allen, Ron Clayton and Ken Brown on the eve of England's Home Championship match against Northern Ireland at Wembley in 1959. Brown and Springett made their débuts in a game won 2–1 by England.

(*Above*) It looks as if Walter Winterbottom is putting his hands together in prayer while welcoming new caps Stan Anderson (centre) and Roger Hunt to the England team before the 1962 match against Austria. The long-running Hunt v. Greaves debate was about to start.

Alf Ramsey

(*Top*) Alf Ramsey was a tracksuit manager from day one of his England reign. Here he is (left) joining in an indoor training session with Bobby Tambling (centre) and Maurice Norman (right) before the first best-forgotten match under his banner against France in 1963. England were beaten 5–2.

(*Above*) Even when it came down to organizing a team photograph, Alf Ramsey liked to be completely in charge. You can just spot Jimmy Greaves coming between Alf and Geoff Hurst in this 1966 training squad get-together.

Sir Alf Ramsey with a replica of the prized Jules Rimet trophy that England won in 1966. This picture was taken at a dinner to mark the twentieth anniversary of England's World Cup Final victory over West Germany at Wembley on July 30, 1966.

Joe Mercer

Joe Mercer, who put the smile back on the face of England football when taking over as caretaker manager for seven matches.

Don Revie

Admiral Don Revie pictured soon after taking over as England manager in 1974. The name of the sportswear manufacturers emblazoned across England tracksuits was considered by many in football to be commercialism gone mad.

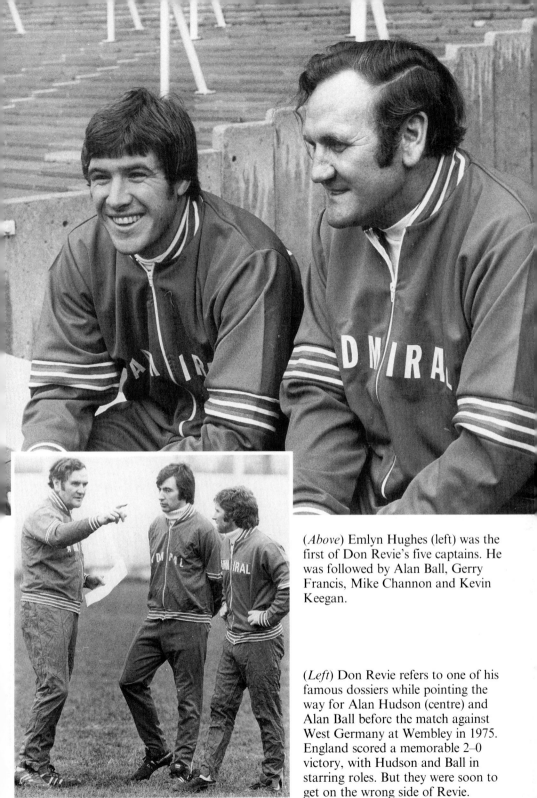

(*Above*) Emlyn Hughes (left) was the first of Don Revie's five captains. He was followed by Alan Ball, Gerry Francis, Mike Channon and Kevin Keegan.

(*Left*) Don Revie refers to one of his famous dossiers while pointing the way for Alan Hudson (centre) and Alan Ball before the match against West Germany at Wembley in 1975. England scored a memorable 2–0 victory, with Hudson and Ball in starring roles. But they were soon to get on the wrong side of Revie.

Kevin Keegan looks close to tears as Don Revie gives a tactical talk before England's World Cup qualifying match against Luxembourg in 1977. It could be captioned 'Cry for me, Argentina' because England did not make it there for the 1978 World Cup finals. Immediately behind Keegan in this picture is coach Bill Taylor, who, sadly, died when working with Ron Greenwood. Everton centre-forward Joe Royle is on the far right.

Don Revie and his faithful right-hand man for club and country, Les Cocker. This picture was taken in June 1977 before the match against Scotland in which England stumbled to their second successive defeat at Wembley. It was the first time England had ever lost consecutive matches at Wembley.

morning the bets had been placed for anything over an hour when Buckingham arrived in the dressing-room. He was humming to himself as he picked up a newspaper, read the back page, looked up and sang, 'Good morning, good morning . . .' and then walked out leaving the players dumbstruck. Another time he told the team, 'Your rhythm is all wrong. I don't want you to attack by going dum-de-dum-de-dum-de-dum and *then* boom! I want you to go dum-dum-de-dum-dum-de-dum-dum and then boom!' Robson has acknowledged that he learnt a lot about management from Buckingham:

> He was a very imaginative man who was a master at taking the pressure off players, and this was a valuable lesson for me. But I also learnt from him that it does not pay to be cruel to players. I remember him once humiliating Rodney Marsh when he was a youngster at Fulham who prided himself on his ball-juggling tricks. He walked into a team meeting and Vic said to him, 'You're nothing but a f———— clown. Piss off.' That stuck with me, and I decided I would never belittle players in front of team-mates if ever I became a manager.

It was Robson who found himself belittled when he first tried his hand at management, with two traumatic experiences. The first was a farce that could have come out of a Monty Python sketch. At the end of his playing career in 1967 he accepted the job of manager of Vancouver Royals in the new North American Soccer League rather than the offer of a managership without the safety net of a contract at his old club, West Bromwich. He moved out to Canada lock, stock and barrel only to find the club on the brink of bankruptcy. The Royals were merged with a team from San Francisco coached by the old Hungarian master Ferenc Puskas, and there was a tug of war over whether he or Robson would be the manager. Bobby had to join Puskas in Madrid where they pooled the players each of them had bought and then tried to make a single team out of them. As Puskas did not speak a word of English, there was a total communications breakdown and Robson was just about to sue for breach of contract when he got an offer he could not resist – to return to Fulham as manager in place of the sacked Vic Buckingham. He never did get his money from the Canadians, and he looks back on the episode as the biggest of several nightmares in his see-sawing football career.

After this false start in Canada, Robson got his managerial career under way at Fulham in January 1968, and lasted just nine months in the job before being booted out. Fulham were bottom of the First Division when he took over and still bottom when they were relegated at the end of the season. A wealthy property developer called Sir Eric Miller joined the Fulham board, and he started interfering in Robson's plans for the team. To give you some idea of what sort of man Miller was, he once got so irritated standing in a queue for a London taxi that he announced that he would buy – yes, buy – the next one that came along. And he did! He put it in his garage along with his Ferrari and Lamborghini. Robson resisted when Miller tried to get him to adopt a similar see-a-player-buy-him approach, and there was a plot concocted behind his back to replace him with Johnny Haynes (who did not really want the job and quit after just one month). Robson read in a newspaper that he was about to be fired in September 1968, and he told me unashamedly that when the news was confirmed he went out on to the deserted Craven Cottage pitch where he had first played as a seventeen-year-old kid and cried his eyes out. Some time later, Sir Eric Miller, with his property empire collapsing, shot himself.

The Vancouver and Fulham experiences were harrowing enough to have put most people off football management for life, but Robson still had deep belief in himself and after three months out of work he was rescued from the dole queue when his old chum Dave Sexton gave him a scouting mission for Chelsea. His first assignment was at Ipswich, who had just lost manager Bill McGarry to Wolves. Robson got such a friendly reception in the Ipswich boardroom that he decided to apply for the job, and was put in charge at Portman Road in January 1969, exactly a year after the start of his unhappy run with Fulham. But Bobby did not get such a friendly reception in the dressing-room and literally had to fight for control. Understandably, he was less than delighted when one of the veteran players he had inherited ordered champagne to celebrate an Ipswich defeat. There was a three-way fist-fight in the dressing-room when another player tore up Robson's team sheet, and as punches flew Bobby had to be pulled away while he was giving as good as he got. Both players involved in the fight were quickly sold, and just as Robson was feeling as if he was getting on top of the job George Best tore the Ipswich defence apart in a League Cup tie at Portman Road. The Ipswich fans were not prepared to accept that it was the brilliance of Best that had been the reason for the defeat, and they started chanting 'Robson out'. It was the sort of demonstratrion never before witnessed at the friendly Suffolk club.

He feared the worse when he was summoned to a board meeting the next day, and could hardly believe his ears when chairman John Cobbold opened up by saying: 'In the presence of our esteemed manager, I would like to make it a matter of record that this board apologises to him for the behaviour of a noisy minority of our fans last night.'

The meeting ended with the board giving him the go-ahead to spend £90,000 on Blackburn Rovers centre-half Allan Hunter. It was the turning point for Robson. He played Hunter alongside a powerful youngster from the north-east called Kevin Beattie, and they developed into the best centre-back partners in the League. After his difficult start, Robson gradually turned the East Anglian club into one of the most respected in Europe with football that was a delight to the eye and a great advertisement for his coaching ability.

Like Alf Ramsey before him, Robson was lucky to have the enthusiastic support of chairman John Cobbold and, later, his brother Patrick. The Cobbold brothers closed ranks and protected their manager when he came under attack for an angry quote that got wide publicity after hooligans had disrupted an Ipswich FA Cup tie at Millwall in March 1978. Robson said off the record – or so he thought – that if he had his way he would turn flame-throwers on the hooligans who were a growing cancer in the game. Jimmy Hill, his old Fulham team-mate, innocently reported the quote on BBC television, and suddenly it was Robson rather than the hooligans who was on the receiving end of a chorus of criticism.

Robson rode the storm, and at the end of that season led out Ipswich at Wembley where they pulled off a shock victory over Arsenal in the FA Cup Final. It was a remarkable performance by a club working on a tiny budget compared with most of their rivals in the First Division.

In his thirteen years at Ipswich, Robson bought only fourteen players for a little over £1 million while bringing £2.5 million into the club by his sales. He showed imagination by nipping across the North Sea to shop in Holland, and in Franz Thijssen and Arnold Muhren he came back with two highly skilled midfield masters who gave Ipswich a new dimension.

His success on a shoestring brought him to the attention of a cluster of chairmen, and he had approaches from nine clubs including Derby, Leeds, Newcastle, Manchester United, Everton and Sunderland and there were also mega-money offers from Bilbao and Barcelona. He turned each of them down, and it was whispered in the village world of football that he was frightened of the challenge of a big club. His loyalty to Ipswich was rewarded with a ten-year contract. 'The only way Bobby Robson would leave Ipswich with our blessing is for the job of England manager,' said Patrick Cobbold.

The words came back to haunt him when for the second time the Suffolk club were asked by the Football Association for the release of their manager. Ipswich had gone close to the elusive treble of League championship, FA Cup and UEFA Cup in 1981, finally having to settle for the UEFA Cup. They were runners-up in the First Division for a second successive year in 1982, and two months later – during the World Cup finals in Spain – Robson agreed to follow the same path as Alf Ramsey into the England manager's job. He was chosen ahead of 'the people's favourite' Brian Clough as successor to Ron Greenwood with whom he had been working closely in a coaching capacity for the England 'B' team. Robson, the man they said was frightened of the big challenges, had taken on the biggest of them all.

Robson's Record

During his eight years years in charge of the England team, Robson's record was:

P	W	D	L	F	A
95	47	30*	18	154	60

Home international matches only:

	P	W	D	L	F	A
v. Scotland	7	4	2	1	8	3
v. Wales	2	1	0	1	2	2
v. Northern Ireland	6	4	2	0	7	0

International matches played in England against overseas opposition:

P	W	D	L	F	A
27	15	8	4	58	16

International matches played outside England against overseas opposition:

P	W	D	L	F	A
53	23	18*	12	79	39

World Cup finals matches:

P	W	D	L	F	A
12	5	4*	3	15	9

*Draws include England's 1990 World Cup semi-final against West Germany which ended at 1–1 after extra time before Germany won 4–3 on penalties.

Robson's international reputation as an outstanding England manager was built on two bold challenges for the ultimate prize of the World Cup, but there were moments in between when the media presented him as as a clown and when he found himself reviled by many fans. It was a depressing time for the game when out-of-control hooligans were showing that Bobby's flame-thrower solution was perhaps not such a bad idea after all.

He was jeered and spat at in Newcastle after electing to build for the future without Kevin Keegan in his team, and he got the same treatment after a disastrous defeat by Denmark in a European Championship match at Wembley on September 21, 1983. At the time, Robson described it as 'the blackest day of my life'. More misery followed when a 2–0 defeat by Russia at Wembley in his twentieth match in charge on June 2, 1984 was greeted by a 'Robson out' demonstration. As he made the long, lonely walk back to the dressing-room he was showered with spit and lager from the louts who were doing so much damage to the reputation of English football.

Nobody could have blamed Robson if he had quit there and then, as the tabloids suggested he should in a no-holds-barred attack that could not have been more vicious had he been a mass murderer. The *Sun* led the way with a strident pro-Clough campaign. His predecessors had all taken heavy criticism from the press, but with Robson it reached an unacceptable personal level that was later repeated when Graham Taylor was the target of spiteful campaigns. What Robson found hardest of all to take was the bombardment that came his way from a legion of former professional footballers and managers who were getting paid for their opinions in the media. I was one of those dishing out heavy comments, but I like to think I was constructive with my criticism and both Ian St John and I went out of our way to show our support for Robson and his players on the way to the World Cup finals of 1986 and 1990. What hurt Robson most of all were the attacks that came from Brian Clough, Emlyn Hughes and, of all people, Sir Alf Ramsey. They were still neighbours in Ipswich but hardly on nodding terms after Alf had ripped into Robson's England team selections. 'I just can't understand why Alf is being so brutal', Bobby told me off-camera during a visit to the *Saint and Greavsie* television studio. 'He's been in my shoes and knows all the problems. I wonder how he would have felt if Walter Winterbottom had gone into print with the same sort of criticism of him?'

The defeat by Russia was England's sixth loss under Robson and the least successful start by any England manager. It would have been easy for him to walk out on a job that had become a nightmare because Barcelona were still keen to have him as their manager, and they were ready to pay him three times his £60,000 FA salary.

But to the amazement of his critics and the admiration of his supporters, including me, he showed he had the guts to stick it out, and he was rewarded in his twenty-first game with an encouraging sign that he was at last getting a formidable team together. Everybody predicted that it would be lambs to the slaughter as he sent an experimental side into the daunting atmosphere of the Maracana Stadium in Rio where only two visiting sides had ever got the better of Brazil. He dug back into his past and revived the 4–2–4 formation that Brazil had given to the world in 1958 and which England had copied with great success when Robson was the midfield partner to Johnny Haynes. That was back in the summertime of our playing careers when he and Johnny provided me with the passes from which I gratefully scored several of my England goals. The bold approach in Brazil – some called it mad – meant playing two wingers in the untried and untested Mark Chamberlain and John Barnes. Just before half-time nineteen-year-old Watford winger Barnes set off on the sort of twisting, turning run that was a Brazilian copyright. He finished his magical mystery tour by steering the ball into the net for as spectacular a goal as ever witnessed at the home of such footballing gods as Pelé and Garrincha.

This incredible goal inspired England to a stunning 2–0 victory, and suddenly things were looking brighter for Robson. He knew that in Peter Shilton, Kenny Sansom, Ray Wilkins, Bryan Robson, Mark Hateley and the untapped Barnes he had the nucleus of an exceptional team, and there was the added bonus that waiting for selection back home in England were players of the calibre of Terry Butcher, Glenn Hoddle, Trevor Francis, Peter Beardsley, Chris Waddle and a young striker by the name of Gary Lineker.

Apart from his on-going struggle to get the media on his side, Robson was weighed down with two other burdens. He found several managers less than helpful when it came to the release of players. 'They pay lip service by saying for public consumption that country should come before club', he confided. 'But several are stabbing me in the back by being quietly obstructive.' The other burden was the escalating problem of hooliganism, and when English clubs were banned from Europe following the 1985 Heysel Stadium tragedy it was the England football team that suffered. Players no longer had European cup matches in which to sharpen their skills and tactical knowledge, and there is no question that the standard of play in English club football went into a decline.

Yet for all this, Robson – with Don Howe and Dave Sexton in support – managed to steer England into the 1986 World Cup finals in Mexico where the infamous handball goal by Maradona prevented them reaching the semi-finals. Highlights of each match are given in Part Two, but even Robson's fiercest critics had to concede that England had exceeded expectations. In six-goal Gary Lineker he had developed a world-class striker, and if skipper Bryan Robson had not been knocked out of action by his recurring shoulder injury England might easily have reached the Final.

Robson built on the foundation that he had laid in Mexico, and apart from a shot-shy performance against Russia in the 1988 European championships England moved with confidence into their 1990 World Cup campaign. They reached the finals in Italy by winning three and drawing three of their six qualifying matches during a run of seventeen matches without defeat.

England were the only finalists not to concede a single goal in the qualifying rounds, and they scored ten themselves. Yet they were still trying to shoot the manager. I remember talking to Bobby after the press had given him a real mauling following a goalless draw against Poland that clinched a place in the World Cup finals. 'You'd think we had failed to qualify for the World Cup', he said.

> Much of the criticism of the team is destructive for the sake of it. They are trying to sell papers off our backs by being as sensational as possible. It's a disgrace, and I don't know how some of the people putting the rubbish in

their papers can live with themselves. They know that what they're writing is not the truth. One reporter has described our players as donkeys. That's an insult to professional footballers who are doing their best for their country. They have got us through to the World Cup finals, and I'll tell you this – they will be really hard to beat in Italy. Just you wait and see.

Robson survived more calls for his head after his personal life had been dragged through the sewer when two red-headed ladies went into lurid details of affairs they alleged to have had with the England manager. He looked to have aged twenty years in the eight years that he reigned as England manager, and clearly all the grey hairs that had sprouted were not because of the demands of the job alone.

On the eve of the World Cup finals, he at last bowed to Fleet Street pressure when he announced that he had accepted a job in Holland with PSV Eindhoven. He would start with them the moment England's World Cup challenge was over. I shared the views of those who considered that the timing of Robson's announcement was not conducive to the England team spirit, but after the way he had been kicked around by the tabloids who could blame him for wanting it made public that he had arranged his own escape and with the reward of a £200,000-a-year contract.

Robson had the last laugh on all his critics as he guided England through to the semi-finals where it took a penalty shoot-out before they were beaten by eventual champions Germany. England officially finished fourth in the tournament , but they were first in the eyes of many for the spirit in which they played the game. The winners of the 'Fair Play' award, they functioned throughout the finals with honest endeavour, and when they found their rhythm following a disjointed opening match against the Republic of Ireland they produced some of the most eye-catching of all the football played. It was a tremendous advertisement for all that Robson believed in, and he had the satisfaction of having unearthed exceptional prospects of the class of Paul Gascoigne, David Platt, Des Walker and Paul Parker to leave to his successor Graham Taylor.

Robson's Players

These were the eighty-six players selected by Robson during his ninety-five international matches as England team manager:

Tony Adams (Arsenal: 17)

Clive Allen (QPR/Tottenham: 5)

Viv Anderson
(Nottingham Forest/Arsenal/
   Manchester Utd: 20)

David Armstrong (Southampton: 2)

Gary Bailey (Manchester Utd: 2)
Mark Barham (Norwich: 2)
John Barnes (Watford/Liverpool: 58)

Peter Beardsley (Newcastle/
  Liverpool: 45)
Dave Beasant (Chelsea: 2)
Luther Blissett (Watford: 14)
Paul Bracewell (Everton: 3)
Steve Bull (Wolverhampton: 11)
Terry Butcher (Ipswich/Rangers: 69)

Mark Chamberlain (Stoke: 8)
Ray Clemence (Tottenham: 2)
Nigel Clough (Nottingham
  Forest: 1)
Steve Coppell (Manchester Utd: 2)
Tony Cottee (West Ham/Everton: 7)
Gordon Cowans (Aston Villa: 9)

Peter Davenport (Nottingham
  Forest: 1)
Alan Devonshire (West Ham: 4)
Kerry Dixon (Chelsea: 8)
Lee Dixon (Arsenal: 1)
Tony Dorigo (Chelsea: 4)
Mike Duxbury
  (Manchester Utd: 10)

John Fashanu (Wimbledon: 2)
Terry Fenwick (QPR/
  Tottenham: 20)
Trevor Francis (Sampdoria: 20)

Paul Gascoigne (Tottenham: 17)
John Gregory (QPR: 6)

Mick Harford (Luton: 2)
Mark Hateley
  (Portsmouth/Milan/Monaco: 31)
Ricky Hill (Luton: 3)
Glenn Hoddle (Tottenham/
  Monaco: 40)
Steve Hodge (Aston Villa/
  Tottenham/Nottingham
  Forest: 22)
Steve Hunt (West Bromwich: 2)

Alan Kennedy (Liverpool: 2)
Sammy Lee (Liverpool: 14)
Gary Lineker (Leicester/Everton/
  Barcelona/Tottenham: 58)

Steve McMahon (Liverpool: 16)
Gary Mabbutt (Tottenham: 13)
Paul Mariner (Ipswich/Arsenal: 9)
Alvin Martin (West Ham: 13)
Brian Marwood (Arsenal: 1)
Tony Morley (Aston Villa: 2)

Phil Neal (Liverpool: 11)

Russell Osman (Ipswich: 5)

Gary Pallister (Middlesbrough: 2)
Paul Parker (QPR: 11)
Stuart Pearce (Nottingham
  Forest: 30)
Mike Phelan (Manchester Utd: 1)
Nick Pickering (Sunderland: 1)
David Platt (Aston Villa: 11)

Cyrille Regis (West Bromwich/
  Coventry: 2)
Peter Reid (Everton: 13)
Graham Rix (Arsenal: 4)
Graham Roberts (Tottenham: 6)
Bryan Robson (Manchester Utd: 65)
David Rocastle (Arsenal: 11)

Kenny Sansom (Arsenal: 59)
David Seaman (QPR: 3)
Peter Shilton (Southampton/
  Derby: 83)
Alan Smith (Arsenal: 4)
Nigel Spink (Aston Villa: 1)
Derek Statham (West Bromwich: 3)
Brian Stein (Luton: 1)
Mel Sterland (Sheffield
  Wednesday: 1)
Trevor Steven (Everton/Rangers: 29)

Gary Stevens (Tottenham: 7)

Gary Stevens (Everton/Rangers: 41)

Danny Thomas (Coventry: 2)

Michael Thomas (Arsenal: 2)

Phil Thompson (Liverpool: 2)

Chris Waddle (Newcastle/ Tottenham/ Marseille: 59)

Des Walker (Nottingham Forest: 25)

Danny Wallace (Southampton: 1)

Paul Walsh (Luton: 3)

Dave Watson (Norwich/Everton: 12)

Neil Webb (Nottingham Forest/ Manchester Utd: 20)

Ray Wilkins (Manchester Utd/ AC Milan: 32)

Steve Williams (Southampton: 6)

Nigel Winterburn (Arsenal: 1)

Peter Withe (Aston Villa: 5)

Tony Woodcock (Arsenal: 18)

Chris Woods (Norwich/Rangers: 16)

Mark Wright (Southampton/ Derby: 30)

The most capped players during Robson's reign, including appearances as substitutes, were Peter Shilton (83), Terry Butcher (69), Bryan Robson (65), Kenny Sansom (59), Chris Waddle (59), John Barnes (58), Gary Lineker (58), Peter Beardsley (45), Gary Stevens (41), Glenn Hoddle (40), Ray Wilkins (32), Mark Hateley (31), Stuart Pearce (30), Mark Wright (30), Trevor Steven (29).

Sixty-four players won their first caps under Robson, who after laying down the burden of the England job did very nicely for himself as a club manager with Eindhoven and then Sporting Lisbon.

The tabloid press no longer had Robson to kick around like a football. But it did not take them long to make his successor, Graham Taylor, the new target for their spiteful attacks.

CHAPTER SEVEN

Graham Taylor

(1990–)

FASTEST TONGUE
IN THE WEST

G raham Taylor took over not only Bobby Robson's job as England
manager but also his unenviable role as the most abused man in
Britain. The tabloid press allowed him only a brief honeymoon
period in the hot seat before pillorying him with the sort of blistering criticism that would have made a weaker man throw in the towel and look for
a less pressurized way of making a living, such as a steeplejack or Prime
Minister!

Mind you, Taylor did not help himself by considering a spate of curious
and confusing team selections, and I could not believe how naive he was in
continually making comments in public that other managers would have
saved for the privacy of the dressing-room. He has a tongue that runs away
with him, and he could learn from Sir Alf Ramsey that there are times
when it pays to keep quiet. One of his players, whose identity I will protect,
described him to me as having 'the fastest tongue in the west'.

Some of his public pronouncements on players, in particular Gary
Lineker, John Barnes and Paul Gascoigne, have made me wince. I grew
up in a playing era when a manager said one thing to you in the dressing-
room and another – much less explosive and explicit – to the press. Taylor
does not come from this school of caution. He goes on record with
comments that are a delight to the headline-seeking reporters but which
must leave his players agonized and astonished. He is a direct, totally
honest character, but it is a fact of footballing life that there are times in
management when it is wisest to be a little less than honest.

I am having to make my assessment of Taylor's reign as England manager
in the aftermath of England's nightmare defeat by Norway in the World Cup
qualifying match in Oslo on June 2, 1993, whereas with his six predecessors
I have been able to make a judgement based on their complete record in the
job. My brutal verdict has to be that after thirty-three months in the job
Taylor was nowhere near getting a team together that could put action where
his mouth is. His early results were satisfactory without being sensational, but

his first major test – the European championship finals in Sweden – was an unmitigated disaster and brought tabloid-led calls for his head.

Taylor inherited from Bobby Robson an England team at its strongest for two decades, but within two years of taking over he appeared to have weakened rather than strengthened it.

By the time this book is on the shelves I hope Taylor will have proved me totally wrong in my opinion that he is not the right man to be in charge of the England team. I have always been of the view that the England manager should be somebody who has played the game at the highest level, with a strong foundation in international football as a player. Neither Taylor nor his right-hand man Lawrie McMenemy even kicked a ball in the (old) First Division let alone for England, and their first experience of the international game was when they took over the running of the England team.

Both are immensely likeable men with strong personalities, but I feel they are handicapped by not having had even the tiniest taste of international football. It meant that both were learning as they went along from the first day of their appointments by the Football Association. I could name half a dozen people who would have been better qualified for the job. Brian Clough, Terry Venables, Steve Coppell, Kevin Keegan, Gerry Francis and Trevor Francis spring easily to mind. And how did the Football Association allow Jack Charlton to get adopted by the Irish when he had made no secret of his desire to manage the England team?

I feel that a manager with a strong international background is more likely to earn the respect and trust of his players. The game at international level is nothing like club football and a completely different approach is necessary, as Taylor and McMenemy have found out by trial and error.

I know I am repeating myself when I say that I have never tried to disguise my distrust and dislike of coaches, and believe they can shackle gifted, spontaneous players by giving over-detailed instructions that are restrictive. Taylor is a coach through and through, and some of his ideas make me feel uneasy. He was a disciple of the long-ball game when first making a name for himself at Watford, and I sense that he would willingly introduce the big-boot tactics in the England team at the expense of the skilled approach to the game if it were not for the fact that he would get eaten alive by know-all critics like me.

Taylor is the Bill Clinton of football. He is the first rock 'n' roller and the first post-war reared manager in the England chair. I have met him during my broadcasting duties and have found him articulate, highly intelligent, very personable, full of bright ideas and deeply caring about the game of football that he clearly loves. He impresses with his knowledge of the game, and there has not been a more conscientious manager of England. Taylor is the sort of bloke you would like to spend a lot of time with away from the public spotlight because he is both entertaining and interesting to listen to, but I have yet to be persuaded that he is the man who should be holding down the most important job in English football.

Taylor,
THE MAN AND THE MANAGER

Born in Worksop, Nottinghamshire, on September 9,1944, Taylor is the son of a sports journalist, Tom, who inspired his early interest in football. His mother, Dorothy, recalls that from first being able to walk he was always to be seen with a ball at his feet on the Newland council estate in Scunthorpe where he grew up.

One of his early primary school reports includes the comment that 'Graham shows great enthusiasm for sport and *is organizing* the football'. He won a scholarship to a grammar school and his father was encouraging him to become a teacher, but Graham had been so badly bitten by the football bug that he talked his parents into letting him leave after one year in the sixth form to start a professional career with Grimsby Town.

His playing career was more about taking part than winning. He played 189 times for the Grimsby first team between 1962 and 1967 as a full-back who was noted for his positional sense and composure under pressure. In 1968 he moved to his local club Lincoln City and played 150 League matches before a recurring hip injury forced him to hang up his boots at the age of twenty-eight. He had impressed the new club chairman Heneage Dove with his enthusiasm and passion for the game, and he was given the job of manager even though half the board were against the appointment because they considered him too young and inexperienced. At the time he was the youngest manager in the Football League.

Taylor made an in-depth study of coaching and also man-management, and he was innovative in the way he approached his job. He showed a tremendous flair for public relations, and made national newspaper headlines with his theme of 'taking the club to the town'. He insisted that all his players should live in Lincoln and get involved in the local community, and he used to organize regular team visits to local factories and foundaries. His philosophy was, 'They come to watch you play on Saturday, so you should see how they work.'

Lincoln City attendances went up and so did the club. They were promoted as Fourth Division champions in 1976 with a record points total of 74 after scoring 111 goals and losing only four matches. 'Our success has stemmed from the back,' said Taylor. 'We concentrate on doing the simple things well and on defending in the opponents' half. Our team is put together like lattice work. When everything moves it must move in synchronization.'

Each of the players' wives was sent a bunch of flowers by Taylor, and his attention to detail both on and off the pitch brought him to the notice of West Bromwich Albion and Watford. West Brom would have been a step up a division, Watford a step back down to the Fourth. It took all the persuasive powers of new Watford chairman Elton John to convince Taylor that his best move was to the Hertfordshire club. He was selected ahead of another candidate for the job, former England captain Bobby Moore.

A combination of Elton's money and Taylor's motivating and organizational powers brought Watford undreamed of success. With former Arsenal manager Bertie Mee called in as a stabilizing force, Taylor set about rebuilding the club from top to bottom. He was a 'hands-on' manager who got involved in every aspect of club affairs and he helped give Watford a new family image at a time when other clubs were struggling to overcome the problems of hooliganism. The biggest change was on the football field where he adopted the controversial long-ball game that had served Wolves so well in the 1950s. No-nonsense clearances from out of defence were converted into goals by a powerhouse attack in which players of the calibre of Luther Blissett and young John Barnes were groomed for stardom by the irrepressible Taylor.

In successive seasons Watford stormed up through the Fourth and Third Divisions and after a pause for breath and a look at their new Second Division surroundings they came up into the First Division in 1982 for the first time in the club's history. A year later Watford were runners-up to Liverpool for the League championship and in 1984 they reached the FA Cup Final at Wembley where they were beaten by Everton. When taking over as manager in 1977 Taylor had told Elton John that he would need to spend a modest £1 million on players to get the club into the First Division, and he went only a few thousand pounds over budget.

He had a close rapport with Elton that went much deeper than the usual manager-chairman relationship. The rock star would often be a house guest of Taylor and his wife, Rita, and family, and the manager would not hesitate to give almost fatherly advice to his chairman about his fitness, his drinking habits and his general lifestyle. On one occasion when Elton went to the Taylor home for Sunday lunch, he found a full bottle of brandy on a plate at his place at the dinner table. 'That's obviously all you're interested in having these days', Taylor said, making the point as strongly as possible that he was drinking too much. Only Taylor would have dared to be that outspoken with the chairman. 'We are as close as brothers', was how Elton put it.

It was when Taylor started to feel that he was losing the momentum that had been given to him by Elton in their peak years together that he started to consider new pastures, and in May 1987 he accepted an offer to take over a challenging salvage job at Aston Villa who had just been relegated to the Second Division.

Working in tandem with demanding and enthusiastic chairman Doug Ellis, Taylor quickly got Villa back to the top table as Second Division runners-up. He built a team that featured the exciting chemistry of David Platt, Tony Daley and Paul McGrath. I had my ear tuned to what was happening at Villa Park in my role as football pundit for Central Television, and it was clear that Taylor was having to walk a minefield of doubts about his wisdom in taking the job. He had heard how 'Deadly' Doug Ellis was said to eat managers for breakfast, and there was a distinct coldness between the two of them after

Taylor had said with typical candour at the club's annual meeting; 'I will not stand for having my wings clipped.'

Villa were in danger of going straight back down into the Second Division, and Ellis – rather than clipping his wings – gave him full freedom and support when a section of the crowd started calling for his head. Taylor rewarded Ellis's faith the following season by pumping the pride back into the famous old club. In February 1990 he steered Villa to the summit of the First Division for the first time in nine years. They were not quite able to sustain the pace to the finishing line, and were beaten to the championship by Liverpool. Taylor talked of this just being the beginning of the Villa revival, but before he could provide action to go with his words he was invited to take over as England manager after Howard Kendall and Terry Venables had been ruled out of contention for the job. Doug Ellis demanded and got £225,000 compensation from the Football Association. 'England are in good hands', he said. 'He has the best form of man-management I have ever come across in football. Graham does not work on fear nor on flattering the players. His method of motivation lies somewhere between the two and it gets results.'

Graham was a member of the ITV World Cup team with me when news of his appointment came through. It meant he had to anchor his views of England's performances under Bobby Robson in Italy, but I was impressed by the way he handled himself in front of the camera and knew that the PR side of things would give him few problems.

My only concern was that he did not have an international footballing pedigree, and I was surprised when he chose Lawrie McMenemy as his number two because he, too, was a stranger to the international scene. It was like appointing men who had no Cabinet experience as Prime Minister and Deputy Prime Minister

I was also surprised when in his first team selection Taylor named Gary Lineker as his skipper. In my opinion it was putting an unnecessary extra burden on a player who had enough on his plate as England's main striker. We were later to learn that the Taylor-Lineker alliance was not the close-knit, happy association it was cracked up to be. An undignified public row surfaced six months after the European championship finals in Sweden, a tournament that finished with Taylor being widely accused of vindictively closing the England career of his captain when he was one goal away from equalling Bobby Charlton's all-time record haul of forty-nine international goals.

Taylor's substitution of Lineker towards the end of a 2–1 defeat by Sweden as England stumbled out of the finals made little sense. Lineker was not alone in concluding that his withdrawal was based on something more than just a tactical change, and all of Taylor's strenuous denials could not stop an avalanche of gossip and innuendo about the strained relationship between manager and captain.

The rift we all suspected was finally confirmed in a Gary Lineker biography,

Strikingly Different by Colin Malam (Stanley Paul), and there followed for public consumption a vicious verbal exchange between Lineker and Taylor that did nothing for the image of either man and was a kick in the teeth for English football. It was like seeing the headmaster and the head boy fighting in the playground.

It has to be said that it was Taylor's fast tongue that laid the foundation to the friction in March 1991 when he criticized Lineker through the media rather than to his face for his disappointing contribution to a crucial match against Ireland. The gap between them became wider when Taylor surprisingly dropped Lineker for the showpiece friendly against France in February 1992. Then there was a deeply wounding 'we only played with ten men' comment from Taylor after a draw with Brazil in May 1992 during which Lineker missed a penalty when a goal would have brought him level with Bobby Charlton's record.

I feel this is when they should have had a private clear-the-air session because they had obviously lost faith and trust in each other. Lineker announced his intention to retire from international football after the European championships, and he continued as captain even though he and Taylor were no longer on the same wavelength.

It seemed to me as an onlooker that Taylor was having problems getting a rapport with well-established international players, who had built their reputations in the Bobby Robson era. He was, in my opinion, premature in ending the international careers of Bryan Robson. Peter Beardsley and Chris Waddle, and despite picking Lineker for twenty-two of his caps it became obvious that he and his captain did not really get along.

The most disturbing aspect of the Taylor-Lineker bust-up was the allegation by the England manager that Lineker's agent, Jon Holmes, had been trying to influence him. Taylor alleged that Holmes openly canvassed for Lineker to be made England captain, and that his England links were used to set up the lucrative deal for his curtain-closing career in Japan. He also charged that Holmes manipulated the hard-hitting press reaction to the omission of Lineker against France.

Holmes, one of the most respected and able of the army of agents now operating in the football world, denied totally the charges made by Taylor. What I cannot understand is why Taylor did not take the obvious way out long before the European championships and make his former Aston Villa midfield motivator David Platt the skipper. I always feel that a captain is best off based in midfield where he can assess situations much better. This is not me showing hindsight vision. I went on record with the opinion that Platt should have been handed the captaincy on the day that Taylor named Lineker as his chief representative on the field of play.

It is not until the end of Taylor's reign as England manager that a proper assessment can be made of him, but the Lineker episode is certain to throw a long, dark shadow over the final judgement.

Taylor's Record

This was Taylor's record after thirty-two matches up to and including the humiliating World Cup qualifying defeat by Norway in Oslo on June 2, 1993:

P	W	D	L	F	A
32	16	12	4	50	24

It is a record that, on paper, stands comparison with those of any of his predecessors,but there were few team performances to get really excited about in the first thirty-three months of Taylor's reign. What was so confusing is that he selected fifty-six players and only once picked an unchanged side. In fairness it should be pointed out that his squad was continually hit by injuries, and he was robbed for long periods of players of the quality of John Barnes, Alan Shearer and the unpredictable Paul Gascoigne.

Gazza was as much an enigma to Taylor as to most other people in football. He just did not seem to know how to come to terms with the unconventional Geordie, who was a footballing genius one minute and a clown the next. It became clear from Taylor's first important match – a European championship qualifier against the Republic of Ireland – that he was not sure how to make the most of Gascoigne's unique talent. He shocked most people, and in particular Ireland's manager Jack Charlton, by leaving Gazza on the touchline bench. Big Jack later confided to me after a 1–1 draw that Gascoigne had been the one player he feared because of his gift for doing the unexpected.

When Gascoigne battled back to fitness after the horrific knee injury collected in the 1991 FA Cup Final, Taylor recalled him to the international stage for the start of England's 1994 World Cup qualifying campaign. Taylor was in ecstasy over Gazza's performances against Norway and Turkey, but then let his tongue run loose again after he had given a sub-standard display against San Marino at Wembley in February 1993. 'I am concerned with Gascoigne's level of fitness and also about his state of mind', he told reporters. ' It doesn't matter how good you are, unless there is a level of fitness you are not able to show people your true ability. Paul's fitness is slipping. '

Taylor made pertinent points about Gascoigne and I shared his concern, but I did not feel he was doing Gazza any favours by pin-pointing his problems so publicly. I know that he and Lawrie McMenemy have had many quiet words with Gazza, trying to help him get the best out of his talent. That in my view is how it should stay – *quiet private words* not to be flourished on every sports page in the land.

Taylor, who could so easily have followed his father as a sports journalist, tries hard to help the media, perhaps too hard. His reward for all his efforts was an all-round mauling after England's abysmal performance in the 1992 European championship finals. I made several visits to the England camp and could see the strain showing on Taylor after unconvincing opening performances against Denmark and France. He was fuming after being kept waiting more than an hour for a brief interview on ITV, and he could not hide his irritation. When Elton Welsby asked him what his team would be for the next match he snapped, 'It's none of your business.' It was most un-Taylor like, and he later got agitated over the way the BBC handled one of his interviews. The master communicator was losing control under the enormous pressure, and he then left himself open to Fleet Street's big guns with his controversial decision to pull off Lineker in the sixty-second minute of a frustrating match against host country Sweden. It meant that England's finest goal scorer of modern times had finished his England career with eighty caps and still one short of Bobby Charlton's all-time goal-scoring record.

The torrent of abuse poured on Taylor after England's elimination from the fnals was more vicious in content than any previous manager had had to face, even including Bobby Robson. The 'Taylor Must Go' campaign was led by the *Sun* who devoted almost its entire back page to a picture of his head as a giant turnip.

I personally would have had to walk out on the job rather than take the insults coming from all angles. Taylor, who had been given fair treatment and encouraging support by the Football Association, went away to think over his future and returned for the new season with a big smile on his friendly face. 'I have recovered from the battering I took,' he told his biggest barracker, the *Sun*.

> Sweden is now out of my head, but when it does creep back I think 'bloody hell'. And when I look back I know I could have handled things differently. It's difficult for me to say this, but I am disappointed with myself. I could have managed it better. Perhaps this was because it was my first major championships. I know this will give ammunition to the people who are against me, but I can only be honest.

Taylor the Talker was back, and full of hope and optimism for the future. As when he was in club management, he likes to be involved with all levels of the game. He has delegated well but keeps his finger on the pulse of what is happening at schoolboy, youth and Under-21 level, and follows with interest the work of FA Director of Coaching, Charles Hughes. But at the end of the day he will be judged solely on what he achieves with the senior England team.

Three months after the débâcle in Sweden England were beaten 1–0 by Spain in Santander. The *Sun* depicted Taylor on their back page as a Spanish onion head. It was enough to make him weep.

Taylor's Players

These were the fifty-six players chosen by Taylor for his first thirty-two matches as England team manager:

Tony Adams (Arsenal: 9)	John Barnes (Liverpool: 13)
	Earl Barrett (Oldham: 1)
David Bardsley (QPR: 2)	David Batty (Leeds: 12)

Peter Beardsley (Liverpool: 4)
Steve Bull (Wolverhampton: 2)

Gary Charles (Nottingham Forest: 2)
Nigel Clough (Nottingham
   Forest: 10)
Gordon Cowans (Aston Villa: 1)
Keith Curle (Manchester City: 3)

Tony Daley (Aston Villa: 7)
Brian Deane (Sheffield Utd: 3)
Lee Dixon (Arsenal: 18)
Tony Dorigo (Chelsea/Leeds: 8)

Les Ferdinand (QPR: 3)

Paul Gascoigne (Tottenham/
   Lazio: 10)
Andy Gray (Crystal Palace: 1)

Mark Hateley (Rangers: 1)
David Hirst (Sheffield Wednesday: 3)
Steve Hodge (Nottingham Forest: 2)

Paul Ince (Manchester Utd: 6)

Rob Jones (Liverpool: 1)

Martin Keown (Everton/Arsenal: 10)

Gary Lineker (Tottenham: 22)

Steve McMahon (Liverpool: 1)
Gary Mabbutt (Tottenham: 3)
Nigel Martyn (Crystal Palace: 2)
Paul Merson (Arsenal: 10)

Gary Pallister (Manchester Utd: 4)

Carlton Palmer (Sheffield
   Wednesday: 15)
Paul Parker (QPR/
   Manchester Utd: 6)
Stuart Pearce (Nottingham
   Forest: 23)
David Platt (Aston Villa/
   Bari/Juventus: 29)

Bryan Robson (Manchester Utd: 3)
David Rocastle (Arsenal: 3)

John Salako (Crystal Palace: 6)
David Seaman (Arsenal: 6)
Lee Sharpe (Manchester Utd: 3)
Alan Shearer (Southampton/
   Blackburn: 6)
Teddy Sheringham (Tottenham: 2)
Andy Sinton (QPR: 8)
Alan Smith (Arsenal: 9)
Trevor Steven (Rangers/Marseille: 6)
Gary Stevens (Rangers: 6)
Paul Stewart (Tottenham: 3)

Geoff Thomas (Crystal Palace: 9)

Chris Waddle (Marseille: 3)
Des Walker (Nottingham Forest/
   Sampdoria: 30)
Mark Walters (Liverpool: 1)
Neil Webb (Manchester Utd: 6)
David White (Manchester City: 1)
Dennis Wise (Chelsea: 5)
Chris Woods (Rangers/Sheffield
   Wednesday: 26)
Ian Wright (Crystal Palace/
   Arsenal: 10)
Mark Wright (Derby/Liverpool: 13)

The most capped players up to and including the World Cup qualifying match against Norway in Oslo on June 2, 1993 – including appearances as substitutes – were: Des Walker (30), David Platt (29), Chris Woods (26), Stuart Pearce

(23), Gary Lineker (22), Lee Dixon (18), Carlton Palmer (15), John Barnes (13), Mark Wright (13), David Batty (12).

David Platt had been a godsend to Taylor. Without his nose for goals, his early record as England manager would not read nearly as well. Platt's four goals against San Marino in a World Cup qualifier in February 1993 took his personal haul to sixteen. Significantly, nine of them had come in the last nine games out of a total of thirteen by the entire team.

The player giving Taylor his biggest headache was his protégé from his Watford days, John Barnes. He was always promising more than he produced for England, and in a bid to give him confidence Taylor went on record to the press before sending Barnes out to play in a comeback match against San Marino: 'What John needs is a kiss and a cuddle to make him feel wanted.'

The master communicator had not chosen his words well. Barnes had a nightmare of a match and the fans seized on Taylor's words and responded by booing and jeering the Liverpool forward every time he touched the ball. It was another case of Taylor's tongue putting unnecessary pressure on one of his players.

As I write, Taylor is still trying to recover from the shock of England's appalling display against Norway in the World Cup qualifying match in Oslo on June 2, 1993. Perhaps ironically, it was the 40th anniversary of the Coronation; I reckon Taylor wanted to crown several of his players who gave less than fully committed performances against an ordinary Norwegian team, made to look extraordinary by what must rank with the all-time worst displays in our international football history.

Although he was let down by his most experienced players, I felt that the blame for England's devastating 2–0 defeat should rest squarely on the shoulders of Taylor, who came up with tactics designed to conquer Norway but which served only to confuse his own team. It was suicidal to play three central defenders at the back, and to anchor David Platt in a negative midfield role after he had shown himself to be England's most effective attacking player in the previous World Cup qualifying games.

Taylor was exposed to the full armoury of the Fleet Street firing squad after the débâcle in Norway, and as I close my notebook on the England football managers I can't help wondering if I should change the title of this book to SHOOT THE MANAGER!

PART TWO

England's complete post-war match record

Winterbottom's teams and match highlights

1: v Northern Ireland, Windsor Park, 28. 9.46. England won 7–2

Swift	Scott	Hardwick*	Wright	Franklin	Cockburn
Finney[1]	Carter[1]	Lawton[1]	Mannion[3]	Langton[1]	

Raich Carter scored in the first minute of what was a memorable match for Middlesbrough team-mates Wilf Mannion and George Hardwick. Mannion illuminated his début with a hat-trick, and Hardwick was made skipper in his first official international appearance. Hardwick was to make thirteen successive appearances for England, all as captain.

2: v Republic of Ireland, Dalymount Park, 30.9.46. England won 1–0

Swift	Scott	Hardwick*	Wright	Franklin	Cockburn
Finney[1]	Carter	Lawton	Mannion	Langton	

Tom Finney saved England's blushes with a scrambled winner 6 minutes from the end as the light started to fade in this Monday evening match. The O'Flanagan brothers – right-wing partners Dr Kevin and Michael – were outstanding for Ireland. Both were also Irish rugby internationals. Manchester City left-half Billy Walsh, playing for Ireland, had been capped by England as a schoolboy.

3: v Wales, Maine Road, 19.10.46. England won 3–0

Swift	Scott	Hardwick*	Wright	Franklin	Cockburn
Finney	Carter	Lawton[1]	Mannion[2]	Langton	

Mannion scored two and laid on the pass for a Tommy Lawton goal against a Welsh defence in which Alf Sherwood was making his full international début at right-back. Over the next ten years he missed only one match for Wales.

4: v Holland, Huddersfield, 27.11.46. England won 8–2

Swift	Scott	Hardwick*	Wright	Franklin	Johnston
Finney[1]	Carter[2]	Lawton[4]	Mannion[1]	Langton	

Lawton scored four goals and might have had eight against a Dutch defence that had no answer to his all-round power. 'Mr Lawton', said Dutch FA President Karel Lotsy after the game, 'you are the world's greatest centre-forward.' Draeger, the Dutch outside-right, wore a hairnet to keep his hair out of his eyes.

5: v **Scotland**, Wembley, 12.4.47. Drew 1–1

Swift	Scott	Hardwick*	Wright	Franklin	Johnston
Matthews	Carter[1]	Lawton	Mannion	Mullen	

With the score deadlocked at 1–1, Raich Carter was racing unchallenged towards the Scottish goal in the dying moments when he heard a whistle and pulled up. The whistle had come from the crowd. Harry Johnston made his 'Home Championship' début, and his Blackpool team-mate Stanley Matthews was preferred to Finney on the right wing.

6: v **France**, Highbury, 3.5.47. England won 3–0

Swift	Scott	Hardwick*	Wright	Franklin	Lowe
Finney[1]	Carter[1]	Lawton	Mannion[1]	Langton	

The selectors continued to dither over whether to play Matthews or Finney. The Preston plumber got the nod this time, making his mark with a goal in a 3–0 canter against a French team whistled and jeered for their shirt-pulling and spoiling tactics.

7: v **Switzerland**, Zurich, 18.5.47. England lost 1–0

Swift	Scott	Hardwick*	Wright	Franklin	Lowe
Matthews	Carter	Lawton	Mannion	Langton	

England's famed and feared attack ran into a Swiss wall defence known as 'The Redoubt'. Switzerland were already perfecting the deep-lying centre-forward tactic that completely baffled England's defenders. Left-winger Jacques Fatton scored the only goal in the 27th minute. It was thirty-three-year-old Raich Carter's final match for England after an international career that stretched back to 1934.

8: v **Portugal**, Lisbon, 27.5.47. England won 10–0.

Swift	Scott	Hardwick*	Wright	Franklin	Lowe
Matthews[1]	Mortensen[4]	Lawton[4]	Mannion	Finney[1]	

The Portuguese substituted their goalkeeper – who went off in tears – and the ball (tossing in a smaller one that they were used to playing with). But no matter what they tried they were outclassed by an England team featuring Matthews and Finney in the same attack for the first time. Mortensen marked his début with four goals, and when Lawton headed the first of his four, legend has it that he complained to Matthews that the lace was facing the wrong way when he centred it.

9: v Belgium, Brussels, 21.9.47. England won 5–2

Swift	Scott	Hardwick*	Ward	Franklin	Wright
Matthews	Mortensen[1]	Lawton[2]	Mannion	Finney[2]	

Many observers considered this the finest match Matthews ever played for England. The 'Wizard of Dribble' laid on all five goals and at the final whistle got a standing ovation from the Belgian crowd.

10: v Wales, Ninian Park, 18.10.47. England won 3–0

Swift	Scott	Hardwick*	Taylor	Franklin	Wright
Matthews	Mortensen[1]	Lawton[1]	Mannion	Finney[1]	

Wales brought in Arsenal's redoubtable defender Walley Barnes for his début, and gave him the thankless task of marking Matthews. 'Stanley ran me dizzy', admitted Barnes, who later became captain of Wales. England were 3–0 up inside the first 15 minutes, with Matthews running riot on the right wing.

11: v Northern Ireland, Goodison Park, 5.11.47. Drew 2–2.

Swift	Scott	Hardwick*	Taylor	Franklin	Wright
Matthews	Mortensen	Lawton[1]	Mannion[1]	Finney	

Three goals came in the last 8 minutes after Northern Ireland had battled to hang on to a 54th minute lead. 'Peter the Great' Doherty headed an 87th minute equalizer for the Irish after Mannion and Lawton had scored in quick succession for England. Mannion had a penalty saved in the 70th minute.

12: v Sweden, Highbury, 19.11.47. England won 4–2

Swift	Scott	Hardwick*	Taylor	Franklin	Wright
Finney	Mortensen[3]	Lawton[1]	Mannion	Langton	

Sweden, including the famous Nordahl brothers – Gunnar, Bertil and Knut – pulled back to 3-2 after England had stormed into a three-goal lead. Mortensen settled it with a classic goal to complete his hat-trick, beating three defenders in a run from the half-way line before firing in an unstoppable 20-yard shot.

13: v Scotland, Hampden Park, 10.4.48. England won 2–0

Swift	Scott	Hardwick*	Wright	Franklin	Cockburn
Matthews	Mortensen[1]	Lawton	Pearson	Finney[1]	

Finney and Mortensen scored a goal each in a rough-house of a match. Goalkeeper Frank Swift insisted on playing on after being knocked out in a collision with 'Flying Scot' Billy Liddell. Swift later collapsed on the railway platform at Manchester and was wheeled off on a porter's trolley for an examination which revealed that he had two broken ribs.

14: v Italy, Turin, 16.5.48. England won 4–0

Swift*	Scott	Howe J	Wright	Franklin	Cockburn
Matthews	Mortensen[1]	Lawton[1]	Mannion	Finney[2]	

Swift recovered from his rib injury to become the first goalkeeper to skipper England. Italy were rated the greatest team in the world, but they were struggling from the 4th minute when Mortensen scored a sensational goal with a screaming shot from an acute angle. Following a series of stunning saves by Swift, Morty laid on a second goal for Lawton, and two individual goals from Finney finished off the Italians in the second half. Jack Howe, making his début at left-back, was the first to play for England while wearing contact lenses.

15: v Denmark, Copenhagen, 26.9.48. Drew 0–0

Swift*	Scott	Aston	Wright	Franklin	Cockburn
Matthews	Hagan	Lawton	Shackleton	Langton	

English hearts stopped when Danish right-winger Johan Ploeger fired in a shot that went through the legs of Frank Swift and into the net, but the linesman's flag was up for offside. England's forwards made little impact against a packed Danish defence on a rain-soaked pitch. Len Shackleton, the Clown Prince, made his début wearing a pair of rugby boots. 'They're more comfortable,' he explained. It was the end of Tommy Lawton's England career after twenty-two games and twenty-three goals, not counting his twenty-five goals in wartime internationals.

16: v Northern Ireland, Windsor Park, 9.10.48. England won 6–2

Swift	Scott	Howe J.	Wright*	Franklin	Cockburn
Matthews[1]	Mortensen[3]	Milburn[1]	Pearson[1]	Finney	

Billy Wright's first of ninety matches as England captain. The two Stanleys – Matthews and Mortensen – dominated the match. Matthews scored the first and helped lay on a hat-trick for his Blackpool team-mate. 'Wor

Jackie' Milburn announced his début with a neatly headed goal. Milburn's JET initials (John Edward Thompson) were suited to his electric pace.

17: v **Wales**, Villa Park, 10.11.48. England won 1–0

Swift	Scott	Aston	Ward	Franklin	Wright*
Matthews	Mortensen	Milburn	Shackleton	Finney[1]	

With Laurie Scott injured, Tim Ward switched to right-back and Mortensen dropped into midfield. Finney scored the winner, but the selectors were unimpressed and he along with Swift, Ward and Shackleton were dropped. Scott's England career was finished by a damaged knee after a run of seventeen successive matches. Alf Ramsey was called in to take his place at right-back.

18: v **Switzerland,** Highbury, 1.12.48. England won 6–0

Ditchburn	Ramsey	Aston	Wright*	Franklin	Cockburn
Matthews	Rowley J.[1]	Milburn[1]	Haines[2]	Hancocks[2]	

Jack Haines and Johnny Hancocks (with size 2 boots) both scored two goals in their international débuts, but the goal that had Highbury roaring came from another débutant, Manchester United's Jack Rowley. He showed why he was rated to have one of the hardest shots in the game with a left-foot drive that bulleted into the net from 35 yards. Haines, who scored both his goals in the first half, never got another chance of a cap after collecting an injury with West Bromwich Albion.

19: v **Scotland**, Wembley, 9.4.49. England lost 1–3

Swift	Aston	Howe J.	Wright*	Franklin	Cockburn
Matthews	Mortensen	Milburn[1]	Pearson	Finney	

The selectors decided to make five changes in the team that beat Switzerland 6–0. With Billy Steel at his most potent, Scotland tore into England after Scottish goalkeeper Jimmy Cowan had almost played England on his own in the opening 20 minutes. Jimmy Mason, Steel and Lawrie Reilly put the Scots on the way to the Home Championship before Milburn snatched a consolation goal.

20: v **Sweden**, Stockholm, 13.5.49. England lost 1–3

Ditchburn	Shimwell	Aston	Wright*	Franklin	Cockburn
Finney[1]	Mortensen	Bentley	Rowley J.	Langton	

Sweden, coached by former Aldershot and Bury winger George Raynor, displayed the team understanding and skill that brought them the 1948

Olympic title. Even without the great Italian-based Gunnar Nordhal, they scored their three goals in the first half during which Ted Ditchburn complained of being blinded by the sun.

21: v Norway, Oslo, 18.5.49. England won 4–1

Swift	Ellerington	Aston	Wright*	Franklin	Dickinson
Finney[1]	Morris[1]	Mortensen	Mannion	Mullen[1 + 1o.g.]	

Frank Swift, one of the all-time great goalkeepers, made his farewell appearance in a comfortable canter against the amateurs of Norway. Derby inside-right Johnny Morris scored on his England début.

22: v France, Paris, 22.5.49. England won 3–1

Williams	Ellerington	Aston	Wright*[1]	Franklin	Dickinson
Finney	Morris[2]	Rowley J.	Mannion	Mullen	

Making his début in the England goal, Bert 'The Cat' Williams was beaten after just 28 seconds by an instant goal from French débutant Georges Moreel. Billy Wright, Wolverhampton team-mate of Williams, scored his first international goal and Morris netted twice, including a late victory-clinching goal.

23: v Republic of Ireland, Goodison Park, 21.9.49. England lost 2–0

Williams	Mozley	Aston	Wright*	Franklin	Dickinson
Harris	Morris	Pye	Mannion	Finney	

England's first home defeat by a non-British team. Nine of the Irish players were with Football League clubs and two from Shamrock Rovers but all of them were born in Ireland. Johnny Carey was a magnificent captain, and Con Martin (penalty) and Peter Farrell scored the goals that produced a stunning result. Derby defender Bert Mozley made his début at right-back on his twenty-sixth birthday. It was an unhappy début, too, for Wolves centre-forward Jesse Pye and Pompey's John Harris, who struck a shot against the bar with the score at 1–0.

24: v Wales, Ninian Park, 15.10.49. England won 4–1

Williams	Mozley	Aston	Wright*	Franklin	Dickinson
Finney	Mortensen[1]	Milburn[3]	Shackleton	Hancocks	

This was the first ever World Cup qualifying match in which England or Wales had taken part. Milburn scored a spectacular hat-trick, and England won comfortably despite having Billy Wright as a limping passenger on the wing.

25: v Northern Ireland, Maine Road, 16.11.49. England won 9–2

| Streten | Mozley | Aston | Watson | Franklin | Wright* |
| Finney | Mortensen[2] | Rowley J.[4] | Pearson[2] | Froggatt J.[1] | |

Jack Rowley, deputizing for the injured Milburn, hammered four goals against an Irish team that had gone down 8–2 against Scotland in their previous match. Pompey's Jack Froggatt scored on his début. England Test cricketer Willie Watson won the first of four caps at right-half, and Bernard Streten got his only England call while playing in the Second Division with Luton. Irish goalkeeper Kelly had to pick the ball out of his net twenty-eight times in five successive international matches.

26: v Italy, White Hart Lane, 30.11.49. England won 2–0

| Williams | Ramsey | Aston | Watson | Franklin | Wright*[1] |
| Finney | Mortensen | Rowley J.[1] | Pearson[1] | Froggatt J. | |

England were outplayed for long periods by an over-elaborate Italian team, and they won thanks to a cracking goal by Rowley and a freak goal by Wright, whose lobbed centre swerved into the net.

27: v Scotland, Hampden Park, 15.4.50. England won 1–0

| Williams | Ramsey | Aston | Wright* | Franklin | Dickinson |
| Finney | Mannion | Mortensen | Bentley[1] | Langton | |

The Scottish FA decided they would send a team to the World Cup finals in Brazil only if they won this match, even though a draw would have been enough for them to qualify. Chelsea centre-forward Roy Bentley, playing a twin spearhead role with Mortensen, scored the winning goal on his international début in a match in which the Scottish players had been put under ridiculous pressure by their own bumbling officials.

28: v Portugal, Luton, 14.4.50. England won 5–3

| Williams | Ramsey | Aston | Wright* | Jones | Dickinson |
| Milburn | Mortensen[1] | Bentley | Mannion | Finney[4] | |

Four goals from Finney, including two from the penalty spot, and a spectacular effort from Stan Mortensen lifted England to victory. But there were worrying signs that the defence was creaking without the steadying influence of Neil Franklin, who had become a soccer mercenary in the outlawed Colombian league after twenty-seven consecutive matches as England's anchorman.

29: v **Belgium,** Brussels, 18.5.50. England won 4–1

Williams	Ramsey	Aston	Wright*	Jones	Dickinson
Milburn (Mullen[1]		Mortensen[1]	Bentley[1]	Mannion[1]	Finney

Wolves' winger Jimmy Mullen became England's first ever substitute when he replaced injured Milburn, and he scored one of the goals as England staged a second-half recovery after trailing 1–0 at half-time. Roy Bentley had a foot in three of the goals and scored himself in this final warm-up before the World Cup finals.

30: v **Chile,** World Cup, Rio de Janeiro, 25.6.50. England won 2–0

Williams	Ramsey	Aston	Wright*	Hughes	Dickinson
Finney	Mannion	Bentley	Mortensen[1]	Mullen[1]	

England made an unconvincing start to their World Cup campaign and were flattered by their 2–0 victory. Laurie Hughes replaced his Liverpool clubmate Bill Jones at centre-half. George Robledo, the Newcastle forward playing for Chile, rattled the England woodwork and neutral observers thought the Chileans unlucky not to get a draw. But an easier match against the USA was to follow!

31: v **USA,** World Cup, Belo Horizonte, 29.6.50. England lost 1–0

Williams	Ramsey	Aston	Wright*	Hughes	Dickinson
Finney	Mannion	Bentley	Mortensen	Mullen	

A deflected shot from Haitian-born centre-forward Larry Gaetjens 8 minutes before half-time gave the United States a victory that caused a shock that could have been measured on the Richter scale. England hit the woodwork three times, and what seemed a certain face-saving goal from a Ramsey free-kick in the closing minutes was miraculously saved by the diving goalkeeper Borghi – a professional baseball catcher. All but three of the Americans were born in the United States, despite reports that England had been beaten by a team from Ellis Island. The goal-scoring hero Gaetjens was later reported to have died in an Haitian jail after helping to organize a guerrilla movement against the island's dictator, 'Papa' Doc. His name will live on in football history.

32: v **Spain,** World Cup, Rio de Janeiro, 2.7.50. England lost 1–0

Williams	Ramsey	Eckersley	Wright*	Hughes	Dickinson
Matthews	Mortensen	Milburn	Baily	Finney	

Spain took the lead through centre-forward Zarra in the 47th minute and then dropped back into deep defence. Even with Matthews and Finney operating,

England could not make the breakthrough and their World Cup challenge was over. Milburn had a legitimate-looking equalizer ruled offside. Alf Ramsey and Bill Eckersley started a fifteen-match full-back partnership, and Tottenham pass-master Eddie Baily got a long-overdue cap.

33: v Northern Ireland, Windsor Park, 7.10.50. England won 4–1

Williams	Ramsey	Aston	Wright*[1]	Chilton	Dickinson
Matthews	Mannion	Lee[1]	Baily[2]	Langton	

Eddie Baily, more noted for his skilful scheming, scored two goals and big Jackie Lee, a Leicestershire cricketer, marked his only international with a goal. Manchester United centre-half Allenby Chilton had to wait until he was thirty-two for this first cap as the selectors continued to hunt for a successor to Neil Franklin.

34: v Wales, Roker Park, 15.11.50. England won 4–2

Williams	Ramsey*	Smith L	Watson	Compton	Dickinson
Finney	Mannion[1]	Milburn[1]	Baily[2]	Medley	

Baily, nicknamed the 'Cheeky Chappie' because of his impersonation of comedian Max Miller, repeated his two-goal act. Arsenal centre-half Leslie Compton made his England début at the age of thirty-eight alongside county cricketing colleague Willie Watson. Les Medley partnered his Tottenham team-mate on the left wing. Lionel Smith, converted from centre-half by Arsenal, came in at left-back.

35: v Yugoslavia, Highbury, 22.11.50. Drew 2–2

Williams	Ramsey*	Eckersley	Watson	Compton	Dickinson
Hancocks	Mannion	Lofthouse[2]	Baily	Medley	

Bolton centre-forward Nat Lofthouse announced his arrival on the inter-national stage with two goals. It was the first time in post-war football that England had gone into action without either Matthews or Finney. Compton deflected the ball into his own net, and Yugoslavia forced a late equalizer to become the first Continental side to avoid defeat in England in a full international.

36: v Scotland, Wembley, 14.4.51. England lost 3–2

Williams	Ramsey	Eckersley	Johnston	Froggatt J.	Wright*
Matthews	Mannion	Mortensen	Hassall[1]	Finney[1]	

Wilf Mannion was carried off with a fractured cheekbone in the 11th minute. With Walter Winterbottom accompanying Mannion to hospital, skipper Billy Wright took the decision to switch Finney to the right to partner Matthews and the two wing wizards often made the Scottish defenders think they were seeing double. The ten men of England made the Scots battle all the way after débutant Harold Hassall had given them a 25th-minute lead. Hibs partners Bobby Johnstone and Lawrie Reilly (twice) netted for Scotland before Finney pulled it back to 3–2.

37: v **Argentina,** Wembley, 9.5.51. England won 2–1

Williams	Ramsey	Eckersley	Wright*	Taylor J.	Cockburn
Finney	Mortensen[1]	Milburn[1]	Hassall	Metcalfe	

Goals in the last 10 minutes from Mortensen and Milburn (following the two he had scored for Newcastle in the FA Cup final four days earlier) gave England a scrambled victory. Eccentric Argentinian goalkeeper Rugilo, nicknamed 'Tarzan', had the crowd roaring with laughter as he swung on the crossbar and clowned his way through the match, which was staged as part of the Festival of Britain celebrations. Fulham centre-half Jim Taylor won the first of two caps at the age of thirty-three.

38: v **Portugal,** Goodison Park, 19.5.51. England won 5–2

Williams	Ramsey*	Eckersley	Nicholson[1]	Taylor J.	Cockburn
Finney[1]	Pearson	Milburn[2]	Hassall[1]	Metcalfe	

Bill Nicholson scored with his first kick in international football, and was never given another chance by the selectors. Alf Ramsey, skippering the side because Billy Wright had been 'rested', mis-hit a back pass that let Portugal in for an equalizer. But then Tom Finney took over and ran the Portuguese into such dizzy array that at the after-match banquet their entire team stood and toasted 'Mr Finney, the Master.'

39: v **France,** Highbury, 3.10.51. Drew 2–2

Williams	Ramsey	Willis	Wright*	Chilton	Cockburn
Finney	Mannion	Milburn	Hassall	Medley[1 +1 o.g.]	

Les Medley's first goal for England and an own goal saved an unimpressive England team from a first home defeat by a foreign side. France were robbed of a deserved victory when Bert Williams made a desperate late save from Grumellon. Arthur Willis, partnering his Spurs team-mate Alf Ramsey, was one of four players – along with Chilton, Henry Cockburn and Wilf Mannion – who never played for England again.

40: v **Wales**, Ninian Park, 20.10.51. Drew 1–1

Williams	Ramsey	Smith L.	Wright*	Barrass	Dickinson
Finney	Thompson	Lofthouse	Baily[1]	Medley	

Eddie Baily saved England from defeat against a Welsh team in which Ivor Allchurch and Trevor Ford were constantly putting England's defence under pressure. Malcolm Barrass was the seventh centre-half tried by the selectors since the defection of Neil Franklin. Tommy Thompson, Aston Villa's diminutive ball-playing inside-right, won the first of two caps.

41: v **Northern Ireland**, Villa Park, 14.11.51. England won 2–0

Merrick	Ramsey	Smith L.	Wright*	Barrass	Dickinson
Finney	Sewell	Lofthouse[2]	Phillips	Medley	

The selectors experimented by giving inside-forwards Jackie Sewell and Len Phillips their first caps either side of Nat Lofthouse, who responded to the new partnership by scoring two goals. Birmingham City goalkeeper Gil Merrick made the short journey to Villa Park for his first of twenty-three caps.

42: v **Austria,** Wembley, 28.11.51. Drew 2–2

Merrick	Ramsey[1]	Eckersley	Wright*	Froggatt J.	Dickinson
Milton	Broadis	Lofthouse[1]	Baily	Medley	

An injury to Finney forced yet another permutation by the selectors, with Gloucester cricketer and Arsenal forward Arthur Milton partnering Ivor Broadis on the right wing. Austria, under the baton of the remarkable Ernst 'Clockwork' Ocwirk, had their early lead cancelled out by a penalty from the ice-cool Ramsey, who then made a goal for Lofthouse with a pin-pointed free-kick. Austria, rated the best side in Europe, saved the match two minutes later with a penalty by Stojaspal. Milton was the last player capped by England at both cricket and football.

43: v **Scotland**, Hampden Park, 5.4.52. England won 2–1

Merrick	Ramsey	Garrett	Wright*	Froggatt J.	Dickinson
Finney	Broadis	Lofthouse	Pearson[2]	Rowley J.	

Neatly taken goals by Stan Pearson stretched England's unbeaten run in full internationals at Hampden Park to fifteen years. His first after 8 minutes was a superb hooked shot. The Scots screamed that they were robbed of a penalty when Merrick pulled down Lawrie Reilly, who managed to score in the last minute.

44: v Italy, Florence, 18.5.52. Drew 1–1

Merrick	Ramsey	Garrett	Wright*	Froggatt J.	Dickinson
Finney	Broadis[1]	Lofthouse	Pearson	Elliott	

Only Wright and Finney remained of the England team that had thrashed Italy 4–0 in Turin in 1948. Broadis gave England a 4th-minute lead that was cancelled out by a spectacular solo effort from Amadei. When bottles were thrown at Lofthouse in the second half, Italian players went to the terraces to remonstrate with the fans. During half-time, a low-flying aircraft dropped twenty-two watches on to the pitch for the players as a present from the match sponsors. 'Sponsorship' would be unheard of in English football for more than twenty years.

45: v Austria, Vienna, 25.5.52. England won 3–2

Merrick	Ramsey	Eckersley	Wright*	Froggatt J	Dickinson
Finney	Sewell[1]	Lofthouse[2]	Baily	Elliott	

The match that earned Nat Lofthouse the nickname 'The Lion of Vienna'. Eight minutes from the end, with the game deadlocked at 2–2, Tom Finney collected a long throw from Gil Merrick and released a pass that sent Lofty clear just inside the Austrian half. He galloped 45 yards with a pack of defenders snapping at his heels, and collided with on-coming goalkeeper Musil as he released a shot. He was flat out unconscious and did not see the ball roll over the goal-line for the winning goal. The Bolton hero was carried off on a stretcher, but, still dazed, returned for the final 5 minutes. He hit a post in the closing moments.

46: v Switzerland, Zurich, 28.5.52. England won 3–0

Merrick	Ramsey	Eckersley	Wright*	Froggatt J.	Dickinson
Allen R.	Sewell[1]	Lofthouse[2]	Baily	Finney	

Billy Wright took over the England caps record from Bob Crompton with this forty-third international appearance. The Swiss were beaten by the same scoring combination that had won the match in Vienna three days earlier – Jackie Sewell one, Lofthouse two. West Bromwich Albion's versatile forward Ronnie Allen won the first of his five caps.

47: v Northern Ireland, Windsor Park, 4.10.52. Drew 2–2

Merrick	Ramsey	Eckersley	Wright*	Froggatt J.	Dickinson
Finney	Sewell	Lofthouse[1]	Baily	Elliott[1]	

Nat Lofthouse scored in the 1st minute and Billy Elliott in the last minute of a dramatic match. Sandwiched in between was the magic of Celtic ball-artist Charlie Tully, who scored twice for Ireland. He beat Merrick from 25 yards and then with his specialist inswinging corner-kick after the Irish team had been reduced by injury to ten men. (In a game for Celtic against Falkirk, Tully netted direct from a corner and was ordered to retake it because the referee was not ready. He immediately repeated the trick and put the ball in the exact same spot in the net!).

48: v Wales, Wembley, 12.11.52. England won 5–2

| Merrick | Ramsey | Smith L. | Wright* | Froggatt J.[1] | Dickinson |
| Finney[1] | Froggatt R. | Lofthouse[2] | Bentley[1] | Elliott | |

Jack Froggatt went off injured after scoring for England. Billy Wright switched to centre-half, with Billy Elliott dropping back from the wing to left-half. Trevor Ford scored two goals for Wales, but they were still outgunned by England's ten men. Redfern Froggatt, Jack's cousin, made his début at inside-right.

49: v Belgium, Wembley, 26.11.52. England won 5–0

| Merrick | Ramsey | Smith L | Wright* | Froggatt J. | Dickinson |
| Finney | Bentley | Lofthouse[2] | Froggatt R.[1] | Elliott[2] | |

Lofthouse kept up his one-man bombardment with a double strike that took his haul to nine goals in five games. Redfern Froggatt scored his first goal for England, and Billy Elliott netted twice against the outplayed Belgians.

50: v Scotland, Wembley, 18.4.53. Drew 2–2

| Merrick | Ramsey | Smith L. | Wright* | Barrass | Dickinson |
| Finney | Broadis[2] | Lofthouse | Froggatt R. | Froggatt J. | |

Lawrie 'Last Minute' Reilly equalized for Scotland with the final kick of the match. It was Reilly's second goal in reply to two from Ivor Broadis. Utility player Jack Froggatt, capped by England at centre-half and as an outside-left, partnered his cousin Redfern on the left wing.

51: v Argentina, Buenos Aires, 17.5.53.
Abandoned at 0–0 after 22 minutes following rain storm

| Merrick | Ramsey | Eckersley | Wright* | Johnston | Dickinson |
| Finney | Broadis | Lofthouse | Taylor T. | Berry | |

The pitch became waterlogged following a cloudburst and British referee Arthur Ellis, up to his ankles in water, had no alternative but to abandon it. 'If we had stayed out any longer we would have needed lifeboats', he said. Three days earlier an Argentinian XI had beaten an FA XI 3-1 in an unofficial international watched by a crowd of 120,000 including Juan Perón and his wife, Eva. The selectors had to wait to see if the new left-wing partnership of Manchester United team-mates Tommy Taylor and Johnny Berry would work at international level.

52: v Chile, Santiago, 24.5.53. England won 2–1

Merrick	Ramsey	Eckersley	Wright*	Johnston	Dickinson
Finney	Broadis	Lofthouse[1]	Taylor T.[1]	Berry	

Tommy Taylor's first goal for England was a freak. His intended cross was turned into the net by Chilean goalkeeper Livingstone, who was the son of a Scot. Lofthouse scored the winning goal after one of a dozen thrusting runs by Finney, and 3 minutes later he headed another Finney cross against the bar.

53: v Uruguay, Montevideo, 31.5.53. England lost 2–1

Merrick	Ramsey	Eckersley	Wright*	Johnston	Dickinson
Finney	Broadis	Lofthouse	Taylor T.[1]	Berry	

World champions Uruguay turned on an exhibition against the old masters, and might have trebled their score but for being over-elaborate with dazzling approach play. Centre-forward Miguez was a box of tricks, and in one run whipped the ball over Billy Wright, ran round him and caught it on his head. Nat Lofthouse and Ivor Broadis struck the woodwork and Tommy Taylor scored in the closing moments after an Alf Ramsey shot had been deflected.

54: v USA, New York City, 8.6.53. England won 6–3

Ditchburn	Ramsey	Eckersley	Wright*	Johnston	Dickinson
Finney[2]	Broadis[1]	Lofthouse[2]	Froggatt R.[1]	Froggatt J.	

The first full international staged in New York was arranged to mark the Queen's Coronation six days earlier. A rain storm forced a twenty-four-hour postponement, and then England – with Finney running riot – avenged the 1–0 World Cup defeat with a comfortable victory in front of a 7,271 crowd at the Yankee Stadium. It was the first time that most of the England team had played under floodlights.

55: v Wales, Ninian Park, 10.10.53. England won 4–1

Merrick	Garrett	Eckersley	Wright*	Johnston	Dickinson
Finney	Quixall	Lofthouse[2]	Wilshaw[2]	Mullen	

Dennis Wilshaw celebrated his first England cap with two goals, and Nat

Lofthouse netted twice for the second successive match. Wales played for much of the game with left-back Alf Sherwood a passenger on the wing after he had been concussed in the 32nd minute. Albert Quixall, worth his weight in gold when sold by Sheffield Wednesday to Manchester United for £45,000 in 1958, made his début at inside-right at the age of twenty.

56: v **Rest of Europe,** Wembley, 21.10.53. Drew 4-4

Merrick	Ramsey[1]	Eckersley	Wright*	Ufton	Dickinson
Matthews S.	Mortensen[1]	Lofthouse	Quixall	Mullen[2]	

An Alf Ramsey penalty in the last minute gave England a draw in a show-piece match to mark the Football Association's ninetieth birthday. Charlton defender Derek Ufton, a solid batsman and understudy at Kent to wicket-keeper Godfrey Evans, won his only cap.

57: v **Northern Ireland**, Goodison Park, 11.11.53. England won 3–1

Merrick	Rickaby	Eckersley	Wright*	Johnston	Dickinson
Matthews S.	Quixall	Lofthouse[1]	Hassall[2]	Mullen	

Recalled after two years, Harold Hassall scored twice playing alongside his Bolton team-mate Nat Lofthouse. It was Hassall's fifth and last cap. West Bromwich right-back Stan Rickaby played in his one and only England match.

58: v **Hungary,** Wembley, 5.11.53. England lost 6–3

Merrick	Ramsey[1]	Eckersley	Wright*	Johnston	Dickinson
Matthews S.	Taylor E.	Mortensen[1]	Sewell[1]	Robb	

England's first defeat by overseas opponents on home territory, and the match that changed the face of English football. The Hungarians, Olympic champions and on a run of twenty-nine successive matches without defeat, played to a flexible 4–2–4 formation and made England's 2–3–5 pattern seem about as outdated as a hansom cab on a motorway. Hidegkuti, a deep-lying centre-forward, nipped in for a hat-trick as two-goal Ferenc Puskas pulled the defence inside out. England were flattered by the 6–3 scoreline. Ramsey, Eckersley, Johnston, Taylor, Mortensen and Robb never played for England again. Ernie Taylor and George Robb were making their débuts.

59: v **Scotland**, Hampden Park, 3.4.54. England won 4–2

Merrick	Staniforth	Byrne R.	Wright*	Clarke H.	Dickinson
Finney	Broadis[1]	Allen R.[1]	Nicholls[1]	Mullen[1]	

Johnny Nicholls had good reason to remember his England début. It was his twenty-third birthday and he celebrated with England's second goal, a flying header from a Finney cross. Playing alongside his West Bromwich Albion team-mate Ronnie Allen, he was one of four débutants, along with Ron Staniforth, Harry Clarke and Manchester United left-back Roger Byrne, who was to prove himself one of the finest players ever to wear the no.3 shirt. Clarke, a towering centre-half, followed Ditchburn, Ramsey, Willis, Nicholson and Medley as members of the Spurs 'push-and-run' team who were capped after the age of thirty.

60: v **Yugoslavia,** Belgrade, 16.5.54. England lost 1–0

Merrick	Staniforth	Byrne R.	Wright*	Owen	Dickinson
Finney	Broadis	Allen R.	Nicholls	Mullen	

Syd Owen was the eleventh centre-half tried since the defection of Neil Franklin to the outlawed Colombian league. Yugoslavia were always the sharper side and deserved their winning goal when a 35-yard free-kick was deflected by Owen into the path of Mitic, who scored from 6 yards.

61: v **Hungary,** Budapest, 23.5.54. England lost 7–1

Merrick	Staniforth	Byrne R.	Wright*	Owen	Dickinson
Harris P.	Sewell	Jezzard	Broadis[1]	Finney	

The biggest defeat in England's ninety-year football history. Just four of the England team had survived from the 6–3 slaughter at Wembley in November: Merrick, Wright, Dickinson and Finney. Fulham centre-forward Bedford Jezzard made a best-forgotten début. Puskas and Kocsis scored two goals each. The unfortunate Peter Harris was winning his second and last cap after a gap of five years. His first cap came in the 2–0 defeat by the Republic of Ireland in 1949.

62: v **Belgium,** World Cup, Basle, 17.6.54. Drew 4–4 after extra-time

Merrick	Staniforth	Byrne R.	Wright*	Owen	Dickinson
Matthews S.	Broadis[2]	Lofthouse[2]	Taylor T.	Finney	

A Jimmy Dickinson own goal during extra-time gave Belgium a draw in a helter-skelter match full of defensive blunders as England made an unimpressive start to their challenge for the World Cup. Billy Wright took over at centre-half when Owen limped to a passenger's role on the wing. For the England skipper it was the start of five distinguished years at the heart of the defence.

63: v **Switzerland,** World Cup, Berne, 29.6.54. England won 2–0

Merrick	Staniforth	Byrne R.	McGarry	Wright*	Dickinson
Finney	Broadis	Taylor T.	Wilshaw[1]	Mullen[1]	

Wolves' left-wing partners Wilshaw and Mullen scored the goals, and their club captain Wright started his first match as England's centre-half. Bill McGarry gave a solid début performance in Wright's old position at right-half.

64: v **Uruguay,** World Cup, Basle, 2.7.54. England lost 4–2

Merrick	Staniforth	Byrne R.	McGarry	Wright*	Dickinson
Matthews S.	Broadis	Lofthouse[1]	Wilshaw	Finney[1]	

Two mistakes by goalkeeper Gil Merrick let defending world champions Uruguay in for goals that turned this quarter-final match in their favour after Lofthouse and Finney had scored to give England hope of causing an upset. Matthews, the man of the match, hit a post and had a shot turned round the post before Uruguay clinched victory in the 77th minute when Merrick failed to save a speculative shot from Ambrois. It was Merrick's final match for England. He had let in thirty goals in his last ten games after conceding only fifteen in his first thirteen internationals.

65: v **Northern Ireland,** Windsor Park, 2.10.54. England won 2–0

Wood	Foulkes	Byrne R.	Wheeler	Wright*	Barlow
Matthews S.	Revie[1]	Lofthouse	Haynes[1]	Pilkington	

Don Revie and Johnny Haynes got their first taste of international football together and scored a goal each. There were five other new caps in a team remodelled following the disappointing performance in the World Cup finals: Ray Wood, Bill Foulkes, Johnny Wheeler, Ray Barlow and Brian Pilkington, who played in place of the injured Finney. Foulkes, Wheeler, Barlow and Pilkington were not capped again after this victory.

66: v **Wales,** Wembley, 10.11.54. England won 3–2

Wood	Staniforth	Byrne R.	Phillips	Wright*	Slater
Matthews S.	Bentley[3]	Allen R.	Shackleton	Blunstone	

Roy Bentley, at last forgiven for his part in the 1950 World Cup humiliation against the United States, sunk Wales with a hat-trick. Two of his goals came from headers at the far post after he had exchanged passes with Matthews. Bentley's Chelsea team-mate Frank Blunstone made his England début on the left wing and Bert Slater played alongside his Wolves skipper Billy Wright in his first international match.

67: v West Germany, Wembley, 1.12.54. England won 3–1

| Williams | Staniforth | Byrne R. | Phillips | Wright* | Slater |
| Matthews S. | Bentley[1] | Allen R.[1] | Shackleton[1] | Finney | |

Len Shackleton, the clown prince, clinched a memorable victory over the world champions with an impudent chip shot as the goalkeeper came racing towards him. He was too much an individualist for the taste of the selectors and never played for England again after a paltry five caps.

68: v Scotland, Wembley, 2.4.55. England won 7–2

| Williams | Meadows | Byrne R. | Armstrong | Wright* | Edwards |
| Matthews S. | Revie[1] | Lofthouse[2] | Wilshaw[4] | Blunstone | |

Matthews was the engineer and Wilshaw the executioner in this annihilation of the Scots. Wilshaw's four goals included the first hat-trick by an England player against Scotland. Duncan Edwards, the human powerhouse from Manchester United, was, at 18 years 183 days, the youngest England player this century. Chelsea right-half Ken Armstrong collected his only cap; he later emigrated to New Zealand for whom he won thirteen caps.

69: v France, Paris, 15.5.55. England lost 1–0.

| Williams | Sillett P. | Byrne R. | Flowers | Wright* | Edwards |
| Matthews S. | Revie | Lofthouse | Wilshaw | Blunstone | |

Peter Sillett, making his début at right-back, conceded the penalty from which the great Raymond Kopa scored the winning goal for France. A month earlier Sillett's penalty goal against Wolves had clinched the League championship for Chelsea. Ron Flowers, making his début alongside his Wolves skipper Billy Wright, had to wait three years for his second cap and then won forty in a row – an unbroken sequence beaten only by Wright's seventy consecutive appearances.

70: v Spain, Madrid, 18.5.55. Drew 1–1

| Williams | Sillett P. | Byrne R. | Dickinson | Wright* | Edwards |
| Matthews S. | Bentley[1] | Lofthouse | Quixall | Wilshaw | |

In a bad-tempered match Nat Lofthouse had his shirt ripped off his back in the first-half, and played throughout the second-half with a numberless shirt. Even Stanley Matthews was drawn into the rough house, and conceded a free-kick with a tackle, the first time anybody could recall him committing a foul. Bentley scored from a Lofthouse pass in the 38th minute and Spain equalized in the 65th minute following a mistake by Duncan Edwards that was as rare as a foul by Matthews.

71: v **Portugal,** Oporto, 22.5.55. England lost 3–1

| Williams | Sillett P. | Byrne R. | Dickinson | Wright* | Edwards |
| Matthews S. | Bentley[1] | Lofthouse (Quixall) | | Wilshaw | Blunstone |

England were disjointed from the moment Lofthouse went off injured, with Quixall coming on as substitute in what was his final England appearance. It was also Bentley's last match for England after twelve appearances in three different shirts over a period of six years. His goal could not save England from their first defeat by Portugal. Matthews and Wright were the only players on the pitch who had featured in the famous 10–0 victory over Portugal in Lisbon eight years earlier.

72: v **Denmark,** Copenhagen, 2.10.55. England won 5–1

| Baynham | Hall | Byrne R. | McGarry | Wright* | Dickinson |
| Milburn | Revie[3] | Lofthouse[1] | Bradford[1] | Finney | |

Goalkeeper Ron Baynham, right-back Jeff Hall and inside-left Geoff Bradford all made débuts. Bradford, a consistent force with Bristol Rovers in the Second Division and winning his only cap, scored the fifth and final goal 8 minutes from the end after a hat-trick from Don Revie (including a penalty) and the usual goal from Lofthouse had floored the Danes. Hall and Byrne were to partner each other at full-back for seventeen successive matches, with only one defeat. They also became partners in tragedy. Hall died from polio a year after Byrne was killed in the 1958 Munich air disaster. The match against Denmark was played on a Sunday to coincide with a British Trades Fair. So as not to weaken club sides for the previous day's League programme, the squad was chosen on a one club, one man basis. In eight instances the players were paired off from the Saturday games so that their clubs were equally weakened.

73: v **Wales,** Ninian Park, 22.10.55. England lost 2–1

| Williams | Hall | Byrne R. | McGarry | Wright* | Dickinson |
| Matthews S. | Revie | Lofthouse | Wilshaw | Finney [(1 o.g.)] | |

Wales conquered England for the first time since 1938 thanks to a headed winning goal from young Swansea winger Cliff Jones, whose Uncle Bryn had scored one of the four goals that beat England seventeen years earlier. England's high-powered attack floundered against a Welsh defence in which the Charles brothers, John and Mel, played side by side.

74: v **Northern Ireland,** Wembley, 2.11.55. England won 3–0

| Baynham | Hall | Byrne R. | Clayton | Wright* | Dickinson |
| Finney[1] | Haynes | Jezzard | Wilshaw[2] | Perry | |

Fulham clubmates Johnny Haynes and Bedford Jezzard played alongside each other for the only time in an England international. Haynes, partnering Tom Finney on the right wing, played farther upfield than usual to confuse his marker, Danny Blanchflower, and it was mainly because of his probing passes that England won comfortably with two goals from Dennis Wilshaw and another from Finney. Jezzard's career was ended a year later by an ankle injury. South African-born Bill Perry came into the attack in place of his Blackpool team-mate Stanley Matthews, and Ronnie Clayton won the first of his thirty-five caps.

75: v **Spain,** Wembley, 30.11.55. England won 4–1

Baynham	Hall	Byrne R.	Clayton	Wright*	Dickinson
Finney[1]	Atyeo[1]	Lofthouse	Haynes	Perry[2]	

The Wembley floodlights were switched on for the first time in an international match 15 minutes from the end of a game in which Spain were always in the dark. Finney missed from the penalty spot in the fifth minute, but then made amends by laying on one goal and scoring another. John Atyeo, the school-teacher from Bristol City, put the finishing touch to a magnificent seven-man passing movement in the 15th minute, and 60 seconds later Bill Perry scored the first of his two goals.

76: v **Scotland**, Hampden Park, 14.4.56. Drew 1–1

Matthews R.	Hall	Byrne R.	Dickinson	Wright*	Edwards
Finney	Taylor T.	Lofthouse	Haynes[1]	Perry	

Haynes silenced the Hampden Roar with a last-minute equalizer, shooting the ball past goalkeeper Tommy Younger after Manchester United teammates Byrne and Taylor had created the opening. Reg Matthews, making his début in front of a 134,000 crowd while a Third Division goalkeeper with Coventry City, almost fainted with nerves just before the kick-off but he pulled himself together and was beaten only on the hour by a mis-hit shot from Aberdeen's Graham Leggat.

77: v **Brazil**, Wembley, 9.5.56. England won 4–2

Matthews R.	Hall	Byrne R.	Clayton	Wright*	Edwards
Matthews S.	Atyeo	Taylor T.[2]	Haynes	Grainger[2]	

It was billed as the 'Old World meets the New' and Brazil arrived with many of the players who two years later won the World Cup in such dazzling fashion. England got off to a flying start with Tommy Taylor and Colin Grainger scoring inside the first 5 minutes. The Brazilians fought back to 2–2, and then Atyeo and Byrne each had a penalty saved by goalkeeper Gylmar. The penalty misses sandwiched a second goal by Taylor, made for him by a Matthews at his magical best against one of the all-time great left-backs, Nilton Santos. There was a farcical hold-up following a dispute over a quickly taken free-kick by Haynes. The ball was caught by Nilton Santos and the Brazilians staged a walk-off protest when the referee awarded a penalty. By the time peace was restored it was no wonder that Atyeo failed with the spot-kick. Colin Grainger crowned a memorable début with a second goal 5 minutes from the end of one of the most exciting and dramatic international matches ever witnessed at Wembley. Johnny Haynes asked Matthews for his autograph before the match. The old maestro's hands were shaking so much with nerves that he was unable to sign. By the end of the match it was Nilton Santos who was shaking at the knees after being given the run-around for one of the few times in his career.

78: v **Sweden,** Stockholm, 16.5.56. Drew 0–0

| Matthews R. | Hall | Byrne R. | Clayton | Wright* | Edwards |
| Berry | Atyeo | Taylor T. | Haynes | Grainger | |

England were lucky to escape with a draw in a match ruined by a near-gale force wind. Goalkeeper Reg Matthews made three stunning saves to stop the Swedes from getting the victory their superior approach play deserved.

79: v **Finland,** Helsinki, 20.5.56. England won 5–1

| Wood | Hall | Byrne R. | Clayton | Wright* | Edwards |
| Astall[1] | Haynes[1] | Taylor T. (Lofthouse[2]) | | Wilshaw | Grainger |

Lofthouse came on as a substitute for the injured Taylor a minute before half-time, and for the twelfth time scored two goals. It lifted his haul to twenty-nine goals, one more than the previous England record set by the great Steve Bloomer before the First World War. Gordon Astall, playing in place of the unavailable Matthews, scored on his début. Best remembered by the players is an Al Jolson impression from Colin Grainger at the after-match banquet. Colin, a nightclub singer, was accompanied on the piano by the Finnish centre-forward, who played professionally with a dance-band.

80: v **West Germany,** Berlin, 26.5.56. England won 3–1

| Matthews R. | Hall | Byrne R. | Clayton | Wright* | Edwards[1] |
| Astall | Haynes[1] | Taylor T. | Wilshaw | Grainger[1] | |

The match that is held up as the finest ever played on the international stage by Duncan Edwards. He strode the pitch like a colossus, scoring a scorcher of a goal from 20 yards in the 20th minute and dominating the entire game both in defence and midfield. Nearly half the 100,000 crowd in the stadium designed by Adolf Hitler were soldiers from the British-occupied zone of Berlin. They staged a delighted pitch invasion when goals from Haynes and Grainger clinched victory. Fritz Walter, the outstanding German skipper, scored a fine individual goal for the team he had led to the World Cup two years earlier.

81: v **Northern Ireland**, Windsor Park, 6.10.56. Drew 1–1

| Matthews R. | Hall | Byrne R. | Clayton | Wright* | Edwards |
| Matthews S.¹ | Revie | Taylor T. | Wilshaw | Grainger | |

A rare goal from Stanley Matthews (his eleventh and last in international football) after just two minutes gave England a dream start, but they were hustled out of their stride by a Northern Ireland team motivated by a dazzling performance from skipper Danny Blanchflower. Jimmy McIlroy equalized after 10 minutes when goalkeeper Reg Matthews palmed a long throw from Peter McParland into his path. McIlroy was faced with an open goal 5 minutes from the end but hit a post.

82: v **Wales**, Wembley, 14.11.56. England won 3–1

| Ditchburn | Hall | Byrne R. | Clayton | Wright* | Dickinson |
| Matthews S. | Brooks¹ | Finney¹ | Haynes¹ | Grainger | |

Goalkeeper Jack Kelsey went off injured shortly after John Charles had headed Wales into an early lead. Right-back Alf Sherwood took over in the Welsh goal, and from then on England were dominant despite the sterling effort of John Charles to turn the tide. Second-half goals from Haynes, débutant Johnny Brooks and the versatile Finney at centre-forward gave England an undistinguished victory.

83: v **Yugoslavia,** Wembley, 28.11.56. England won 3–0

| Ditchburn | Hall | Byrne R. | Clayton | Wright* | Dickinson |
| Matthews S. | Brooks¹ | Finney | Haynes (Taylor T.²) | | Blunstone |

Johnny Haynes was heavily tackled off the ball by Yugoslav right-back Belin in the 30th minute, and was unable to continue. His substitute, Tommy Taylor, scored two second-half goals. Matthews ran the Yugoslav left-back into such a state of confusion that he finally resorted to rugby tackling him in a bid to stop his dribbling runs.

84: v Denmark, Molineux, 5.12.56. England won 5–2

| Ditchburn | Hall | Byrne R. | Clayton | Wright* | Dickinson |
| Matthews S. | Brooks | Taylor T.³ | Edwards² | Finney | |

This World Cup qualifying match was distinguished by a hat-trick from Tommy Taylor and two spectacular goals from his Manchester United team-mate Duncan Edwards, who played at inside-left in place of the injured Haynes.

85: v Scotland, Wembley, 6.4.57. England won 2–1

| Hodgkinson | Hall | Byrne R. | Clayton | Wright* | Edwards¹ |
| Matthews S. | Thompson T. | Finney | Kevan¹ | Grainger | |

Duncan Edwards snatched victory for England six minutes from the end with a blistering 25-yard shot that crashed into the net off a post. Goalkeeper Alan Hodgkinson had to pick the ball out of his net just a minute into his international début. Scottish winger Tommy Ring had taken advantage of a Matthews slip to race unchallenged into the England penalty area before beating the on-coming Hodgkinson. Derek Kevan, making his début in preference to Johnny Haynes, equalized in the 62nd minute. Scottish fans were convinced they were robbed when Willie Fernie bundled the ball into the net after it had been dropped by Hodgkinson following a jolting Lawrie Reilly shoulder-charge. The referee ruled that the goalkeeper had both feet off the ground when contact was made.

86: v Republic of Ireland, Wembley, 8.5.57. England won 5–1

| Hodgkinson | Hall | Byrne R | Clayton | Wright* | Edwards |
| Matthews S. | Atyeo² | Taylor T.³ | Haynes | Finney | |

A second Tommy Taylor hat-trick in successive matches – all his goals coming in the first half – and two from John Atyeo crushed an outgunned Irish team in this World Cup qualifying match.

87: v Denmark, Copenhagen, 15.5.57. England won 4–1

| Hodgkinson | Hall | Byrne R. | Clayton | Wright* | Edwards |
| Matthews S. | Atyeo¹ | Taylor T.² | Haynes¹ | Finney | |

Denmark took the lead in the 25th minute, with Haynes equalizing just before half-time. It was not until the final 15 minutes that England got on top. Tommy Taylor scored twice to take his haul in four matches to ten goals and Atyeo also got on the scoresheet. It was the international swan-song of 'Mr Football' Stanley Matthews, who was retired from the world stage at the age of forty-two and twenty-two years after the first of his fifty-four caps. He also played in 29 war-time internationals.

88: v Republic of Ireland, Dalymount Park, 19.5.57. Drew 1–1

| Hodgkinson | Hall | Byrne R. | Clayton | Wright* | Edwards |
| Finney | Atyeo[1] | Taylor T. | Haynes | Pegg | |

England were shocked by a third-minute goal from Alf Grinstead, and struggled to make any impact against an Irish defence in which goalkeeper Tommy Godwin and centre-half Charlie Hurley were outstanding. The game was into its last minute when Finney fired over a perfect cross for Atyeo to head an equalizer that gave England a point that clinched their place in the World Cup finals. David Pegg, who was to die in the Munich air crash, won his only cap in place of the originally named Matthews.

89: v Wales, Ninian Park, 19.10.57. England won 4–0

| Hopkinson | Howe | Byrne R. | Clayton | Wright* | Edwards |
| Douglas | Kevan | Taylor T. | Haynes[2] | Finney[1 +1 o.g.] | |

Wales were in trouble from the moment early in the game when left-back Mel Hopkins passed the ball wide of goalkeeper Jack Kelsey and into his own net. Missing the powerful influence of the absent John Charles, Wales caved in to two goals from Haynes and a brilliant strike from Finney. Goalkeeper Eddie Hopkinson, right-back Don Howe and outside-right Bryan Douglas – the 'new Matthews' – all made impressive débuts. There was another débutant: Harold Shepherdson was having his first match as trainer, a job he would hold for sixteen years.

90: v Northern Ireland, Wembley, 6.11.57. England lost 3–2

| Hopkinson | Howe | Byrne R. | Clayton | Wright* | Edwards[1] |
| Douglas | Kevan | Taylor T. | Haynes | A'Court[1] | |

Skipper Danny Blanchflower and goalkeeper Harry Gregg were carried off shoulder high by celebrating Irish fans after this unexpected victory that ended England's sixteen-match unbeaten run. Gregg had saved at least three certain goals with a series of blinding saves. Jimmy McIlroy gave Ireland a first-half lead with a penalty shot that hit a post and then went into the net off the back of goalkeeper Hopkinson. Liverpool winger Alan A'Court, making his début in place of the injured Finney, equalized soon after half-time before McCrory and Simpson – with a goal disputed by England – put Ireland 3–1 clear. Edwards pulled back a goal, but the Irish went on to their first victory over England since 1927.

91: v France, Wembley, 27.11.57. England won 4–0

| Hopkinson | Howe | Byrne R. | Clayton | Wright* | Edwards |
| Douglas | Robson R.[2] | Taylor T.[2] | Haynes | Finney | |

Bryan Douglas had a storming game, and three of the four goals came from his crosses. Bobby Robson, winning his first cap, scored two goals, as did Tommy Taylor. Tragically, they were to be Taylor's last for England. Three months later, on Febuary 6, 1958, Taylor, along with Roger Byrne, David Pegg, Geoff Bent, Eddie Colman, Mark Jones and Liam Whelan, perished in the Munich air crash as Manchester United returned from a European Cup tie in Belgrade. Several days after the crash, the untapped genius Duncan Edwards died of his injuries. The United and England teams had been ripped apart.

92: v **Scotland**, Hampden Park, 19.4.58. England won 4–0

Hopkinson	Howe	Langley	Clayton	Wright*	Slater
Douglas[1]	Charlton R.[1]	Kevan[2]	Haynes	Finney	

Bobby Charlton, a Munich survivor, electrified the first of his 106 England appearances with a classic goal when he connected with a Finney cross on the volley to send it flashing into the Scotland net from the edge of the penalty area. His wonder strike came in the 62nd minute after Douglas had headed England into a first-half lead and then laid on the first of two goals for Derek Kevan. Jim Langley made a commendable début in place of the sadly missed Roger Byrne, with Bill Slater taking on the impossible job of following Duncan Edwards.

93: v **Portugal,** Wembley, 7.5.58. England won 2–1

Hopkinson	Howe	Langley	Clayton	Wright*	Slater
Douglas	Charlton R.[2]	Kevan	Haynes	Finney	

Two goals from Bobby Charlton – the second a scorching shot similar to that which rocked the Scots – rescued England from the brink of defeat. Portugal created enough chances to have won the game, but their finishing was feeble. Jim Langley failed to score from the penalty spot, one of only two misses throughout his career.

94: v **Yugoslavia**, Belgrade, 11.5.58. England lost 5–0

Hopkinson	Howe	Langley	Clayton	Wright*	Slater
Douglas	Charlton R.	Kevan	Haynes	Finney	

All the confidence and cohesion built up in the England team pre-Munich had disappeared, and they found this World Cup warm-up match in Belgrade too hot to handle in more ways than one. The match was played in a heat wave with temperatures in the high nineties, and three of the Yugoslav goals came in the last 10 minutes with several of the England players close to exhaustion. The match was a personal nightmare for Jim

Langley, who was run ragged by the right-winger Petacavoc, who scored three goals.

95: v **USSR,** Moscow, 18.5.58. Drew 1–1

McDonald	Howe	Banks T.	Clamp	Wright*	Slater
Douglas	Robson R.	Kevan[1]	Haynes	Finney	

For this final match before the World Cup, Eddie Clamp came in at right-half to make an all-Wolves half-back line with clubmates Billy Wright and Bill Slater. Colin McDonald took over in goal and Tommy Banks was called in at left-back. After the jolting defeat in Yugoslavia, England gave a much more disciplined performance in the new Lenin Stadium, and a Derek Kevan goal just before half-time gave them a draw against a Russian side rated one of the best in Europe. England might have won but for the goalkeeping of the great 'Man in Black' Lev Yashin, and the intervention of the woodwork when first Finney and then Kevan struck shots against a post. The shock after the match was that Brian Clough, Middlesbrough's untried goal master, was told he was not needed for the World Cup squad.

96: v **USSR,** World Cup, Gothenburg, 8.6.58. Drew 2–2

McDonald	Howe	Banks T.	Clamp	Wright*	Slater
Douglas	Robson R.	Kevan[1]	Haynes	Finney[1]	

Finney coolly placed a penalty wide of Lev Yashin 6 minutes from the final whistle to give England a draw in their opening World Cup match against a Russian team much changed from the side they had played in Moscow the previous month. The Russians had led 2–0 with 20 minutes to go, and it looked all over for England until Douglas created a goal for Kevan. After Finney had scored the equalizer from the penalty spot, a furious Lev Yashin got hold of the referee and spun him around like a top. Incredibly, the incensed goalkeeper was allowed to stay on the field. In the closing moments a crushing tackle on Finney damaged his knee and put him out of the rest of the tournament.

97: v **Brazil,** World Cup, Gothenburg, 11.6.58. Drew 0–0

McDonald	Howe	Banks T.	Clamp	Wright*	Slater
Douglas	Robson R.	Kevan	Haynes	A'Court	

This was the only match in which Brazil failed to score, and it was due mainly to the defensive tactics worked out by Winterbottom's assistant Bill Nicholson who had watched their opening match against Austria. Bill Slater played a key role, sticking close to their ball master Didi and not allowing him to settle ino his usual rhythm. The result forced the Brazilians to rethink, and they were persuaded to call up two exceptional but untested individualists: Garrincha and Pelé. The rest is World Cup history! Slater finished the match with bruises on the inside of both knees where he had kept banging them together to stop Didi pulling off his favourite trick of threading the ball through an opponent's legs.

98: v **Austria,** World Cup, Boras, 15.6.58. Drew 2–2

McDonald	Howe	Banks T.	Clamp	Wright*	Slater
Douglas	Robson R.	Kevan[1]	Haynes[1]	A'Court	

England, needing to beat Austria to qualify for the quarter-finals, were trailing 1–0 at half-time to an extraordinary goal scored from 35 yards by left-half Koller. Johnny Haynes equalized ten minutes into the second-half, and then the Austrians regained the lead following a corner. Kevan pulled England level again 10 minutes from the end, and 5 minutes later they celebrated what they thought was a winning goal after Bobby Robson had breasted down the ball and shot all in one sweet movement. The referee ruled that he had handled the ball. The draw meant England had to play off against Russia, their third meeting in a month.

99: v **USSR,** World Cup, Gothenburg, 17.6.58. England lost 1–0

McDonald	Howe	Banks T.	Clayton	Wright*	Slater
Brabrook	Broadbent	Kevan	Haynes	A'Court	

Chelsea winger Peter Brabrook came in for his début along with Wolves inside-forward Peter Broadbent. Brabrook almost became an instant hero with a shot that struck the Russian post and then bounced into Yashin's hands. In the second half he had a goal disallowed before the Russians scored the winning goal when Ilyin's shot went in off a post to put England out of the World Cup. When he led a dejected England team back to London, Winterbottom was met at the airport by his young son, Alan, who asked the question on the lips of thousands of football fans: 'Daddy, why didn't you play Bobby Charlton?'

100: v **Northern Ireland**, Windsor Park, 4.10.58. Drew 3–3

McDonald	Howe	Banks T.	Clayton	Wright*	McGuinness
Brabrook	Broadbent	Charlton R.[2]	Haynes	Finney[1]	

Northern Ireland and England concocted a thriller on a waterlogged, mud-heap of a pitch. Bobby Charlton, playing at centre-forward, scored with two thunderbolt shots to add fuel to the arguments that he should have been let off the leash in the World Cup. Twenty-year-old Wilf McGuinness, another of the Busby Babes from Old Trafford, won the first of what would surely have been many England caps but for a broken leg virtually ending his career two years later.

101: v USSR, Wembley, 22.10.58. England won 5–0

McDonald	Howe	Shaw G	Clayton	Wright*	Slater
Douglas	Charlton R.[1]	Lofthouse[1]	Haynes[3]	Finney	

This was hollow revenge against the Russians for the defeat in the match that really mattered. Johnny Haynes, the pass master, turned goal snatcher with his one and only hat-trick. The selectors dipped into the past and brought back the old lion Nat Lofthouse after two years in the wilderness. He revealed a flash of his old power with a crashing left-foot shot for the fifth goal despite a Russian defender having a handful of his shirt. Bobby Charlton's goal came from the penalty spot. The BBC television 'Sportsview' team led by Kenneth Wolstenholme had been campaigning to have Haynes replaced. When they reported the match and Johnny's hat-trick, they appeared in front of the cameras in sackcloth and ashes.

102: v Wales, Villa Park, 26.11.58. Drew 2–2

McDonald	Howe	Shaw G.	Clayton	Wright*	Flowers
Clapton	Broadbent[2]	Lofthouse	Charlton R.	A'Court	

Arsenal winger Danny Clapton was given the impossible job of following Tom Finney, who won his seventy-sixth and final cap against Russia (Finney remains in the minds and memories of many pros of the 'forties and 'fifties as the greatest player ever to pull on an England shirt). Like Haynes, Peter Broadbent was more a schemer than a scorer but – standing in for the injured hat-trick hero – he twice netted equalizing goals against a spirited Welsh team.

103: v Scotland, Wembley, 11.4.59. England won 1–0

Hopkinson	Howe	Shaw G.	Clayton	Wright*	Flowers
Douglas	Broadbent	Charlton R.[1]	Haynes	Holden	

Billy Wright made his 100th international appearance, and after an acrobatic header from Bobby Charlton had won the match the England skipper was carried shoulder high to the Wembley dressing-rooms by his teammates Don Howe and Ronnic Clayton. Haynes collected a painful memento when a fierce tackle by Dave Mackay left him with a broken little finger on his left hand. Bolton winger Doug Holden won the first of his five caps.

104: v Italy, Wembley, 6.5.59. Drew 2–2

| Hopkinson | Howe | Shaw G. | Clayton | Wright* | Flowers |
| Bradley[1] | Broadbent | Charlton R.[1] | Haynes | Holden | |

England were reduced to ten men when Ron Flowers went off with a broken nose with England leading 2–0. The goals were scored by Manchester United team-mates Bobby Charlton and Warren Bradley, a schoolmaster who was making his début on the right wing. By the time Flowers returned to the defence seventeen minutes later the young, experimental Italian team had drawn level. The Italians were fielding the first all home-born team for twenty years. When they stood to attention before the match they were astonished to hear the Mussolini-era national anthem, which had been banned since the war.

105: v Brazil, Rio de Janeiro, 13.5.59. England lost 2–0

| Hopkinson | Howe | Armfield | Clayton | Wright* | Flowers |
| Deeley | Broadbent | Charlton R. | Haynes | Holden | |

Charlton and Haynes rapped shots against the post after England had gone 2–0 down to early goals against a Brazilian team that featured both Didi and Pelé in a rare appearance together. Watched by a crowd of 150,000, Jimmy Armfield was given a chasing he will not forget by Julinho in what was a baptism of fire for the Blackpool defender. He was called in to partner Don Howe in an out-of-club position at left-back. Norman Deeley, the small, direct Wolves winger, was the fifth player to wear the no. 7 shirt since the departure of the one and only Finney. Goalkeeper Eddie Hopkinson saved two certain goals from Pelé, but could do nothing to stop a thunderbolt from Julinho. As he lay on the ground a posse of Brazilian radio commentators rushed on to the pitch to try to interview him. It is just as well that they could not translate his direct comments delivered in Lancastrian tones.

106: v Peru, Lima, 17.5.59. England lost 4–1

| Hopkinson | Howe | Armfield | Clayton | Wright* | Flowers |
| Deeley | Greaves[1] | Charlton R. | Haynes | Holden | |

Jimmy Greaves arrived on the international stage with a neatly taken second-half goal, drawing the goalkeeper off his line before slotting a left-foot shot just inside a post. But it was the only bright moment in a miserable England performance. The Peruvians were helped to four goals by mistakes from a strangely lethargic England defence.

107: v **Mexico,** Mexico City, 24.4.59. England lost 2–1

Hopkinson	How	Armfield	Clayton	Wright*	McGuinness (Flowers)
Holden (Bradley)		Greaves	Kevan[1]	Haynes	Charlton R.

The British newspapermen covering the match reported that seismic tremors shook the ground during the match, but none of the England players felt the earthquake. Perhaps they were too exhausted from chasing around in the thin air when not properly acclimatized and under a searing midday sun. England scored first through Derek Kevan, but were worn out within the hour and despite officially using substitutes for the first time were run off their feet in the last half hour.

108: v **USA,** Los Angeles, 28.5.59. England won 8–1

Hopkinson	Howe	Armfield	Clayton	Wright*	Flowers[2]
Bradley[1]	Greaves	Kevan[1]	Haynes[1]	Charlton R.[3]	

This runaway victory in Billy Wright's 105th and final match helped wipe out the memory of the 1–0 defeat by the United States in the 1950 World Cup finals, but at one stage it looked as if another embarrassment was on its way. The Americans had an early goal disallowed and then took the lead, and at 1–1 at half-time the reporters were preparing head-chopping stories that were hurriedly rewritten as Bobby Charlton led a second-half goal rush with a hat-trick. The only forward who did not get his name on the scoresheet was one James Peter Greaves.

109: v **Wales**, Ninian Park, 17.10.59. Drew 1–1

Hopkinson	Howe	Allen A.	Clayton*	Smith T.	Flowers
Connelly	Greaves[1]	Clough	Charlton R.	Holliday	

Brian Clough at long last got the England chance his stack of goals with Middlesbrough deserved. Into the team with him from the England Under-23 squad came Tony Allen, John Connelly, Cloughie's clubmate Eddie Holliday and, taking the place of Billy Wright, Birmingham centre-half Trevor Smith. It was a mix that did not work, and it was a Greaves goal that saved England from defeat against a Welsh team operating without either of the Charles brothers. Smith spent much of his début limping with a calf muscle injury, and he could not prevent twenty-year-old Graham Moore from scoring for Wales.

110: v **Sweden,** Wembley, 28.10.59. England lost 3–2

Hopkinson	Howe	Allen A.	Clayton*	Smith T.	Flowers
Connelly[1]	Greaves	Clough	Charlton R.[1]	Holliday	

An unchanged team was given a second chance, but a defeat by Sweden signalled the end of the international road for Hopkinson, Smith and Clough. They carried the can for a performance that brought rare jeers from England supporters. Swedish centre-forward Simonsson made such an impression that the next day he was signed by Real Madrid.

111: v Northern Ireland, Wembley, 18.11.59. England won 2–1

Springett	Howe	Allen A.	Clayton*	Brown	Flowers
Connelly	Haynes	Baker¹	Parry¹	Holliday	

Joe Baker, the Englishman from Hibernian with the broad Scottish accent, and Bolton's Ray Parry were two of nine new caps tried in three matches. Baker gave England the lead with a brilliantly worked goal which was equalized with 3 minutes to go by Billy Bingham. The match was into its final seconds when Parry snatched the winner. West Ham centre-half Ken Brown gave a good account of himself in the middle of the England defence, but was quickly dumped as the selectors continued their hunt for a successor to Billy Wright. Ron Springett marked his first game in the England goal with a save from a Jimmy McIlroy penalty.

112: v Scotland, Hampden Park, 19.4.60. Drew 1–1

Springett	Armfield	Wilson	Clayton*	Slater	Flowers
Connelly	Broadbent	Baker	Parry	Charlton R.¹	

Tottenham brought the club-or-country issue to boiling point by refusing to release their three Scots, Dave Mackay, Bill Brown and John White, for this match. The referee awarded fifty-five free-kicks and three penalties, two of which were missed. Bobby Charlton converted from the penalty spot, and failed to find the net with a second twice-taken penalty. Graham Leggat, partnered by Ian St John and Denis Law, scored Scotland's goal. Ray Wilson, starting his distinguished England career at left-back, played on despite collecting a broken nose in the second minute, and Joe Baker battled on with a dislocated shoulder.

113: v Yugoslavia, Wembley, 11.5.60. Drew 3–3

Springett	Armfield	Wilson	Clayton*	Swan	Flowers
Douglas¹	Haynes¹	Baker	Greaves¹	Charlton R.	

England were trailing 3–2 with 90 seconds to go when Joe Baker headed the ball against the bar, and Johnny Haynes swept in the rebound. Straight from the kick-off an England attack ended with Baker again heading against the bar, but this time there was nobody able to turn the ball back into the goal. An England victory would have been an injustice to a Yugoslavia side that played some excellent football, with two-goal Galic continually turning the defence inside out. It was a tough début for the latest candidate for the no. 5 shirt, Peter Swan of Sheffield Wednesday. He replaced Bill Slater, who heard that he was dropped just a few minutes before being told that he had been elected 'Footballer of the Year'.

114: v **Spain,** Madrid, 15.5.60. England lost 3–0

Springett	Armfield	Wilson	Robson R.	Swan	Flowers
Brabrook	Haynes*	Baker	Greaves	Charlton R.	

Johnny Haynes took over from the dropped Ronnie Clayton as captain. The rain in Spain was mainly on the pitch and England got bogged down in a midfield that was a mass of mud. Alfredo di Stefano played a reluctant part in the Spanish victory. He wanted to save himself for Real Madrid's European Cup Final date with Eintracht Frankfurt at Hampden Park four days later. He had a long-running argument on the touchline that he wanted to come off, but was persuaded to play on and help Martinez clinch victory with two goals in the last ten minutes. Di Stefano and his colleagues Gento and del Sol then flew off to Glasgow to join the Real team that conjured one of the great performances of all time in their 7–3 victory over Eintracht.

115: v **Hungary,** Budapest, 22.5.60. England lost 2–0

Springett	Armfield	Wilson	Robson R.	Swan	Flowers
Douglas	Haynes*	Baker	Viollett	Charlton R.	

England missed a sackful of goals because of feeble finishing, but the approach play was an encouraging sign of things to come. Florian Albert, Hungary's new centre-forward discovery, scored both goals in the second-half. Dennis Viollett, Manchester United's quick and clever inside-forward, won the first of two caps.

116: v **Northern Ireland**, Belfast, 8.10.60. England won 5–2

Springett	Armfield	McNeil	Robson R.	Swan	Flowers
Douglas[1]	Greaves[2]	Smith R.[1]	Haynes*	Charlton R.[1]	

The start of one of the most impressive sequences of results in England football history. Bobby Smith scored with his second kick in international football after Haynes had rolled a short free-kick into his path. Robson and Haynes were impressive midfield partners in a 4–2–4 formation, and the front four – Douglas, Greaves, Smith and Bobby Charlton – looked as potent a force as England had fielded for ten years. Middlesbrough's powerfully built Mick McNeil replaced injured Ray Wilson at left-back.

117: v Luxemburg, Luxemburg, 19.10.60. England won 9–0

| Springett | Armfield | McNeil | Robson R. | Swan | Flowers |
| Douglas | Greaves³ | Smith R.² | Haynes*¹ | Charlton R.³ | |

Greaves and Charlton helped themselves to hat-tricks in this World Cup qualifying match against outclassed Luxemburg. Bobby Smith notched two, but the goal of the game was a thundering shot from skipper Haynes.

118: v Spain, Wembley, 26.10.60. England won 4–2

| Springett | Armfield | McNeil | Robson R. | Swan | Flowers |
| Douglas¹ | Greaves¹ | Smith R.² | Haynes* | Charlton R. | |

As in Madrid five months earlier, torrential rain turned the pitch into a miniature lake, but this time it was England who kept their feet better against an exceptional Spanish team that included their big shots di Stefano, del Sol, Suarez and Gento. England started and finished their victory romp with classic goals, the first from Greaves and the second from Bobby Smith, who delicately chipped the ball over the goalkeeper's head from 20 yards to break the Spanish spirit after they had twice battled back to equalize. One of the outstanding features of the game was the duel between Armfield and Gento, with the Blackpool full-back emerging triumphant against one of the greatest wingers of all time.

119: v Wales, Wembley, 23.11.60. England won 5–1

| Hodgkinson | Armfield | McNeil | Robson R. | Swan | Flowers |
| Douglas | Greaves² | Smith R.¹ | Haynes*¹ | Charlton R.¹ | |

Greaves scored the first of his two goals in the second minute and Wales were never allowed to recover from this jolting start. The five-goal haul took England's total to twenty-three in four matches. Winterbottom had pledged to go through the season with an unchanged team, but injury to Ron Springett brought a recall for Alan Hodgkinson.

120: v Scotland, Wembley, 15.4.61. England won 9–3

| Springett | Armfield | McNeil | Robson R.¹ | Swan | Flowers |
| Douglas¹ | Greaves³ | Smith R.² | Haynes*² | Charlton R. | |

The peak performance by Winterbottom's new team. Bobby Robson started the ball rolling with a 20-yard shot that left goalkeeper Frank Haffey flapping at empty air in the 9th minute. Greaves struck twice, putting the finishing touches to moves masterminded by Haynes. The Scots, including players of the quality of Billy McNeill, Dave Mackay and Ian St John, pulled back to 3–2 early in the second-half before they were sunk under a storm of five goals in eleven minutes. Haffey was picked on by the Scots as the scapegoat for the defeat, and he was cruelly dubbed 'Slap-Haffey'. But neutral observers considered this an exceptional display by England in general and Haynes in particular. He pulled the Scottish defence apart with a procession of precise passes, and was chaired off the pitch by team-mates at the end of the nine-goal slaughter. Greaves (12) and Smith (7) had scored nineteen goals between them in five matches at the start of a partnership that was later to flourish for Tottenham.

121: v **Mexico**, Wembley, 10.5.61. England won 8–0

Springett	Armfield	McNeil	Robson R.[1]	Swan	Flowers[1]
Douglas[2]	Kevan	Hitchens[1]	Haynes*	Charlton R.[3]	

Smith was injured and Greaves suspended by Chelsea (for refusing to go on a club tour to Israel on the eve of his move to AC Milan), but the goal floodgates were still kicked open by England. Gerry Hitchens made a sensational start to his England career, scoring with his first shot after just 90 seconds. Bobby Charlton, a blond bombshell on the left wing, hammered his first international hat-trick as England took their goals tally to an astonishing forty in six matches.

122: v **Portugal**, Lisbon, 21.5.61. Drew 1–1

Springett	Armfield	McNeil	Robson R.	Swan	Flowers[1]
Douglas	Greaves	Smith R.	Haynes*	Charlton R.	

A mix-up between goalkeeper Ron Springett and Bobby Robson let Portugal in for the first goal of the match just after half-time in a World Cup qualifier played in extreme heat. Ron Flowers crashed in the vital equalizer 9 minutes from the end from a free-kick that took a slight deflection on the way into the net.

123: v **Italy**, Rome, 24.5.61. England won 3–2

Springett	Armfield	McNeil	Robson R.	Swan	Flowers
Douglas	Greaves[1]	Hitchens[2]	Haynes*	Charlton R.	

The Italians, parading the gifted Argentinian-born Omar Sivori as the ace in their pack, took control after the shock of going behind to an early goal by Gerry Hitchens. Sivori equalized with a flashing shot after side-stepping a challenge, and Italy's domination was rewarded with a second goal that convinced Sivori victory was complete and he started playing to the crowd. But his exhibitionism proved premature. Greaves raced 40 yards to lay on an equalizer for Hitchens, whose performance persuaded Inter Milan that they should buy him. Greaves, due to join AC Milan, capped a magnificent performance when 5 minutes from the end he raced on to a Haynes pass and steered the ball wide of Italy's substitute goalkeeper. He had come on for Buffon, who was carried off after a brave dive at the feet of Haynes had left him with a broken nose. Haynes led the England players on a lap of honour at the end as the 100,000 crowd whistled and hooted both them and their own players. It was a famous victory to rank alongside the 1948 triumph in Turin.

124: v Austria, Vienna, 27.5.61. England lost 3–1

Springett	Armfield	Angus	Miller	Swan	Flowers
Douglas	Greaves[1]	Hitchens	Haynes*	Charlton R.	

England's run of eight matches without defeat (W7 D1 L0 F44 A11) ended in the Prater Stadium. The Austrians played a clever retreating defensive game and concentrated on hitting England with quick counter-attacks. Greaves equalized their early goal, but the England defence – in which Burnley team-mates John Angus and Brian Miller were winning their only caps – lacked its usual understanding and they conceded two late goals against an enterprising Austrian attack.

125: v Luxemburg, Highbury, 28.9.61. England won 4–1

Springett	Armfield*	McNeil	Robson R.	Swan	Flowers
Douglas	Fantham	Pointer1	Viollett[1]	Charlton R.[2]	

With Greaves and Hitchens otherwise engaged in Italy and Haynes injured, Johnny Fantham, Ray Pointer and Dennis Viollett teamed up together for the first time in this World Cup qualifier. It was a combination that struggled to get into gear against the part-timers of Luxemburg, who had been swamped 9–0 in the first meeting. The Highbury crowd continually booed and slow-handclapped England, but they were finally silenced by two long-range goals from Charlton – one from his left foot and the other from his right. The following month the same Luxemburg team caused one of the greatest of all upsets in the World Cup qualifying rounds when they beat Portugal 4–2.

126: v Wales, Ninian Park, 14.10.61. Drew 1–1

Springett	Armfield	Wilson	Robson R.	Swan	Flowers
Connelly	Douglas[1]	Pointer	Haynes*	Charlton R.	

Bryan Douglas, having switched from the wing to the role of inside forward between Burnley team-mates John Connelly and Ray Pointer, scored the goal that gave England a draw in what Welsh idol John Charles described as 'the toughest international match in which I've played'. England's walking wounded at the end included Pointer (concussion), Flowers (gashed face) and Armfield (pulled muscle).

127: v **Portugal,** Wembley, 25.10.61. England won 2–0

| Springett | Armfield | Wilson | Robson R. | Swan | Flowers |
| Connelly[1] | Douglas | Pointer[1] | Haynes* | Charlton R. | |

Portugal needed to win to qualify for the World Cup finals ahead of England, but their hopes died as Connelly and Pointer scored a goal each inside the first 10 minutes. Eusebio, the new shooting star of Benfica, rattled the England woodwork with two shots in the closing stages.

128: v **Northern Ireland**, Wembley, 22.11.61. Drew 1–1

| Springett | Armfield | Wilson | Robson R. | Swan | Flowers |
| Douglas | Byrne | Crawford | Haynes* | Charlton R.[1] | |

The selectors tried yet another attack combination, this time pairing Ipswich centre-forward Ray Crawford with Johnny 'Budgie' Byrne, who was making a name for himself in the Third Division with Crystal Palace. They were never comfortable with each other against an Irish team in which Danny Blanchflower was in imperious form. The game was decorated with a goal each from Bobby Charlton and Jimmy McIlroy, and the Irish could claim to have been unlucky only to get a draw.

129: v **Austria,** Wembley, 4.4.62. England won 3–1

| Springett | Armfield | Wilson | Anderson | Swan | Flowers[1] |
| Connelly | Hunt[1] | Crawford[1] | Haynes* | Charlton R. | |

England avenged the defeat in Vienna of the previous year thanks mainly to the midfield domination of Haynes, who kept picking holes in the massed Austrian defence with low, angled passes. Five goal chances fell to the feet of Roger Hunt, who was making his début along with Sunderland's rugged Stan Anderson. Hunt was able to score from only one of the opportunities, and the London press started the Greaves v. Hunt debate that was to last throughout their careers. It is worth pointing out here that Jimmy and Roger have nothing but the highest respect for each other and that the 'bitter rivalry' between them was manufactured by the media.

130: v **Scotland**, Hampden Park, 14.4.62. England lost 2–0

| Springett | Armfield | Wilson | Anderson | Swan | Flowers |
| Douglas | Greaves | Smith R. | Haynes* | Charlton R. | |

For the first time in fifteen games, England failed to score and this was as much due to the tight Scottish defence as the misfiring of the England attack that had new Tottenham team-mates Greaves and Smith back in harness. The Scots were determined to avenge their 9–3 hammering of 1961, and 'Slim' Jim Baxter, Pat Crerand and John White gave them midfield control, while Denis Law and Ian St John were a couple of buzzsaws in attack. A Davie Wilson goal in the 13th minute and a penalty by Eric Caldow in the closing moments gave Scotland their first home victory over England since 1937. Haynes claimed a goal when his shot bounced down off the underside of the bar, but the referee waved play on. For the first time for thirty-five years England had failed to win a match in the Home Championship. All the flair, the panache and the confidence of a year ago seemed to have disintegrated.

131: v **Switzerland,** Wembley, 9.5.62. England won 3–1

| Springett | Armfield | Wilson | Robson R. | Swan | Flowers[1] |
| Connelly[1] | Greaves | Hitchens[1] | Haynes* | Charlton R. | |

Only a series of stunning saves by Ron Springett saved England from defeat after they had swept to a 3–1 lead in the first half hour with goals from Ron Flowers, Gerry Hitchens and John Connelly. Hitchens and Greaves smacked shots against the woodwork, but England became caught in the clutches of complacency and the Swiss staged a second-half revival that brought the best out of Springett.

132: v **Peru,** Lima, 20.5.62. England won 4–0

| Springett | Armfield | Wilson | Moore | Norman | Flowers[1] |
| Douglas | Greaves[3] | Hitchens | Haynes* | Charlton R. | |

The final warm-up match before the 1962 World Cup finals was notable for a hat-trick from Greaves and the cool, commanding début performance of twenty-one-year-old West Ham wing-half Bobby Moore. Ron Flowers gave England the lead from the penalty spot before Greaves scored his three goals. Jimmy also put a shot against a post and Johnny Haynes hit the crossbar. Springett saved a spot-kick to become the first England goalkeeper to make two penalty saves. Maurice Norman made his bow at the heart of the defence after Peter Swan had pulled out with tonsilitis.

133: v **Hungary,** World Cup, Rancagua, 31.5.62. England lost 2–1

| Springett | Armfield | Wilson | Moore | Norman | Flowers[1] |
| Douglas | Greaves | Hitchens | Haynes* | Charlton R. | |

A depressing start to the World Cup. Ron Springett was deceived by the flight of a harmless-looking 15-yard shot from Tichy in the 20th minute, and from then on England were struggling to get into the game on a wet, slippery surface that made every step a challenge. Fifteen minutes into the second-half a goal-bound Greaves shot was handled on the line, and Flowers scored from the penalty spot. Flowers was then reluctantly responsible for Hungary's winning goal. He slipped on the soaked turf and left Florian Albert free to race away and score with a low shot.

134: v **Argentina,** World Cup, Rancagua, 2.6.62. England won 3–1

Springett	Armfield	Wilson	Moore	Norman	Flowers[1]
Douglas	Greaves[1]	Peacock	Haynes*	Charlton R.[1]	

Alan Peacock, evading the brutal attentions of Argentine captain Ruben Navarro, thought he had started his international career with an early goal when he headed a Charlton cross wide of the goalkeeper. But Navarro managed to push the ball out with his hand. Ice-cool Flowers scored from the spot for the third successive match. Charlton then crashed in one of his specials, and midway through the second half Greaves made it 3–0 after the goalkeeper had failed to hold a Douglas cross. A defensive muddle let Sanfillipo in for a late consolation goal.

135: v **Bulgaria**, World Cup, Rancagua, 7.6.62. Drew 0–0

Springett	Armfield	Wilson	Moore	Norman	Flowers
Douglas	Greaves	Peacock	Haynes*	Charlton R.	

This was probably the most boring, sterile match England had ever contested. They needed only a draw to qualify for the quarter-finals ahead of Argentina, and as Bulgaria showed no inclination to win the match England were content to sit back and make sure they made no mistakes. The result was that the ball hardly left the midfield area and neither goalkeeper was tested.

136: v **Brazil,** World Cup, Vina del Mar, 10.6.62. England lost 3–1

Springett	Armfield	Wilson	Moore	Norman	Flowers
Douglas	Greaves	Hitchens[1]	Haynes*	Charlton R.	

England's World Cup life was snuffed out by a Brazilian team minus Pelé but with 'Little Bird' Garrincha at his bewildering best. The ball-conjuring winger put Brazil in the lead 13 minutes before half-time when he moved like a whippet to head in a Zagallo corner. England hit back with an equalizer 6 minutes later, Hitchens sweeping the ball home after a Greaves header had hit the bar. Garrincha decided the match early in the second-half. His free-kick from 25 yards was too hot to handle for Springett, and as he pushed the ball out Vava followed up to head it into the net. Then Garrincha, the man with two left feet, sent a viciously swerving shot curling out of Springett's reach and into the roof of the net.

137: v France, Hillsborough, 3.10.62. Drew 1–1

Springett	Armfield*	Wilson	Moore	Norman	Flowers[1]
Hellawell	Crowe	Charnley	Greaves	Hinton	

Walter Winterbottom was working out his notice, Johnny Haynes was recovering from injuries received in a car smash and Bobby Charlton was still not fit after a hernia operation. Mike Hellawell, Chris Crowe, Ray Charnley and Alan Hinton were brought together in an experimental forward line that never looked like clicking in this European championship qualifying match. A Ron Flowers penalty saved England from defeat against a French team skippered by the old fox Raymond Kopa. Maurice Norman was booed every time he touched the ball on the home ground of Peter Swan, the man he had replaced at centre-half.

138: v Northern Ireland, Windsor Park, 20.10.62. England won 3–1

Springett	Armfield*	Wilson	Moore	Labone	Flowers
Hellawell	Hill F.	Peacock	Greaves[1]	O'Grady[2]	

Mike O'Grady, twenty-year-old Huddersfield winger and the fifth son of an Irishman, was the latest player tried at outside-left. He must have shaken the skeletons of his ancestors as he sank Northern Ireland with two goals. Greaves, another player with deep Irish roots, also scored in a match that featured the début at centre-half of Brian Labone.

139: v Wales, Wembley, 22.11.62. England won 4–0

Springett	Armfield*	Shaw G.	Moore	Labone	Flowers
Connelly[1]	Hill F.	Peacock[2]	Greaves[1]	Tambling	

Walter Winterbottom's final match. Alf Ramsey watched from the stand in readiness to take over. There was a crowd of only 27,500 – the lowest to date for a Wembley international – to see England romp to a comfortable victory. Bobby Tambling made his début in the no. 11 shirt. Alan Peacock scored two goals, John Connelly one and Greaves netted the last goal of Winterbottom's reign. In the dressing-room after the match skipper Jimmy Armfield presented Walter with a set of crystal cut-glass goblets on behalf of the players. The toast was, 'Walter Winterbottom, master manager'.

Ramsey's teams and match highlights

140: v **France**, Paris, 27.2.63. England lost 5-2

Springett	Armfield*	Henry	Moore	Labone	Flowers
Connelly	Tambling[1]	Smith[1]	Greaves	Charlton R.	

Alf Ramsey's first match – a European championship qualifier – was a personal nightmare for goalkeeper Ron Springett. He was responsible for three of the French goals, his most costly error coming after England had pulled back from 3-0 to 3–2 with goals from Bobby Tambling and the recalled Bobby Smith. Springett did not try to make any excuses, but Ramsey pointed out that he had been kicked in the ribs when conceding the first goal. Ron Henry, Tottenham's skilful left-back, had an uncomfortable night against a flying French winger in his one and only England appearance.

141: v **Scotland**, Wembley, 6.4.63. England lost 2–1

Banks	Armfield*	Byrne G.	Moore	Norman	Flowers
Douglas1	Greaves	Smith	Melia	Charlton R.	

Both teams were down to ten men within 5 minutes following a collision between Bobby Smith and Scottish skipper Eric Caldow, who was carried off with a triple fracture of the leg. By the time Smith limped back on with his bruised knee bandaged, 'Slim' Jim Baxter had twice beaten England's new goalkeeper Gordon Banks, first after a misplaced pass by Armfield and then from the penalty spot. Bryan Douglas scored 10 minutes from the end, but the Scots deserved a victory that was masterminded by Baxter. Liverpool team-mates Gerry Byrne and Jimmy Melia made their debuts. It was the first match played at the 'new' Wembley with a £500,000 roof that ran right round the stadium like a giant lip.

142: v **Brazil**, Wembley, 8.5.63. Drew 1–1

Banks	Armfield*	Wilson	Milne	Norman	Moore
Douglas1	Greaves	Smith	Eastham	Charlton R.	

There was no Pelé, but Pépé popped up with a first-half 'banana' free-kick from 25 yards that deceived Gordon Banks and swung into the roof of the England net. Douglas scrambled a late equalizer. Gordon Milne was the first defensive 'ball-winning' midfield player selected by Ramsey, a role that would ultimately go to Nobby Stiles. George Eastham followed his father, George senior, as an England international, and they were the first father and son to win England caps.

143: v Czechoslovakia, Bratislava, 20.5.63. England won 4–2

Banks	Shellito	Wilson	Milne	Norman	Moore*
Paine	Greaves[2]	Smith[1]	Eastham	Charlton R.[1]	

The first victory under the Ramsey baton, and what an impressive scalp. Czechoslovakia had been runners-up in the 1962 World Cup final and included European footballer of the year Josef Masopust in their midfield. Greaves, Smith and Charlton scored the goals, and Ken Shellito and Terry Paine made impressive débuts. A knee injury would virtually end Shellito's career within the year. Bobby Moore captained England for the first time in place of the injured Armfield.

144: v East Germany, Leipzig, 2.6.63. England won 2–1

Banks	Armfield*	Wilson	Milne	Norman	Moore
Paine	Hunt[1]	Smith	Eastham	Charlton R.[1]	

Roger Hunt, playing in place of tonsilitis-victim Greaves, scored a spectacular equalizer from 30 yards after Banks had conceded a soft goal midway through the first half. Bobby Charlton netted the second-half winner after a series of goalmouth misses against an outpowered East German team.

145: v Switzerland, Basle, 5.6.63. England won 8–1

Springett	Armfield*	Wilson	Kay[1]	Moore	Flowers
Douglas[1]	Greaves	Byrne J.[2]	Melia[1]	Charlton R.[3]	

A hat-trick from Bobby Charlton and two goals from Johnny Byrne helped England bury the Swiss under an avalanche of goals. Everton midfield dynamo Tony Kay scored in his only international appearance before the careers of both he and his former Sheffield Wednesday team-mate Peter Swan were wrecked by a bribery and betting scandal.

146: v Wales, Ninian Park, 12.10.63. England won 4–0

Banks	Armfield*	Wilson	Milne	Norman	Moore
Paine	Greaves[1]	Smith[2]	Eastham	Charlton R.[1]	

The double act of Greaves and Smith was unstoppable. Greaves made a goal in the 5th minute for Smith who then returned the compliment before Jimmy laid on a second goal for his Tottenham team-mate. Bobby Charlton finished off the Welsh with his thirty-first goal for England, beating the record jointly held by Nat Lofthouse and Tom Finney.

147: v Rest of World, Wembley, 23.10.63. England won 2–1

Banks	Armfield*	Wilson	Milne	Norman	Moore
Paine1	Greaves[1]	Smith	Eastham	Charlton R.	

Rest of the World: Yashin Santos D. Schnellinger Pluskal Popluhar Masopust Kopa Law di Stefano Eusebio Gento (Subs: Soskic, Eyzaguirre, Baxter, Seeler, Puskas)

Jinking Jimmy Greaves was the star turn on the Wembley stage in this prestige match to celebrate the centenary of the Football Association. He might have had a first-half hat-trick but for the magnificent goalkeeping of Russia's 'Man in Black' Lev Yashin. Terry Paine gave England a first-half lead which was cancelled out by Denis Law, and it was Greavsie who conjured up the winner with just 3 minutes of a memorable match left.

148: v Northern Ireland, Wembley, 20.11.63. England won 8–3

Banks	Armfield*	Thomson	Milne	Norman	Moore
Paine[3]	Greaves[4]	Smith[1]	Eastham	Charlton R.	

Four goals from Greaves and a hat-trick from Terry Paine lit up this first match under the Wembley floodlights, and Bobby Smith scored once in what was to be his final international. Smith (12) and Greaves (19) between them collected thirty-one goals in just thirteen matches together. Wolves full-back Bobby Thomson made a sound début.

149: v Scotland, Hampden Park, 11.4.64. England lost 1–0

Banks	Armfield*	Wilson	Milne	Norman	Moore
Paine	Hunt	Byrne J.	Eastham	Charlton R.	

Roger Hunt and Johnny Byrne deputized for injured Greaves and Smith. Alan Gilzean, who was to take over from Smith as partner to Greaves at Spurs, scored the only goal of the match after Gordon Banks had misjudged a 72nd-minute corner-kick from Davie Wilson that got held up in the near-gale force wind.

150: v Uruguay, Wembley, 6.5.64. England won 2–1

Banks	Cohen	Wilson	Milne	Norman	Moore*
Paine	Greaves	Byrne J.[2]	Eastham	Charlton R.	

George Cohen came in at right-back for the injured Jimmy Armfield, and partnered Ray Wilson for the first time. Ramsey's 1966 World Cup defence was taking shape. Johnny Byrne scored both England goals in an uninspiring match.

151: v **Portugal**, Lisbon, 17.5.64. England won 4–3

Banks	Cohen	Wilson	Milne	Norman	Moore*
Thompson	Greaves	Byrne J.[3]	Eastham	Charlton R.[1]	

Johnny Byrne completed a memorable hat-trick in the final moments with a beautifully disguised chip shot from the edge of the penalty area that went over the heads of three defenders and the goalkeeper and into the net. Portugal, who had led twice through the towering Torres – a 6 ft 7 in centre-forward – and Eusebio, could not believe it. Liverpool dribbler Peter Thompson won his first of sixteen caps as he tried to prove to Ramsey that he did need wingers.

152: v **Republic of Ireland**, Dublin, 24.5.64. England won 3–1

Waiters	Cohen	Wilson	Milne	Flowers	Moore*
Thompson	Greaves[1]	Byrne J.[1]	Eastham[1]	Charlton R.	

Goals from George Eastham and Johnny Byrne gave England a 2-1 half-time lead and Jimmmy Greaves wrapped it up in the 55th minute when he put the finishing touch to a classic five-man move down the right wing involving Milne, Thompson, Byrne and Eastham. Noel Cantwell switched from left-back to the middle of the Irish defence in a bid to control Byrne, who was at his brilliant best as he tormented his markers with subtle touches and clever changes of pace.

153: v **USA**, New York, 27.5.64. England won 10–0

Banks	Cohen	Thomson	Bailey	Norman	Flowers*
Paine[2]	Hunt[4]	Pickering[3]	Eastham (Charlton R.[1])	Thompson	

Everton centre-forward Fred Pickering started his international career with a hat-trick and Roger Hunt scored four goals as England ran riot against an overwhelmed United States team. Mike Bailey, driving captain of Charlton before his move to Wolves, had a comfortable début and would have won many more caps but for breaking a leg four months later.

154: v **Brazil**, Rio de Janeiro, 30.5.64. England lost 5–1

Waiters	Cohen	Wilson	Milne	Norman	Moore*
Thompson	Greaves[1]	Byrne J.	Eastham	Charlton R.	

Alf Ramsey preferred Tony Waiters to Gordon Banks in goal for this

'Little World Cup' tournament match against the world champions. Greaves equalized a first-half goal that Pelé created for Rinaldo, and then midway through the second-half Pelé took over and pulverized England with a purple patch that produced three goals in 5 minutes. Twice he earned free-kicks just outside the penalty area while dancing through the England defence juggling the ball like a circus performer. Waiters was completely deceived by swerving free-kicks from Rinaldo and Julinho, and then Pelé contributed a magical goal of his own, pushing the ball through the legs of first Bobby Moore and then Maurice Norman before sending a long-range shot screaming into the net. Diaz scored goal number five after Pelé had again confused the England defence 2 minutes from the end.

155: v **Portugal**, São Paulo, 4.6.64. Drew 1–1

Banks	Thomson	Wilson	Flowers	Norman	Moore*
Paine	Greaves	Byrne J.	Hunt[1]	Thompson	

Portugal were down to ten men when centre-forward José Torres was sent off for attempting to hit the referee shortly after Roger Hunt had equalized a goal by Peres. Jimmy Greaves and Johnny Byrne hit the woodwork, and Byrne had a goal disallowed but England failed to take advantage of having an extra man.

156: v **Argentina**, Rio de Janeiro, 6.6.64. England lost 1–0

Banks	Thomson	Wilson	Milne	Norman	Moore*
Thompson	Greaves	Byrne J.	Eastham	Charlton R.	

England held Argentina for an hour until Rojas scored in a breakaway raid seconds after Greaves had missed a clear chance at the opposite end of the pitch. The Argentinians, with skipper Antonio Rattin in commanding form, then played strolling possession football to frustrate England and to clinch victory in the 'Little World Cup' tournament.

157: v **Northern Ireland**, Windsor Park, 3.10.64. England won 4–3

Banks	Cohen	Thomson	Milne	Norman	Moore*
Paine	Greaves[3]	Pickering[1]	Charlton R.	Thompson	

Greaves scored a first half hat-trick as England rushed to a 4-0 half-time lead, but the second half belonged to George Best and Ireland. The young Manchester United winger tied the defenders into knots, and inspired the Irish into a fight back that had England hanging on to a one-goal lead at the final whistle. Ramsey gave his team a rocket for becoming complacent.

158: v **Belgium**, Wembley, 21.10.64. Drew 2–2

Waiters	Cohen	Thomson	Milne	Norman	Moore*
Thompson	Greaves	Pickering[1]	Venables	Hinton[1]	

Ramsey experimented with a new left-wing partnership of Terry Venables and Alan Hinton against a Belgian side that included eight players from their league champions Anderlecht. It was Hinton whose shot was deflected into the net for an equalizing goal in the 70th minute. For Venables, selection completed a unique collection of England caps at all levels – schools, youth, amateur, Under-23 and full.

159: v **Wales**, Wembley, 18.11.64. England won 2–1

Waiters	Cohen	Thomson	Bailey	Flowers*	Young
Thompson	Hunt	Wignall[2]	Byrne J.	Hinton	

Mike Bailey, Ron Flowers and Gerry Young formed a makeshift half-back line because of injuries. There was also an experimental inside-forward trio, with Frank Wignall the spearhead to Roger Hunt and Johnny Byrne. Wignall scored both England goals before Cliff Jones netted for Wales.

160: v **Holland**, Amsterdam 9.12.64. Drew 1–1

Waiters	Cohen	Thomson	Mullery	Norman	Flowers*
Thompson	Greaves[1]	Wignall	Venables	Charlton R.	

Alan Mullery made his debut in midfield alongside Terry Venables, a partnership that they would soon renew at Tottenham. It was another Tottenham star, Greaves, who scored 4 minutes from the end to force a draw in this match to celebrate the seventy-fifth anniversary of the Dutch Football Association.

161: v **Scotland**, Wembley, 10.4.64. Drew 2–2

Banks	Cohen	Wilson	Stiles	Charlton J.	Moore*
Thompson	Greaves[1]	Bridges	Byrne J.	Charlton R.[1]	

England did well to salvage a draw from a game in which they were reduced to only nine fit players. Ray Wilson went off at half-time with torn rib muscles, and Johnny Byrne – dropping back to replace Wilson at left-back – became a limping passenger with a knee injury that virtually finished his international career. Ramsey blooded Barry Bridges, Nobby Stiles and Jack Charlton (with brother Bobby on the left wing). It was the first time that England's 1966 World Cup defence paraded together. Bobby Charlton and Greaves gave England a commanding 2–0 lead inside the first 35 minutes. Denis Law scored for Scotland 5 minutes before half-time with a viciously swerving shot, and Ian St John equalized midway through the

Ron Greenwood

'The only way is up, gentlemen . . .' 'Reverend' Ron Greenwood makes a point in his first press conference after taking over as England manager in 1977.

(*Above*) Ron Greenwood appears to be trying to put his England players in a hypnotic trance before his first match against Switzerland in 1977. The result was a goalless draw.

(*Right*) Ron Greenwood might have been predicting the score of England's match against Northern Ireland in Belfast in 1979. England won 5–1 to virtually clinch a place in the 1980 European championship finals.

Bobby Robson

Bobby Robson starts spreading the word as he begins his reign as England manager in 1982. On the receiving end are Trevor Francis and, with his back to the camera, Kenny Sansom.

(*Above*) The Robsons, both Geordies but not related – manager Bobby with his 'Captain Marvel' Bryan.

(*Left*) Thumbs up in Mexico as Bobby Robson celebrates England's 3–0 victory over Paraguay in the 1986 World Cup finals.

(*Left*) It looks as though the strain of the job is beginning to tell as Bobby Robson urges greater effort during a training session at Bisham Abbey in 1987.

(*Below*) One of the lowest points for Bobby Robson and his coach Don Howe. England are on their way to a 3–1 defeat by the USSR and exit from the 1988 European championship finals in Frankfurt.

Graham Taylor

No, Graham Taylor is not singing a song. He's pleading for total effort from the players for his first match as England manager against Hungary in 1990. England won 1–0.

OPPOSITE
 (*Above*) Graham Taylor directs an England training session and points the way for what he hopes will be a place in the World Cup finals..(*Right*) Graham Taylor and Lawrie McMenemy, a formidable double act. McMenemy is happy to take a back seat, but his wise counselling is often sought by Taylor.

Graham Taylor has a quiet word with Paul Gascoigne before England's European championship match against the Republic of Ireland in Dublin in 1990. Taylor shocked everybody by leaving England's most gifted player on the touchline.

second half after Cohen had cleared a Davie Wilson shot off the line.

162: v **Hungary**, Wembley, 5.5.65. England won 1–0

Banks	Cohen	Wilson	Stiles	Charlton J.	Moore*
Paine	Greaves[1]	Bridges	Eastham	Connelly	

Ramsey's international playing career had ended the last time the Hungarians visited Wembley for their famous 6–3 victory in 1953. The revenge for which he had waited so long was given to him by a Greaves goal in the 16th minute. Bobby Charlton failed a late fitness test and John Connelly was recalled for the first time since Ramsey's desperate first match against France.

163: v **Yugoslavia**, Belgrade, 9.5.65. Drew 1–1

Banks	Cohen	Wilson	Stiles	Charlton J.	Moore*
Paine	Greaves	Bridges[1]	Ball	Connelly	

Ramsey's jigsaw came closer to completion when Alan Ball made his début, showing the energy and enthusiasm that was to make him such a vital member of the 1966 World Cup squad. Barry Bridges, Chelsea's jet-paced centre-forward, headed England's equalizer after the Yugoslavs had taken a 15th-minute lead. England were the first foreign side to avoid defeat in Yugoslavia in a full international.

164: v **West Germany**, Nuremberg 12.5.65. England won 1–0

Banks	Cohen	Wilson	Flowers	Charlton J.	Moore*
Paine[1]	Ball	Jones	Eastham	Temple	

Derek Temple, Everton's flying winger, was called into England's injury-weakened side for what was his only cap. It was his surging run and cross that laid on the winning goal for Terry Paine in the 37th minute. Ramsey experimented with a variation of a 4–3–3 formation, with Mick Jones leading the attack for the first time.

165: v **Sweden**, Gothenburg, 16.5.65. England won 2–1

Banks	Cohen	Wilson	Stiles	Charlton J.	Moore*
Paine	Ball[1]	Jones	Eastham	Connelly[1]	

Alan Ball scored his first goal in international football and John Connelly snatched the winner in a game in which the mudheap of a pitch got the better of most of the players. Nobby Stiles lost his contact lenses and a special lubricant had to be flown in from London on match day so that he could wear a spare pair. He and Ball dominated the midfield.

166: v **Wales**, Ninian Park, 2.10.65. Drew 0–0

Springett	Cohen	Wilson	Stiles	Charlton J.	Moore*
Paine	Greaves	Peacock	Charlton R.	Connelly	

Goalkeeper Ron Springett was recalled for his first game since his night-mare match in France in Ramsey's first game as England manager. He played impressively enough in a goalless game to book a place in the 1966 World Cup squad as an understudy to his successor Gordon Banks.

167: v **Austria**, Wembley, 20.10.65. England lost 3–2

Springett	Cohen	Wilson	Stiles	Charlton J.	Moore*
Paine	Greaves	Bridges	Charlton R.[1]	Connelly[1]	

England were twice in front through Bobby Charlton and John Connelly, but slack defensive play let the Austrians in for two late goals. It was to be England's last defeat before the World Cup.

168: v **Northern Ireland**, Wembley, 10.11.65. England won 2–1

Banks	Cohen	Wilson	Stiles	Charlton J.	Moore*
Thompson	Baker[1]	Peacock[1]	Charlton R.	Connelly	

Joe Baker, deputizing for hepatitis-victim Greaves, put England in the lead in the 19th minute. The Irish equalised 60 seconds later when Willie Irvine turned a George Best centre through the legs of an embarrassed Gordon Banks. Persistent rain made the surface treacherous, and the Irish defenders were slithering around when Alan Peacock scored England's winner in the 70th minute.

169: v **Spain**, Madrid, 8.12.65. England won 2–0

Banks	Cohen	Wilson	Stiles	Charlton J.	Moore*
Ball	Hunt[1]	Baker[1] (Hunter)		Eastham	Charlton R.

One of the most significant games in Ramsey's reign as manager. He gave full rein to his 4–3–3 formation for the first time following the experiment in Nuremberg, and the resounding victory convinced him that he had found the tactics best suited to England for the World Cup. Joe Baker gave England an early lead on a pitch soaked by melting snow, and then limped off in the 35th minute with a pulled muscle. Norman Hunter became the first England player to make his début as a substitute. Roger Hunt clinched victory with a classic goal on the hour after a sweeping length-of-the-pitch passing movement involving George Cohen, Bobby Charlton and Bobby Moore.

170: v Poland, Liverpool, 5.1.66. Drew 1–1

Banks	Cohen	Wilson	Stiles	Charlton J.	Moore*[1]
Ball	Hunt	Baker	Eastham	Harris	

Bobby Moore scored one of the two goals that decorated his 108 international appearances to cancel out Poland's lead on a glue-pot pitch at Goodison. Moore put the finishing touch to a late move started by Burnley winger Gordon Harris, deputizing for the injured Bobby Charlton, and it was Jack Charlton who made the final pass that created the opening for England's skipper.

171: v West Germany, Wembley, 23.2.66. England won 1–0

Banks	Cohen	Newton (Wilson)	Moore*	Charlton J.	Hunter
Ball	Hunt	Stiles[1]	Hurst	Charlton R.	

This was to prove a dress rehearsal for the World Cup Final just five months later. Nobby Stiles, wearing the no. 9 shirt but playing in midfield, scored the only goal of the match and of his international career. Geoff Hurst made an impressive England début, and Keith Newton's first England game ended just before half-time when he limped off to be replaced by substitute Ray Wilson. The Germans claimed an equalizer when Heiss turned in a cross from Held, but the referee disallowed it after consulting a flag-waving linesman. The shape of things to come!

172: v Scotland, Hampden Park, 2.4.66. England won 4–3

Banks	Cohen	Newton	Stiles	Charlton J.	Moore*
Ball	Hunt[2]	Charlton R.[1]	Hurst[1]	Connelly	

Geoff Hurst scored his first goal for England in the 19th minute to start a spree that excited the 134,000 crowd but made purists wince at the procession of defensive blunders. Hunt made it 2–0 for England before Denis Law threw himself forward in typical dare-devil style to head Scotland's first goal just before half-time. Hunt made it 3–1 early in the second half, and then Celtic's jinking winger Jimmy Johnstone pulled it back to 3–2 before a thunderbolt shot from Bobby Charlton restored the two-goal lead. Johnstone, turning the England defence inside out with his dribbling runs, scored the final goal 6 minutes from the end with a delicate curling shot that deceived goalkeeper Gordon Banks.

173: v Yugoslavia, Wembley, 4.5.66. England won 2–0

Banks	Armfield*	Wilson	Peters	Charlton J.	Hunter
Paine	Greaves[1]	Charlton R.[1]	Hurst	Tambling	

Jimmy Greaves, back in the England team after his hepatitis-forced four-month lay-off, scored the first goal in the 9th minute. Bobby Charlton celebrated being elected 'Footballer of the Year' by wrapping up England's victory with another of his screaming long-range shots. Martin Peters, the player who would be described by Ramsey as 'ten years ahead of his time', twice went close to marking his début with a goal.

174: v Finland, Helsinki, 26.6.66. England won 3–0

| Banks | Armfield* | Wilson | Peters[1] | Charlton J.[1] | Hunter |
| Callaghan | Hunt[1] | Charlton R. | Hurst | Ball | |

Martin Peters scored his first goal for England and the first of the match at the start of a final warm-up tour before the World Cup finals. Alan Ball failed from the penalty spot in a game remembered more for the many missed chances than those that were eventually taken by Jack Charlton and Roger Hunt.

175: v Norway, Oslo, 29.6.66. England won 6–1

| Springett | Cohen | Byrne G. | Stiles | Flowers | Moore*[1] |
| Paine | Greaves[4] | Charlton R. | Hunt | Connelly[1] | |

Jimmy Greaves scored four goals for the second time in his international career against a Norwegian team that was out of its depth. FA and Chelsea chairman Joe Mears, a long-time friend and supporter of Greaves, died of a heart attack in Oslo the day after the match.

176: v Denmark, Copenhagen, 3.7.66. England won 2–0

| Bonetti | Cohen | Wilson | Stiles | Charlton J.[1] | Moore* |
| Ball | Greaves | Hurst | Eastham[1] | Connelly | |

Goals from Jack Charlton and George Eastham gave England their sixth successive victory. Goalkeeper Peter Bonetti had his first taste of international football and performed well on a bumpy pitch that led to many errors in front of him.

177: v Poland, Chorzow, 5.7.66. England won 1–0

| Banks | Cohen | Wilson | Stiles | Charlton J. | Moore* |
| Ball | Greaves | Charlton R. | Hunt[1] | Peters | |

A beautifully struck shot by Roger Hunt in the 13th minute was enough to give England victory in this final match before the World Cup finals. This would prove to be the line-up that just twenty-five days later would win the World Cup for England, with just one exception: Hurst in place of Greaves.

178: v **Uruguay**, World Cup, Wembley, 11.7.66. Drew 0–0

Banks	Cohen	Wilson	Stiles	Charlton J.	Moore*
Ball	Greaves	Charlton R.	Hunt	Connelly	

A dull and uninspiring start to the World Cup. Uruguay played with nine men back in defence and defied all England's attempts to break them down. It was the first time in twelve matches that England had failed to score. John Connelly was Ramsey's one winger.

179: v **Mexico**, World Cup, Wembley, 16.7.66. England won 2–0

Banks	Cohen	Wilson	Stiles	Charlton J.	Moore*
Paine	Greaves	Charlton R.[1]	Hunt[1]	Peters	

Ramsey had not yet completely abandoned wingers. Terry Paine was preferred to Connelly in this second game, with Peters taking the place of Alan Ball in midfield. Bobby Charlton unleashed one of his 25-yard specials for the first goal, and Roger Hunt clinched victory after having what looked a good goal ruled offside.

180: v France, World Cup, Wembley, 20.7.66. England won 2–0

Banks	Cohen	Wilson	Stiles	Charlton J.	Moore*
Callaghan	Greaves	Charlton R.	Hunt[2]	Peters	

Two smartly taken Roger Hunt goals gave England a confidence booster on their way into the World Cup quarter-finals. Ian Callaghan became the third winger tried by the England manager. Jimmy Greaves finished the match with a deep gash on his left shin, and Stiles was booked for a crunching tackle on French striker Simon. Ramsey ignored calls that he should drop Stiles.

181: v **Argentina**, World Cup, Wembley, 23.7.66. England won 1–0

Banks	Cohen	Wilson	Stiles	Charlton J.	Moore*
Ball	Hurst[1]	Charlton R.	Hunt	Peters	

Argentina shelved their superior skills and instead concentrated on what seemed a premeditated policy of disrupting England with a spate of petty fouls. Their captain Antonio Rattin arrogantly challenged just about every decision that the referee made and waved his arms around like a traffic policeman. Finally the referee, a little West German called Rudlof Kreitlin, could take no more of Rattin's disruptive tactics and ordered him off. It was almost comical to see the tiny figure of the referee staring up at the tall, stately looking Rattin and demanding that he leave the field. It was also very sad. It took ten minutes of argument and touchline interpretations before Rattin finally walked. Geoff Hurst, making his tournament début in place of the injured Greaves, headed the winning goal from a Martin Peters cross to the near post. It had made-in-West Ham written all over it. For Banks, it was a record seventh successive England appearance without conceding a goal. This was the first match in which England played without a recognized winger. Ramsey's 'Wingless Wonders' were off the launching pad.

182: v Portugal, World Cup semi-final, Wembley, 26.7.66. England won 2–1

Banks	Cohen	Wilson	Stiles	Charlton J.	Moore*
Ball	Hurst	Charlton R.[2]	Hunt	Peters	

This was the classic match of the 1966 World Cup. It lacked the drama of the Final, but the football played by both teams had rarely been bettered at Wembley. The match belonged more to Bobby Charlton than anybody. He moved with the grace of a Nureyev and the power of a panther. His reward was two superb goals, one drilled low into the net from a rebound after a Roger Hunt shot had been blocked, and the second, a real beauty, rifled high into the net from 25 yards. Seven minutes from the end England's magnificent defence conceded their first goal of the tournament when Eusebio scored from the penalty spot after Jack Charlton had handled a header from José Torres.

183: v West Germany, World Cup Final, Wembley, 30.7.66. England won 4–2 (after extra time)

Banks	Cohen	Wilson	Stiles	Charlton J.	Moore*
Ball	Hurst[3]	Charlton R.	Hunt	Peters[1]	

Ramsey decided to stick with an unchanged team. No place for Greaves. West Germany took the negative approach of putting Franz Beckenbauer on man-to-man marking duty against Bobby Charlton, so the two most creative players on the pitch cancelled each other out. A rare Ray Wilson mistake on a wet surface let Helmut Haller in for a 13th-minute goal, which was equalized 6 minutes later when Hurst headed in a perfectly flighted free-kick from his West Ham team-mate Bobby Moore. Just after the hour a Hurst shot was blocked and it was another West Hammer, Peters, who smacked the rebound smartly into the net to make it 2–1. England were 1 minute from the World Cup when Jack Charlton was adjudged to have fouled Germany's skipper Uwe Seeler. During a goalmouth scramble that followed the free-kick defender Hans Weber forced the ball into the net. Ten minutes into extra-time, the inexhaustible Alan Ball made one of his many scampering runs past left-back Schnellinger and centred the ball. Hurst turned and fired a first-time shot against the under-side of the bar, and England claimed the ball had crossed the goal-line. Swiss referee Georg Dienst awarded a controversial goal after consulting the Russian linesman Bakhramov. To this day, the Germans dispute the decision. Hurst ended all arguments in the final seconds when he ran on to a clearance from Bobby Moore and hammered a left foot shot past goalkeeper Hans Tilkowski to complete the first ever World Cup hat-trick. England were champions of the world.

184: v **Northern Ireland**, Windsor Park, 22.10.66. England won 2–0

Banks	Cohen	Wilson	Stiles	Charlton J.	Moore*
Ball	Hurst	Charlton R.	Hunt[1]	Peters[1]	

The Irish, with George Best and Derek Dougan in menacing mood, battled hard to overcome Engand in their first match as world champions, but they were sunk by a goal in each half by first Hunt and then Peters. The match became bad tempered and in the closing minutes Linfield winger Ferguson was ordered off.

185: v **Czechoslovakia**, Wembley, 2.11.66. Drew 0–0

Banks	Cohen	Wilson	Stiles	Charlton J.	Moore*
Ball	Hurst	Charlton R.	Hunt	Peters	

This was the sixteenth match since the summer of 1965 in which England had not conceded a goal. The Czechs came only to defend, and their nine-man blanket defence smothered the England attack.

186: v **Wales**, Wembley, 16.11.66. England won 5–1

Banks	Cohen	Wilson	Stiles	Charlton J.[1]	Moore*
Ball	Hurst[2]	Charlton R.[1]	Hunt	Peters[1] o.g.	

The Charlton brothers were both on the score-sheet and Geoff Hurst netted twice against a Welsh team that telegraphed their tactics by continually trying to play long balls to their twin strikers Wyn Davies and Ron Davies. Apart from a consolation headed goal by Wyn Davies, the England defence comfortably controlled the Welsh attack by shutting out their supply line from the wings.

187: v **Scotland**, Wembley, 15.4.67. England lost 3–2

Banks	Cohen	Wilson	Stiles	Charlton J.[1]	Moore*
Ball	Greaves	Charlton R.	Hurst[1]	Peters	

Scotland claimed they were world champions after handing England their first defeat in twenty matches, but it was something of a hollow victory against a team reduced to eight fit players. Jack Charlton hobbled at centre-foward for much of the match with a broken toe, Ray Wilson was a limping passenger after getting a kick on the ankle, and Jimmy Greaves was reduced to half pace by a knock in his comeback match. Denis Law was at his tormenting best and gave Scotland the lead after 28 minutes, and it remained at 1–0 until a four-goal rush in the last 12 minutes. Bobby Lennox made it 2–0 before Jack Charlton bravely pulled one back. Gordon Banks was beaten at the near post by Jim McCalliog for Scotland's third goal and then Hurst headed home a Bobby Charlton cross.

188: v **Spain**, Wembley, 24.5.67. England won 2–0

Bonetti	Cohen	Newton	Mullery	Labone	Moore*
Ball	Greaves[1]	Hurst	Hunt[1]	Hollins	

John Hollins won his only cap for England and played a prominent part in the first goal. His centre to the far post was headed down by Ball into the path of Hunt, whose shot was blocked and Greaves banged in the rebound; it was his fourty-fourth and final goal for England. Hunt scored England's second goal in a match played for much of the time in a torrential downpour.

189: v **Austria**, Vienna, 27.5.67. England won 1–0

Bonetti	Newton	Wilson	Mullery	Labone	Moore*
Ball[1]	Greaves	Hurst	Hunt	Hunter	

Sir Alf Ramsey's fiftieth match since he took over and his thirty-third victory. It was also a milestone match for Harold Shepherdson, who was on the touchline for his hundreth match as England trainer. A neatly worked goal by Alan Ball in the 20th minute won the match.

190: v **Wales**, Ninian Park, 21.10.67. England won 3–0

Banks	Cohen	Newton	Mullery	Charlton J.	Moore*
Ball[1]	Hunt	Charlton R.[1]	Hurst	Peters[1]	

The match turned on a magnificent save by Gordon Banks. Wales were having the better of the early play in a rainstorm when his Stoke teammate Roy Vernon fired a shot from point-blank range. Somehow Banks managed to fist the ball off target, and from then on England took command. Martin Peters and Bobby Charlton scored a goal each and Alan Ball netted from the penalty spot.

191: v **Northern Ireland**, Wembley, 22.11.67. England won 2–0

Banks	Cohen	Wilson	Mullery	Sadler	Moore*
Thompson	Hunt	Charlton R.[1]	Hurst[1]	Peters	

Versatile David Sadler made his début at centre-half against a Northern Ireland team missing their two key forwards Best and Dougan. Goals from Hurst and Bobby Charlton clinched victory in an undistinguished match.

192: v **USSR**, Wembley, 6.12.67. Drew 2–2

Banks	Knowles	Wilson	Mullery	Sadler	Moore*
Ball[1]	Hunt	Charlton R.	Hurst	Peters[1]	

Ray Wilson was given a rare chasing on a snow-carpeted pitch by flying Russian winger Chislenko. Alan Ball gave England an early lead, but two goals from 'Red Rocket' Chislenko put Russia in command. Bobby Moore and Ray Wilson combined to make an opening for Martin Peters, who headed an equalizer. Cyril Knowles made an assured debut out of position at right-back.

193: v **Scotland**, Hampden Park, 24.2.68. Drew 1–1

Banks	Newton	Wilson	Mullery	Labone	Moore*
Ball	Hurst	Summerbee	Charlton R.	Peters[1]	

England needed a draw to qualify for the European championship quarter-finals, Scotland a win. Peters produced one of his most impressive performances for England, scoring their goal with a superbly controlled swerving shot and going close on three other occasions. John Hughes headed Scotland's equalizer when Godon Banks slipped on the treacherous surface that was a mixture of mud and ice. Charlie Cooke had a brilliant 20-minute spell when he ran the England defence dizzy, but the Scottish strikers could not cash in on his creative work. Mike Summerbee made a quietly impressive début.

194: v **Spain**, Wembley, 3.4.68. England won 1–0

Banks	Knowles	Wilson	Mullery	Charlton J.	Moore*
Ball	Hunt	Summerbee	Charlton R.[1]	Peters	

Bobby Charlton crashed the ball into the net from a short free-kick taken by Martin Peters to equal the forty-four-goal England record held by Jimmy Greaves. Spain threatened to snatch a last minute equalizer in this first leg European championship quarter-final tie, but Banks pulled off a spectacular save from a lightning back-heel by Amancio.

195: v **Spain**, Madrid, 8.5.68. England won 2–1

Bonetti	Newton	Wilson	Mullery	Labone	Moore*
Ball	Peters[1]	Charlton R.	Hunt	Hunter[1]	

When Geoff Hurst pulled out at the last minute with a damaged toe, Ramsey selected Norman Hunter for this return leg of the European championship quarter-finals. As the team was announced with 'Bites Yer Legs' included Alan Ball looked to the sky and said with hands clasped, 'For what they are about to receive ...' Amancio brought the scores level on aggregate in the first minute of the second half, but Peters quickly restored England's one-goal advantage when he headed in a Ball corner. Ten minutes from the end Roger Hunt collected an Alan Mullery throw and his cross was thrashed into the net by Hunter, using what was rated one of the most under-used right boots in football.

196: v **Sweden**, Wembley, 22.5.68. England won 3–1

Stepney	Newton	Knowles	Mullery	Labone	Moore*
Bell	Peters[1]	Charlton R.[1] (Hurst)	Hunt[1]	Hunter	

Alex Stepney played his only game in the England goal one week before helping Manchester United win the European Cup on the same pitch. Colin Bell also made his first appearance, and helped inspire goals from Peters, Hunt and Charlton, who became the new record holder with forty-five goals before limping off.

197: v **West Germany**, Hanover, 1.6.68. England lost 1–0

Banks	Newton	Knowles	Hunter	Labone	Moore*
Ball	Bell	Summerbee	Hurst	Thompson	

England's unbeaten record against the Germans, which had lasted sixty-seven years, ended when Brian Labone deflected a Franz Beckenbauer shot wide of Gordon Banks 8 minutes from the end. It was a goal that silenced the jeers of the German spectators who had been barracking their own team as England made and missed a string of chances.

198: v **Yugoslavia**, Florence, 5.6.68. England lost 1–0

Banks	Newton	Wilson	Mullery	Labone	Moore*
Ball	Peters	Charlton R.	Hunt	Hunter	

Dragan Dzajic, Yugoslavia's world-class winger, snapped up the goal that won this European Nations Cup semi-final after Bobby Moore had failed to reach a high cross 5 minutes from the end. It was a bruising, angry battle in which the Yugoslavs kicked anything that moved, and in the final moments Alan Mullery became the first player ever sent off while playing for England. He got his marching orders for retaliating after being on the receiving end of a brutal tackle.

199: v USSR, **Rome**, 8.6.68. England won 2–0

| Banks | Wright | Wilson | Stiles | Labone | Moore* |
| Hunter | Hunt | Charlton R.[1] | Hurst[1] | Peters | |

Goals from Bobby Charlton and Geoff Hurst lifted England to victory in this play-off for third place in the European championship finals. The Russians had been deadlocked with Italy after extra-time in a goal-less semi-final. Italy went through to the final on the toss of a coin and then beat Yugoslavia 2–0 in a replay after a 1–1 draw.

200: v **Romania**, Bucharest, 6.11.68. Drew 0–0

| Banks | Wright (McNab) | Newton | Mullery | Labone | Moore* |
| Ball | Hunt | Charlton R. | Hurst | Peters | |

Tommy Wright, who had partnered his Everton team-mate Ray Wilson at full-back against Russia, now had Blackburn's Keith Newton playing with him at left-back. England's World Cup heroes Cohen and Wilson had both had their international careers ended by injuries after playing together in twenty-seven matches. Wright and Newton, who would later continue their partnership at club level with Everton, hardly had time to get to know each other before Wright went off injured in the 10th minute to be replaced by Arsenal's Bob McNab who, despite playing out of position, gave a sound début performance in a dreary, defence-dominated match.

201: v **Bulgaria**, Wembley, 11.12.68. Drew 1–1

| West | Newton (Reaney) | McNab | Mullery | Labone | Moore* |
| Lee | Bell | Charlton R. | Hurst[1] | Peters | |

Francis Lee made his first England appearance alongside his Manchester City team-mate Colin Bell, and his thrusting runs down the right wing were a continual source of danger to a packed Bulgarian defence. There were also first England caps for goalkeeper Gordon West and Leeds full-back Paul Reaney, who came on as a substitute for injured Keith Newton. Geoff Hurst scored England's goal, and the Bulgarians replied with a great solo goal by centre-forward Asparoukhov.

202: v **Romania**, Wembley, 15.1.69. Drew 1–1

| Banks | Wright | McNab | Stiles | Charlton J.[1] | Hunter |
| Radford | Hunt | Charlton R.* | Hurst | Ball | |

A memorable match for the Charlton brothers. Bobby captained the team in injured Bobby Moore's absence in what was his ninetieth international, and big Jack scored England's goal. It was John Radford's first game for England and Roger Hunt's last. Hunt was sick of the criticism being aimed at him during an unsuccessful press campaign to get Jimmy Greaves recalled, and he asked Ramsey not to consider him for any more matches.

203: v **France**, Wembley, 12.3.69. England won 5–0

| Banks | Newton | Cooper | Mullery | Charlton J. | Moore* |
| Lee[1] | Bell | Hurst[3] | Peters | O'Grady[1] | |

Geoff Hurst was again a hat-trick hero, this time two of his goals against an outclassed French side coming from the penalty spot. Francis Lee scored his first goal for England and Mike O'Grady, recalled after six years in the wilderness, was also on the mark. Terry Cooper was Keith Newton's new left-back partner as Ramsey continued his search for a duo to compare with Cohen and Wilson.

204: v **Northern Ireland**, Windsor Park, 3.5.69. England won 3–1

| Banks | Newton | McNab | Mullery | Labone | Moore* |
| Ball | Lee[1] | Charlton R. | Hurst[1] | Peters[1] | |

The scoreline flattered England. Goalkeeper Gordon Banks was under long periods of pressure after Eric McMordie had cancelled out an early Martin Peters goal. With Newton doing an excellent containing job on George Best, England began to gain command and goals from Lee and Hurst wrapped up the game for them, but not before Banks had made two splendid saves against the always dangerous Derek Dougan. Live television cut the attendance to 23,000.

205: v **Wales**, Wembley, 7.5.69. England won 2–1

| West | Newton | Cooper | Moore* | Charlton J. | Hunter |
| Lee[1] | Bell | Astle | Charlton R.[1] | Ball | |

Wyn Davies gave Wales the lead and they were looking the better team when England were awarded a penalty that Francis Lee fired against the woodwork. The miss seemed to inspire rather than depress the Manchester City striker, and he laid on the equalizer for Bobby Charlton following a smart exchange of wall passes and then notched the winner after a Jeff Astle drive had been cleared off the line.

206: v **Scotland**, Wembley, 10.5.69. England won 4–1

Banks	Newton	Cooper	Mullery	Labone	Moore*
Lee	Ball	Charlton R.	Hurst²	Peters²	

The old West Ham double-act of Hurst and Peters sunk the Scots with two goals each. Colin Stein scored to make it 2–1, and the final scoreline was harsh on a Scottish team powerfully driven from midfield by Billy Bremner and Archie Gemmill.

207: v **Mexico**, Mexico City, 1.6.69. Drew 0–0

West	Newton (Wright)	Cooper	Mullery	Labone	Moore*
Lee	Ball	Charlton R.	Hurst	Peters	

Goalkeeper Gordon West played impressively as deputy for Gordon Banks, and then astonished Ramsey by asking not to be considered for any more internationals because he suffered so much from home-sickness. The England team struggled in the second-half as Mexico's high altitude took its toll, and Ramsey noted that he would need to give them several weeks to acclimatize before the 1970 World Cup finals.

208: v **Uruguay**, Montevideo, 8.6.69. England won 2–1

Banks	Wright	Newton	Mullery	Labone	Moore*
Lee¹	Bell	Hurst¹	Ball	Peters	

Gordon Banks, back in the England goal following a round-trip home to England for the funeral of his father, had to be at his best to keep out the Uruguay attack after Francis Lee had scored an early goal. Banks was beaten by a diving header from Cubilla, but Hurst collected the winner ten minutes from the end following neat approach work by Ball and Lee.

209: v **Brazil**, Rio de Janeiro, 12.6.69. England lost 2–1

Banks	Wright	Newton	Mullery	Labone	Moore*
Ball	Bell¹	Charlton R.	Hurst	Peters	

Colin Bell gave England a 1–0 half-time lead and victory hopes were high when Banks saved a penalty from Brazilian skipper Carlos Alberto that briefly silenced the 160,000 crowd. Alan Mullery policed Pele so well that he made hardly any impact on the match, but England tired in the final 20 minutes and they were brought to their knees by late goals from Tostao and Jairzinho.

210: v Holland, Amsterdam, 5.11.69. England won 1–0

Bonetti	Wright	Hughes	Mullery	Charlton J.	Moore*
Lee (Thompson)		Bell¹	Charlton R.	Hurst	Peters

Colin Bell scored the goal that defeated a Dutch team that played the more skilful football but without being able to provide the finishing touch to their impressive approach work. Emlyn Hughes made a sound start to his England career at left-back.

211: v Portugal, Wembley, 10.12.69. England won 1–0

Bonetti	Reaney	Hughes	Mullery	Charlton J.¹	Moore*
Lee	Bell (Peters)	Astle	Charlton R.	Ball	

Francis Lee, noted as one of the deadliest of all penalty takers, missed his second spot-kick in an England shirt. England were awarded the penalty after Jeff Astle had been brought down. Lee stumbled as he ran up to take the kick and sliced the ball wide. It took centre-half Jack Charlton to show the forwards how to get the ball into the net on a pitch made slow by heavy rain.

212: v Holland, Wembley, 14.1.70. Drew 0–0

Banks	Newton	Cooper	Peters	Charlton J.	Hunter
Lee (Mullery)	Bell	Jones (Hurst)	Charlton R.*	Storey-Moore	

England were slow-handclapped and jeered by their fans who did not appreciate that Holland were an emerging power in world football. The Dutch team included such quality players as Cruyff, Van Hanegem, Krol and Keizer, and England's defenders had to work flat out to hold them. Mick Jones, playing his first international match for four years, was substituted by Hurst after 70 minutes. Ian Storey-Moore, making his one and only England appearance, had a good-looking headed goal disallowed.

213: v Belgium, Brussels, 25.2.70. England won 3–1

Banks	Wright	Cooper	Moore*	Labone	Hughes
Lee	Ball²	Osgood	Hurst¹	Peters	

Alan Ball was rewarded for one of his typically non-stop performances with two goals. Geoff Hurst scored the other goal against a punchless Belgium team which had Paul van Himst as their one world-class player. Chelsea's graceful but unpredictable Peter Osgood made a quietly satisfactory début in snowy conditions.

214: v **Wales**, Ninian Park, 18.4.70. Drew 1–1

Banks	Wright	Hughes	Mullery	Labone	Moore*
Lee[1]	Ball	Charlton R.	Hurst	Peters	

Ramsey was shaping his tactics for the coming defence of the World Cup, and had settled on a 4–4–2 formation with Francis Lee and Geoff Hurst as the two front runners supported from midfield by Alan Mullery, Alan Ball, Bobby Charlton and Martin Peters. There was press criticism of the system after England had struggled to hold Wales, Lee salvaging a draw with a spectacular solo goal after Dick Krzywicki had given the Welsh a well-deserved lead.

215: v **Northern Ireland**, Wembley, 21.4.70. England won 3–1

Banks	Newton (Bell)	Hughes	Mullery	Moore*	Stiles
Coates	Kidd	Charlton R.[1]	Hurst[1]	Peters[1]	

Bobby Charlton led the team out in his hundredth appearance in an England shirt and celebrated with his forty-eighth goal. Peters, now of Tottenham, and Hurst were also on the mark to give England a comfortable victory. George Best, Charlton's gifted Manchester United clubmate, gave Northern Ireland a rare moment of supremacy when he took advantage of dithering in the England defence to turn a half chance into a goal.

216: v **Scotland**, Hampden Park, 25.4.70. Drew 0–0

Banks	Newton	Hughes	Stiles	Labone	Moore*
Thompson (Mullery)	Ball	Astle	Hurst	Peters	

It was England's final game before flying off for the World Cup warm-up games in South America, and the Scots were determined to give them a morale-sapping defeat as a farewell present. England were equally determined not to be beaten and the game became bogged down in a midfield stalemate. It produced the first goalless draw between Scotland and England since 1872.

217: v **Colombia**, Bogota, 20.5.70. England won 4–0

Banks	Newton	Cooper	Mullery	Labone	Moore*
Lee	Ball[1]	Charlton R.[1]	Hurst	Peters[2]	

England arrived in Bogota after two weeks of altitude training in Mexico. Ramsey fielded what he considered his World Cup team and two goals from Peters and one each from Bobby Charlton and Alan Ball gave England a comfortable victory at an altitude of 8,600 ft. England were a goal up in just 90 seconds.

218: v **Ecuador**, Quito, 24.5.70. England won 2–0

Banks	Newton	Cooper	Mullery	Labone	Moore*
Lee[1] (Kidd[1])	Ball	Charlton R. (Sadler)		Hurst	Peters

England literally went up into the clouds for this final warm-up match before the World Cup. Quito is more than 9,000 ft above sea-level, and the
ball swerved around like a boomerang. Lee gave England the lead and was
then substituted in the 70th minute by Brian Kidd, who scored a second
goal. Ironically, Kidd had been told he was one of six players not included in the final World Cup squad of twenty-two. It was during a stop-over
in Bogota on the flight back to Mexico that Bobby Moore was arrested
on a trumped-up jewel-theft charge: (see page 46).

219: v **Romania**, World Cup, Guadalajara, 2.6.70. England won 1–0

Banks	Newton (Wright)	Cooper	Mullery	Labone	Moore*
Lee (Osgood)	Ball	Charlton R.	Hurst[1]	Peters	

A Geoff Hurst goal in the 70th minute – the ball going through the legs of
the Romanian goalkeeper – was enough to give England a winning send-off
to their World Cup defence. Moore, back with the squad after his harrowing experience in Colombia, was the outstanding defender on the pitch.

220: v **Brazil**, World Cup, Guadalajara, 7.6.70. England lost 1–0

Banks	Wright	Cooper	Mullery	Labone	Moore*
Lee (Astle)	Ball	Charlton R. (Bell)		Hurst	Peters

An amazing save by Gordon Banks from a tenth minute header by Pelé
inspired England, and they held the world champions-to-be for an hour.
Then a Pelé dummy completely threw the England defence and Banks was
left unprotected as Jairzinho ran on to the ball from the right and rammed
a shot into the corner of the net. Jeff Astle, joining the action as a late
substitute for Francis Lee, had the best chance of the match when he was
in possession in front of an open goal, but he shot wide and England's
chance of saving the game had gone.

221: v **Czechoslovakia**, World Cup, Guadalajara, 11.6.70. England won 1–0

Banks	Newton	Cooper	Mullery	Charlton J.	Moore*
Bell	Charlton R. (Ball)	Astle (Osgood)	Clarke[1]	Peters	

Allan Clarke volunteered for penalty duty in his first England international appearance, and showed an ice-cool temperament as he slotted home a disputed 48th-minute spot-kick that clinched a place in the World Cup quarter-finals. The only time the Czechs looked like scoring was when a speculative shot from 25 yards by right-back Dobias swerved in the thin air. Banks, at full stretch, managed to tip it on to the bar and as as he turned the ball rebounded into his arms.

222: v West Germany, World Cup, Léon, 14.6.70. England lost 3–2 (after extra time)

Bonetti	Newton	Cooper	Mullery¹	Labone	Moore*
Lee	Ball	Charlton R. (Bell)		Hurst	Peters¹ (Hunter)

England were in command for 69 minutes thanks to goals from Alan Mullery and Martin Peters in stifling conditions. Franz Beckenbauer pulled the Germans back into the game with a shot that goalkeeper Peter Bonetti would have saved nine times out of ten. Bonetti had been called into the team at the last minute after Gordon Banks was forced to pull out with a mystery stomach illness. Ramsey immediately sent on Colin Bell as substitute for Bobby Charlton, who was being saved for a semi-final that never came England's way. German substitute Jurgen Grabowski was running rings round exhausted left-back Terry Cooper, and Ramsey decided on a second substitution, sending on Norman Hunter for Peters in a bid to stiffen the defence. A freak header by Uwe Seeler sent the ball on an arc over the wrong-footed Bonetti to send the game into extra-time just as in the 1966 World Cup Final, but this time it was the Germans who came out on top. Hurst had a goal disallowed, and then Gerd Muller rammed in the winner after Grabowski had beaten Cooper and crossed for Loehr to head the ball down into 'Der Bomber's' path. England's reign as world champions was over, as was the great international career of Bobby Charlton after a record 106 caps.

223: v East Germany, Wembley, 25.11.70. England won 3–1

Shilton	Hughes	Cooper	Mullery	Sadler	Moore*
Lee¹	Ball	Hurst	Clarke¹	Peters¹	

Peter Shilton won the first of his world record 125 caps against an East German team that promised much more than they finally produced. The Germans had scored sixteeen goals winning their previous four matches, but they could make little impression against an experimental England defence as Ramsey started rebuilding with the 1974 World Cup in mind.

224: v Malta, Valletta, 3.2.71. England won 1–0

Banks	Reaney	Hughes	Mullery*	McFarland	Hunter
Ball	Chivers	Royle	Harvey	Peters[1]	

Alan Mullery was skipper in place of Bobby Moore, who had been suspended by his West Ham club following the 'Blackpool Affair' (see
page 76). Martin Chivers, Roy McFarland and Everton team-mates Joe
Royle and Colin Harvey made their debuts in a European championship
qualifying match played on an iron-hard pitch that Gordon Banks described as 'the worst I have ever seen.' It had a sand surface that had been
rolled flat by a steam-roller. Martin Peters scored the only goal after half
a dozen chances had been missed.

225: v Greece, Wembley, 21.4.71. England won 3–0

Banks	Storey	Hughes	Mullery	McFarland	Moore*
Lee[1]	Ball (Coates)	Chivers[1]	Hurst[1]	Peters	

Greece arrived for this European championship qualifying match without
any of their star players from Panathinaikos, who were being saved for a
European Cup semi-final. A superbly struck goal by Martin Chivers was
all that separated the teams at half-time, and it took late headed goals by
Hurst and Lee to clinch victory and silence the jeers of a frustrated crowd.

226: v Malta, Wembley, 12.5.71. England won 5–0

Banks	Lawler[1]	Cooper	Moore*	McFarland	Hughes
Lee[1]	Coates	Chivers[2]	Clarke[1]	Peters (Ball)	

Allan Clarke scored one penalty and missed another and Martin Chivers
netted twice and might have had five goals. Francis Lee was on the mark,
and Chris Lawler decorated his début with a spectacular long-range goal
from 30 yards. But it was not enough to please the spectators who jeered
and slow-handclapped England's performance in this return European
championship match.

227: v Northern Ireland, Windsor Park, 15.5.71. England won 1–0

Banks	Madeley	Cooper	Storey	McFarland	Moore*
Lee	Ball	Chivers	Clarke[1]	Peters	

George Best had an opportunist goal disallowed after flicking the ball
away from Gordon Banks as the England goalkeeper threw it up in preparation for a kicked clearance. Allan Clarke's winning goal brought offside
claims from the Irish defenders who also insisted that Francis Lee had handled the ball before passing to Clarke. It was not Ireland's lucky day.

228: v **Wales**, Wembley, 19.5.71. Drew 0–0

Shilton	Lawler	Cooper	Smith	Lloyd	Hughes
Lee	Coates	Hurst	Brown (Clarke)		Peters*

Ramsey's experimental side played like passing strangers in the face of a fierce challenge from Wales. England included new caps Larry Lloyd, Tommy Smith and Tony Brown, whose only appearance for England lasted just 74 minutes. Francis Lee had a goal ruled offside in the 43rd minute.

229: v **Scotland**, Wembley, 22.5.71. England won 3–1

Banks	Lawler	Cooper	Storey	McFarland	Moore*
Lee (Clarke)	Ball	Chivers²	Hurst	Peters¹	

Martin Peters headed England into the lead before Alan Ball gifted Scotland an equalizer with a suicidal back-pass into the path of Hugh Curran. Ball made amends with a storming performance in midfield, and two Martin Chivers goals gave England victory and the home international championship.

230: v **Switzerland**, Basle, 13.10.71. England won 3–2

Banks	Lawler	Cooper	Mullery	McFarland	Moore*
Lee	Madeley	Chivers¹	Hurst¹ (Radford)		Peters ¹ o.g.

Two rare mistakes by Gordon Banks let Switzerland in for equalizers after England had twice taken the lead through goals by Hurst and Chivers in the first half of this European championship qualifier. It was just looking as if the Swiss would escape with a draw when a Chivers cross was deflected into the net for a 79th minute winner.

231: v **Switzerland**, Wembley, 10.11.71. Drew 1–1

Shilton	Madeley	Cooper	Storey	Lloyd	Moore*
Summerbee¹ (Chivers)	Ball	Hurst	Lee (Marsh)	Hughes	

Mike Summerbee gave England the lead in the 9th minute, but then they struggled to contain a lively Swiss team that deserved their equalizer, hammered in from 25 yards by Odermatt in the 26th minute. It was a swinging shot that spun into the net off Shilton's hands. England's passing was often careless.

232: v **Greece**, Athens, 1.12.71. England won 2–0

Banks	Madeley	Hughes	Bell	McFarland	Moore*
Lee	Ball	Chivers¹	Hurst¹	Peters	

A cannonball shot from Geoff Hurst midway through the first half put England in charge of a match dominated by the attacking midfield trio of Ball, Bell and Peters. Martin Chivers wrapped up the victory with a last-minute goal to clinch England's place in the quarter-finals of the European championship. Francis Lee twice hit the post.

233: v West Germany, Wembley, 29.4.72. England lost 3–1

Banks	Madeley	Hughes	Bell	Moore*	Hunter
Lee[1]	Ball	Chivers	Hurst (Marsh)	Peters	

Derby manager Brian Clough pulled injured Roy McFarland out of the England squad at the last minute, and Ramsey's gamble of playing Bobby Moore at centre-half was a tactical disaster in this European championship quarter-final. Moore and Norman Hunter were always struggling at the heart of the defence against the dynamic Gerd Müller, who fed off a procession of passes from the gifted Gunther Netzer. Francis Lee equalized a 26 minute goal by Uli Hoeness, and outplayed England clung on until 6 minutes from the end when Netzer scored from the penalty spot. Müller then made it 3–1 with a devastating shot on the turn.

234: v West Germany, Berlin, 13.5.72. Drew 0–0

Banks	Madeley	Hughes	Storey	McFarland	Moore*
Ball	Bell	Chivers	Marsh (Summerbee)	Hunter (Peters)	

Franz Beckenbauer was outstanding as the German defence shut out England's attack in a match played in a non-stop \downpour. The Germans, content to protect their two-goal lead from the first leg, came closest to breaking the deadlock when a 40-yard free-kick from Gunther Netzer smacked against the bar. England, with Norman Hunter and Peter Storey making their presence felt, conceded twenty-seven free-kicks and were described by German manager Helmut Schoen as 'brutal'.

235: v Wales, Ninian Park, 20.5.72. England won 3–0

Banks	Madeley	Hughes[1]	Storey	McFarland	Moore*
Summerbee	Bell[1]	Macdonald	Marsh[1]	Hunter	

England cruised to a comfortable victory in a bruising match in which Peter Storey and Terry Yorath, two of the hardest men in the League, had a personal feud, with Norman Hunter often joining in on Storey's side. Leading 1–0 from a first-half goal by Emlyn Hughes, England clinched victory with two goals in a minute midway through the second half. Rodney Marsh scored with a first-time volley from 18 yards, and then Mike

Summerbee laid on the third goal for his Manchester City team-mate Colin Bell. Malcolm Macdonald made a bright début.

236: v **Northern Ireland**, Wembley, 23.5.72. England lost 1–0

Shilton	Todd	Hughes	Storey	Lloyd	Hunter
Summerbee	Bell*	Macdonald (Chivers)	Marsh	Currie (Peters)	

This was England's first defeat by Northern Ireland since 1957. Terry Neill, the Irish player-manager winning his fiftieth cap, scored the only goal of the match from close range following a Danny Hegan corner in the 33rd minute. Colin Bell skippered England in the absence of Bobby Moore, and Tony Currie and Colin Todd won their first caps. It was the first match since the 1966 World Cup that England kicked off without one of the heroes of '66 in the starting line-up.

237: v **Scotland**, Hampden Park, 27.5.72. England won 1–0

Banks	Madeley	Hughes	Storey	McFarland	Moore*
Ball[1]	Bell	Chivers	Marsh (Macdonald)		Hunter

The referee called captains Bobby Moore and Billy McNeill together and ordered them to tell their players to calm things down after forty-six free-kicks had been awarded in the first 30 minutes. An Alan Ball goal in the 28th minute gave England victory in this daggers-drawn centenary match between the two countries. Scottish FA President Hugh Nelson described the game as 'a disgrace'.

238: v **Yugoslavia**, Wembley, 11.10.72. Drew 1–1

Shilton	Mills	Lampard	Storey	Blockley	Moore*
Ball	Channon	Royle[1]	Bell	Marsh	

Mick Mills, Frank Lampard, Jeff Blockley and Mike Channon made their international débuts. They looked set for a winning start when Joe Royle scored his first goal for England in the 40th minute, but Yugoslav centre-forward Franjo Vladic snatched an equalizer 5 minutes after half-time and Peter Shilton had to be at his best as skilful winger Dragan Djazic started to pull the uncertain England defence apart. The Yugoslavs missed three clear-cut chances in the closing stages.

239: v **Wales**, Ninian Park, 15.11.72. England won 1–0

Clemence	Storey	Hughes	Hunter	McFarland	Moore*
Keegan	Chivers	Marsh	Bell[1]	Ball	

Colin Bell cashed in on clever approach work by Alan Ball to score the decisive winning goal in the first-half of this World Cup qualifying match. Liverpool team-mates Ray Clemence and Kevin Keegan made quiet débuts in what was Sir Alf Ramsey's 100th match as manager.

240: v Wales, Wembley, 24.1.73. Drew 1–1

Clemence	Storey	Hughes	Hunter[1]	McFarland	Moore*
Keegan	Bell	Chivers	Marsh	Ball	

A long-range shot from Norman Hunter in the 42nd minute beat his Leeds team-mate Gary Sprake in the Welsh goal to salvage a World Cup point. John Toshack had given Wales the lead in the 23rd minute, and England's forwards floundered against a Welsh defence in which Sprake, Peter Rodrigues and Mike England were outstanding.

241: v Scotland, Hampden Park, 14.2.73. England won 5–0

Shilton	Storey	Hughes	Bell	Madeley	Moore*
Ball	Channon[1]	Chivers[1]	Clarke[2]	Peters [1] o.g.	

England were three goals clear in 15 minutes, and skated to an easy victory on a treacherous, snow-carpeted pitch. The match was played to celebrate the centenary of the Scottish Football Association, but England – with Bobby Moore making his 100th appearance – wrecked the party. It was a nightmare start to Willie Ormond's job as new Scottish manager.

242: v Northern Ireland, Goodison Park, 12.5.73. England won 2–1

Shilton	Storey	Nish	Bell	McFarland	Moore*
Ball	Channon	Chivers[2]	Richards	Peters	

The game should have been played in Belfast but was switched to Goodison Park at the request of the Irish FA. A rare mistake by goalkeeper Pat Jennings let Martin Chivers in for his first goal in the 9th minute, and another mistake – this time by Terry Neill – set Chivers up for the winning goal nine minutes from the end. Dave Clements scored for Ireland from the penalty spot after a foul by Peter Storey in the 22nd minute. John Richards won his only cap. England's disjointed display brought them jeers and slow handclaps from the Goodison crowd.

243: v Wales, Wembley, 15.5.73. England won 3–0

Shilton	Storey	Hughes	Bell	McFarland	Moore*
Ball	Channon[1]	Chivers[1]	Clarke	Peters[1]	

England scored three goals and had two others disallowed as they pulled the Welsh defence apart in this Home Championship match. Allan Clarke did not get his name on the scoresheet, but he was the outstanding player on the pitch as he combined neatly with Mike Channon and Martin Chivers. It was England's first victory at Wembley for two years.

244: v Scotland, Wembley, 19.5.73. England won 1–0

Shilton	Storey	Hughes	Bell	McFarland	Moore*
Ball	Channon	Chivers	Clarke	Peters[1]	

Martin Peters headed in a beautifully flighted free-kick from Alan Ball in the 54th minute to give England victory in a match that could easily have been won by the Scots but for two magnificent saves by Peter Shilton.

245: v Czechoslovakia, Prague, 27.5.73. Drew 1–1

Shilton	Madeley	Storey	Bell	McFarland	Moore*
Ball	Channon	Chivers	Clarke[1]	Peters	

Allan Clarke saved England from defeat with a last-minute equalizer after collecting the ball from his Leeds team-mate Paul Madeley. The Czechs led from the 56th minute when Novak steered the ball into the net off a post. England looked unfamiliar in yellow shirts and royal-blue shorts.

246: v Poland, Chorzow, 6.6.73. England lost 2–0

Shilton	Madeley	Hughes	Storey	McFarland	Moore*
Ball	Bell	Chivers	Clarke	Peters	

A disastrous defeat for England in a vital World Cup qualifying match. Poland went ahead in the 9th minute when a Lubanski shot found its way into the net off the foot of Bobby Moore and the arm of Peter Shilton. Early in the second half Moore made an uncharacteristic hash of a tackle against Lubanski, who raced clear to make it 2–0. To compound England's misery Alan Ball was sent off following an angry clash 12 minutes from the final whistle.

247: v USSR, Moscow, 10.6.73. England won 2–1

Shilton	Madeley	Hughes	Storey	McFarland	Moore*	Currie
Channon (Summerbee)	Chivers[1]	Clarke (Macdonald)	Peters (Hunter [1 o.g.])			

Just four days after the disappointment of defeat in Poland, England showed their character with a victory made harder by the stifling, humid conditions in the Lenin Stadium. Chivers powered England into the lead in the 9th minute, and 10 minutes after half-time a clever dummy by Martin Peters so confused Russian defender Khurtislava that he turned the ball into his own net. The Russians pulled back a goal in the 66th-minute from the penalty spot. Tony Currie was an impressive deputy for Alan Ball.

248: v **Italy**, Turin, 14.6.73. England lost 2–0

Shilton	Madeley	Hughes	Storey	McFarland	Moore*
Currie	Channon	Chivers	Clarke	Peters	

Bobby Moore set a new appearances record in his 107th match for England, but he was unable to celebrate a victory. Anastasi gave Italy the lead in the 37th minute, and Capello made it 2–0 7 minutes after half-time as the England defenders stood waiting for an offside whistle that never came. It was Italy's first victory against England.

249: v **Austria**, Wembley, 26.9.73. England won 7–0

Shilton	Madeley	Hughes	Bell1	McFarland	Hunter
Currie[1]	Channon[2]	Chivers[1]	Clarke[2]	Peters*	

England over-ran an Austrian defence that had no answer to the combined power of Mike Channon, Martin Chivers and Allan Clarke – the 'top Cs', with Tony Currie also getting in on the goal spree. It was Currie, Colin Bell and Martin Peters who dictated the pace and pattern of the match from midfield. Channon scored the first goal in the 10th minute, and Clarke struck twice before half-time. Channon and Chivers added goals early in the second half, and Currie made it 6–0 in the 64th minute with a rasping shot from the edge of the area. Bell completed the goal avalanche three minutes from the end. 'England can still teach the world how to play', said Austrian manager Leopold Stastny.

250: v **Poland**, Wembley, 17.10.73. Drew 1–1

Shilton	Madeley	Hughes	Bell	McFarland	Hunter
Currie	Channon	Chivers (Hector)		Clarke[1]	Peters*

England had thirty-five goal attempts to two by Poland, but it was the Poles who went through to the World Cup finals at England's expense. Poland had the man of the match in goalkeeper Tomaszewski, who was labelled a clown by Brian Clough. He gave England nothing to laugh about as he saved at least four goals with eccentric but effective goalkeeping. It was Poland who took the lead in the 55th minute in a rare breakaway raid. Norman Hunter, the most feared tackler in English football, mistimed a challenge out on the touchline and the ball was transferred to unmarked Domarski, whose low shot went under the diving Shilton. Allan Clarke equalized from the penalty spot 8 minutes later. England were denied the victory they needed to clinch a place in the World Cup finals when late substitute Kevin Hector headed wide from close range in the last minute of the most frustrating match of Ramsey's reign.

251: v **Italy**, Wembley, 14.11.73. England lost 1–0

Shilton	Madeley	Hughes	Bell	McFarland	Moore*
Currie	Channon	Osgood	Clarke (Hector)		Peters

Italy scored their first ever win in England when Capello netted the only goal of the match in a counter attack in the 87th minute. England dominated the game for long periods but could not find a way through Italy's brilliantly organized defence. It was to be Bobby Moore's 108th and final cap.

252: v **Portugal**, Lisbon, 3.4.74. Drew 0–0

Parkes	Nish	Pejic	Dobson	Watson	Todd
Bowles	Channon	Macdonald (Ball)		Brooking	Peters*

Alf Ramsey's final match as manager. Because of FA Cup commitments and withdrawals, he gave first caps to Phil Parkes, Mike Pejic, Martin Dobson, Dave Watson, Stan Bowles and Trevor Brooking. There was a lot of promising football played up to the penalty area, but the finishing continually let England down. Ramsey was sacked three weeks later.

Mercer's teams and match highlights

253: v Wales, Ninian Park, 11.5.74. England won 2–0

Shilton	Nish	Pejic	Hughes*	McFarland	Todd
Keegan[1]	Bell	Channon	Weller	Bowles[1]	

Joe Mercer's first match as caretaker manager brought a satisfactory rather than spectacular victory against Wales. Keith Weller, making an impressive début, set up the first goal in the 35th minute. His shot was pushed by goalkeeper John Phillips into the path of Stan Bowles, who slipped the ball into the net from close range for his first goal for England. It was a game of firsts, with Kevin Keegan scoring the first of his twenty-one international goals.

254: v. Northern Ireland, Wembley 15.5.74. England won 1–0

Shilton	Nish	Pejic	Hughes*	McFarland (Hunter)	Todd
Keegan	Weller[1]	Channon	Bell	Bowles (Worthington)	

A late headed goal by Keith Weller at last broke the Northern Ireland resistance, with goalkeeper Pat Jennings pulling off a series of magnificent saves. England's defence became disorganized after centre-half Roy McFarland limped off in the 36th minute with an achilles injury that put him on the sidelines for six months. Keegan clipped the bar with a shot just before half-time. Frank Worthington made his England bow as a substitute for Stan Bowles in the 64th minute.

255: v Scotland, Hampden Park, 18.5.74. England lost 2–0

Shilton	Nish	Pejic	Hughes*	Hunter (Watson)	Todd
Channon	Bell	Worthington (Macdonald)		Weller	Peters

Own goals by Mike Pejic and Colin Todd deflated an England team that struggled to cope with the pace and skill of a Scottish attack in which Peter Lorimer, Jimmy Johnstone, Kenny Dalglish and Joe Jordan were outstanding. Pejic deflected a Jordan shot into the England net in the 5th minute, and a harmless-looking cross was diverted past goalkeeper Peter Shilton by Todd in the 31st minute. England were vulnerable at the heart of the defence until Dave Watson replaced Norman Hunter as a conventional centre-half.

256: v **Argentina**, Wembley, 22.5.74. Drew 2–2

Shilton	Hughes*	Lindsay	Todd	Watson	Bell
Keegan	Channon¹	Worthington¹	Weller	Brooking	

Argentina equalized with a last-minute penalty by Mario Kempes after the Argentinian referee adjudged that Kempes had been fouled by skipper Emlyn Hughes. There were moments in the second half when the game threatened to get out of control as England's players started to get drawn into personl feuds in retaliation for a spate of reckless tackles. England were flattered by a 2–0 lead following goals by Mike Channon and Frank Worthington either side of the interval. Hughes, who had got involved in a skirmish with the Argentinians as they came off at half-time, blocked the ball in the 58th minute. It ran into the path of Kempes who fired an unstoppable shot into the net to give a glimpse of the goal-scoring ability that would power Argentina to the World Cup in 1978. Alec Lindsay made a sound début as full back partner to his Liverpool team-mate Hughes.

257: v **East Germany**, Leipzig, 29.5.74. Drew 1–1

Clemence	Hughes*	Lindsay	Todd	Watson	Dobson
Keegan	Channon¹	Worthington	Bell	Brooking	

England hit the woodwork four times before Streich gave the East Germans a fortunate lead in the 67th minute. Just 60 seconds later Mike Channon cancelled it out with a free-kick hammered low through the defensive wall from 20 yards. Martin Dobson, Colin Bell and Trevor Brooking dominated the match in midfield. Dobson was winning the second of five caps under three different managers.

258: v **Bulgaria**, Sofia, 1.6.74. England won 1–0

Clemence	Hughes*	Lindsay	Todd	Watson	Dobson
Brooking	Bell	Keegan	Channon	Worthington¹	

Frank Worthington won the match in the 44th minute with a classically constructed goal. Kevin Keegan flicked on a Ray Clemence goalkick and Worthington brought it under control and then rifled it into the net all in one sweet movement. Colin Todd and Dave Watson were outstanding in a fine all-round team performance, with Keegan, Channon and Worthington pulling the Bulgarian defence inside out with their pace and clever interchanging of passes and positions.

259: v Yugoslavia, Belgrade, 5.6.74. Drew 2–2

Clemence	Hughes*	Lindsay	Todd	Watson	Dobson
Keegan[1]	Channon[1]	Worthington (Macdonald)		Bell	Brooking

Joe Mercer's farewell match got off to a cracking start when Mike Channon forced the ball into the net in the sixth minute after the goalkeeper had failed to hold a Trevor Brooking shot following a Kevin Keegan corner-kick. The Yugoslavians fought back to equalize and then take the lead after misunderstandings in the England defence. Keegan, who had been arrested at Belgrade airport two days earlier (see page 52), had the satisfaction of heading the equalizer in the 75th minute to give a happy ending to the Joe Mercer interlude.

Don Revie's teams and match highlights

260: **Czechoslovakia,** Wembley, 30.10.74. England won 3-0

Clemence	Madeley	Hughes*	Dobson (Brooking)	Watson	Hunter
Bell[2]	Francis G.	Worthington (Thomas)		Channon[1]	Keegan

Don Revie boldy opened his career as England manager by making a double substitution in the 70th minute of this European championship qualifier. Revie sent on Dave Thomas and Trevor Brooking for Frank Worthington and Martin Dobson, and it was Thomas who created the first goal when his cross was headed in by Mike Channon. Two more goals followed in the next nine minutes. Channon found Bell with a superb diagonal pass, and he steered it into the net with a well-placed shot. Then the inspired Channon crossed the ball for Bell to head in the third goal that sent choruses of 'Land of Hope and Glory' thundering around Wembley for an England team newly decked out in shirts with red and blue shoulder stripes.

261: v **Portugal,** Wembley, 20.11.74. Drew 0–0

Clemence	Madeley	Watson	Hughes*	Cooper (Todd)	Brooking
Francis G.	Bell	Thomas	Channon	Clarke (Worthington)	

The 'Land of Hope and Glory' anthem gave way to boos and jeers as England struggled to make any impact against a disciplined and resolute Portuguese defence. Terry Cooper, recalled by his old club boss after three years in the international wilderness, broke down with a nagging injury and Colin Todd played exceptionally well as a makeshift left-back. There was a lack of understanding between the midfield and the front line, with a procession of passes going astray on the rain-sodden surface.

262: v **West Germany,** Wembley, 12.3.75. England won 2-0

Clemence	Whitworth	Gillard	Bell[1]	Watson	Todd
Ball*	Macdonald[1]	Channon	Hudson	Keegan	

England celebrated the 100th international match played at Wembley by handing West Germany their first defeat since the 1974 World Cup triumph. New skipper Alan Ball inspired magnificent performances from his midfield partners Colin Bell and, in particular, Alan Hudson. They paralyzed the German defence with their pin-point passing on a soaked pitch, and it was Bell who gave England a 25th minute lead with a deflected shot following a Hudson free-kick. Macdonald, whose pace was always a problem for an experimental German team, scored his first goal for England in the 66th minute when he raced to the far post to head in a cross from Bell. Steve Whitworth and Ian Gillard made sound débuts as new full-back partners.

263: v **Cyprus,** Wembley, 16.4.75. England won 5–0

| Shilton | Madeley | Watson | Todd | Beattie | Bell |
| Ball* | Hudson | Channon (Thomas) | | Macdonald[5] | Keegan |

Malcolm Macdonald scored all five goals in an extraordinary display of finishing. He became the first player to score five at Wembley and his feat equalled the five-goal haul by Tottenham's Willie Hall for England against Northern Ireland at Old Trafford in 1938. Macdonald scored his first in the second minute, made it 2–0 in the 35th minute and added two more early in the second half against an outplayed Cypriot team. He finished off his one-man spectacular with a brilliantly headed goal in the closing stages. Macdonald's team-mates came off at the end wondering how between them they had managed to miss at least six more goals.

264: v **Cyprus,** Limassol, 11.5.75. England won 1–0

| Clemence | Whitworth | Beattie (Hughes) | Watson | Todd | Bell |
| Thomas (Tueart) | Ball* | Channon | Macdonald | Keegan[1] | |

England had to be content with a 6th-minute winning goal from a Kevin Keegan header in this European championship return match. A bumpy pitch led to many of the England passes missing their target in a scrappy match during which goalkeeper Ray Clemence was hardly tested. Kevin Beattie, winning his second cap, limped off with a groin injury just before half-time and Dennis Tueart came on as a 73rd-minute substitute for Dave Thomas.

265: v **Northern Ireland,** Belfast, 17.5.75. Drew 0–0

| Clemence | Whitworth | Hughes | Bell | Watson | Todd |
| Ball* | Viljoen | Macdonald (Channon) | Keegan | Tueart | |

England equalled their record of six consecutive clean sheets in an emotional return to Belfast for the first time in four years. The Irish defence in which goalkeeper Pat Jennings, right-back Pat Rice and centre-half Allan Hunter were outstanding, allowed the England forwards little time and space in which to work.

266: v Wales, Wembley, 21.5.75. Drew 2–2

Clemence	Whitworth	Gillard	Francis G.	Watson	Todd
Ball*	Channon (Little)		Johnson²	Viljoen	Thomas

David Johnson made a memorable debut, scoring both of England's goals including an 85th minute equalizer that stole victory from a spirited Welsh team. Johnson gave England an 8th-minute lead, but Wales were rewarded for their persistence with two goals 10 minutes into the second-half. The first was scored by John Toshack, who then laid on a second for Arfon Griffiths. Aston Villa's Brian Little, sent on as a substitute in the 70th minute, found Johnson with a centre from which he headed the goal that ended Welsh hopes of a first ever win at Wembley. South African Colin Viljoen, Johnson's Ipswich team-mate, made his second and final appearance for England.

267: v Scotland, Wembley, 24.5.75. England won 5–1

Clemence	Whitworth	Beattie¹	Bell¹	Watson	Todd
Ball*	Channon	Johnson¹	Francis G.²	Keegan (Thomas)	

England scored twice in the first seven minutes, the opening goal from Gerry Francis a spectacular shot that rocketed into the net from 25 yards. Scotland never recovered from this shattering start despite some superb play by Kenny Dalglish. Colin Bell made it 3–0 5 minutes before half-time before Bruce Rioch pulled one back from the penalty spot in the last minute of the half. Ball, Bell and Francis were in unstoppable form, and it was Francis who made it 4–1 in the 63rd minute with a deflected shot after Ball had pushed a free-kick through Bell's legs into his path. Kevin Keegan, a bundle of energy in the England attack, rammed a shot against the bar 10 minutes later and Johnson steered the rebound into the net to complete the rout of a dispirited Scottish side.

268: v Switzerland, Basle, 3.9.75. England won 2–1

Clemence	Whitworth	Todd	Watson	Beattie	Bell
Currie	Francis G.*	Channon¹	Johnson (Macdonald)	Keegan¹	

Kevin Keegan scored from close range in the 8th minute and had a penalty saved 3 minutes later. David Johnson laid on a second goal for Mike Channon in the 19th minute and England looked on course for a comfortable victory. But they got caught in the clutches of complacency, and the Swiss were allowed back in the game after sloppy marking had allowed Muller the freedom of the penalty area for a headed goal in the 30th minute. England's defence was often at full stretch in the second half, but the best scoring chances fell to the feet of substitute Malcolm Macdonald who missed the target twice in the closing stages.

269: v Czechoslovakia, Bratislava, 30.10.75. England lost 2–1

Clemence   Madeley   Gillard   Francis G.*   McFarland (Watson) Todd

Keegan   Channon¹(Thomas)   Macdonald   Clarke   Bell

This European championship qualifier had kicked off 24 hours earlier but was abandoned after 19 minutes because of fog. The Czechs trailed 1–0 to a Mike Channon goal after 26 minutes, but the clever Masny laid on an equalizer a minute before half-time and then a winner in the opening minute of the second half. England were unsettled by the no-holds-barred physical approach of the Czechs, and started to retaliate with reckless tackles of their own in a game that was often brutal. The only player ordered off by a lenient referee was the Czech reserve goalkeeper, who was sent to the dressing-room for disputing a decision from the substitute's bench.

270: v Portugal, Lisbon 19.11.75. Drew 1–1

Clemence   Whitworth   Beattie   Francis G.*   Watson   Todd

Keegan   Channon¹   Macdonald (Thomas)   Brooking   Madeley (Clarke)

England went a goal down in their final European championship qualifier to a 16th minute free-kick by Rodrigues that swerved viciously on its way into the net from 25 yards. The Portuguese missed two easy chances before Mike Channon equalised with a free-kick that deflected into the net off a defender 3 minutes before half-time. England needed a victory to boost their fading chances of reaching the European quarter-finals, but they kept running blindly into an offside trap. The draw left the Czechs needing only a draw in Cyprus to qualify ahead of England. They beat the Cypriots in a canter and went on to win the championship.

271: v Wales, Wrexham, 24.3.76. England won 2–1

Clemence   Cherry (Clement)   Mills   Neal   Thompson   Doyle

Keegan*   Channon (Taylor¹)   Boyer   Brooking   Kennedy¹

Crystal Palace striker Peter Taylor became the first Third Division player capped since Johnny Byrne, then also with Palace, in 1961. Taylor came on as a substitute for Mike Channon and scored the second victory-clinching goal ten minutes from the end of a match staged to mark the centenary of the Welsh FA. An experimental England side included seven other new caps: Trevor Cherry, Phil Neal, Phil Thompson, Mike Doyle, Phil Boyer, Ray Kennedy and Dave Clement. Kennedy, one of five Liverpool players in the team, gave England the lead in the 70th minute after a Trevor Brooking centre had been headed out. Alan Curtis scored for Wales in the last minute.

272: v **Wales,** Cardiff, 8.5.76. England won 1–0

Clemence	Clement	Mills	Towers	Greenhoff	Thompson
Keegan	Francis G.*	Pearson	Kennedy	Taylor[1]	

England were fortunate not to be three goals down before Peter Taylor scored the only goal of a scrappy match with a low shot from twenty yards in the 59th minute. Eight of England's players between them had just ten caps, with Tony Towers, Brian Greenhoff and Stuart Pearson making their débuts.

273: v **Northern Ireland,** Wembley, 11.5.76. England won 4–0

Clemence	Todd	Mills	Thompson	Greenhoff	Kennedy
Keegan (Royle)	Francis G.*[1]	Pearson[1]	Channon[2]	Taylor (Towers)	

Mike Channon, dropped against Wales, responded to his recall with two goals. His first came from the penalty spot just 90 seconds after skipper Gerry Francis had opened the scoring with a superbly taken goal in the 35th minute. Stuart Pearson made it 3–0 after the England defence had snuffed out an Irish revival early in the second-half, and Channon rounded off an impressive all-round display when he drove the ball wide of goalkeeper Pat Jennings and into the roof of the net following a clever flick pass by Kevin Keegan.

274: v **Scotland,** Hampden Park, 15.5.76. England lost 2–1

Clemence	Todd	Mills	Thompson	McFarland (Doyle)	Kennedy
Keegan	Francis G.*	Pearson (Cherry)		Channon[1]	Taylor

The game that is a skeleton in goalkeeper Ray Clemence's cupboard. He allowed a half-hit shot from Kenny Dalglish to roll through his legs for

Scotland's winning goal in the 49th minute. Mike Channon had given England an 11th minute lead following enterprising play by Roy McFarland, and Bruce Rioch equalized 6 minutes later when he headed an Eddie Gray corner-kick powerfully wide of Clemence. A spectacular 40-yard run by Dalglish ended with Clemence snatching the ball from him in the penalty area, a complete contrast to what was to happen in the second half.

275: v **Brazil,** Los Angeles, 23.5.76. England lost 1–0

Clemence	Todd	Doyle	Thompson	Mills		Francis G.*
Cherry	Brooking	Keegan	Pearson	Channon		

A last-minute goal by substitute Roberto gave Brazil a flattering victory in this opening match in the United States Bicentennial Tournament. England dominated the match for long periods, but their finishing lacked the accuracy of their approach play.

276: v **Italy,** New York, 28.5.76. England won 3–2

Rimmer (Corrigan)	Clement	Neal (Mills)	Thompson¹	Doyle	Towers
Wilkins	Brooking	Royle	Channon*²	Hill	

England were two goals down inside the first 20 minutes, but they struck back to win with three goals in the opening 7 minutes of the second half. Channon was in inspiring form as captain, and his two goals sandwiched a headed goal by Phil Thompson from a Gordon Hill corner. England beat Team America 3–1 three days later in Philadelphia, but it was not considered a full international. Keegan (2) and Gerry Francis scored the goals against a side including Bobby Moore, Tommy Smith and Pelé.

277: v **Finland,** Helsinki, 13.6.76. England won 4–1

Clemence	Todd	Mills	Thompson	Madeley	Cherry
Keegan²	Channon¹	Pearson¹	Brooking	Francis G.*	

Kevin Keegan was outstanding as England got off to a flying start in their 1978 World Cup campaign. Keegan laid on the first goal in the 14th minute for Stuart Pearson, who returned the compliment after the Finns had forced an equalizer against the run of play. Mike Channon made it 3–1 in the 57th minute and Keegan wrapped it up 3 minutes later with a superb solo goal.

278: v **Republic of Ireland,** Wembley, 8.9.76. Drew 1–1

Clemence	Todd	Madeley	Cherry	McFarland	Greenhoff
Keegan*	Wilkins	Pearson[1]	Brooking	George (Hill)	

England were flattered by their lead when Stuart Pearson steered a Kevin Keegan cross into the net from close range a minute before half-time. Gerry Daly equalized from the penalty spot following a foul on Steve Heighway. The Irish were always the more inventive side and England were lucky to escape with a draw.

279: v **Finland,** Wembley, 13.10.76. England won 2–1

Clemence	Todd	Beattie	Thompson	Greenhoff	Wilkins
Keegan*	Channon	Royle[1]	Brooking (Mills)		Tueart[1] (Hill)

England spurted into the lead with a 3rd-minute goal from Denis Tueart, but finished with chants of 'Rubbish' ringing in their ears after they had made a hash of a World Cup match in which they needed a resounding win against unrated opponents. The Finns played above themselves, and equalized early in the second half before Joe Royle headed a 52nd-minute winner fom Mike Channon's centre.

280: v **Italy,** Rome, 17.11.76. England lost 2–0

Clemence	Clement (Beattie)	Mills	Greenhoff	McFarland	Hughes
Keegan*	Channon	Bowles	Cherry	Brooking	

Italy, including six Juventus players, were a class above England in this crucial World Cup qualifying match. A goal in each half by Antognoni and Bettega was enough to settle it for Italy, who virtually booked their tickets for the finals in Argentina.

281: v **Holland,** Wembley, 9.2.77. England lost 2–0

Clemence	Clement	Beattie	Doyle	Watson	Madeley (Pearson)
Keegan*	Greenhoff (Todd)		Francis T.	Bowles	Brooking

Holland produced what many considered was the finest display at Wembley by a visiting team since Hungary beat England 6–3 in 1953. The two Johanns – Cryuff and Neeskens – dictated the pace and pattern of thc match and it was Jan Peters, playing in only his second international, who nipped in for two goals in 10 minutes in the first half. Trevor Francis made his début for an Engand team that spent much of the game chasing shadows.

282: v **Luxemburg,** Wembley, 30.3.77. England won 5–0

| Clemence | Gidman | Cherry | Kennedy[1] | Watson | Hughes |
| Keegan*[1] | Channon[2] | Royle (Mariner) | | Francis T.[1] | Hill |

Four goals in the last half-hour kept alive England's faint hopes of qualifying for the 1978 World Cup finals. Kevin Keegan had given England a 10th-minute lead, but then they became too anxious against the Luxemburg part-time professionals. Gilbert Dresch was sent off in the 85th minute for a foul on Mike Channon. He became only the second player sent off in a Wembley international, following Antonio Rattin into the black history book.

283: v **Northern Ireland,** Belfast, 28.5.77. England won 2–1

| Shilton | Cherry | Mills | Greenhoff | Watson | Todd |
| Wilkins (Talbot) | | Channon*[1] | Mariner | Brookin | Tueart[1] |

Denis Tueart ducked low to head in a Brian Talbot cross in the 86th minute to give England a winning goal against the run of play. Northern Ireland had taken a 5th-minute lead through Chris McGrath against an England team weakened by the absence of Liverpool players who had helped the Merseyside club win the European Cup three days earlier. Mike Channon equalized in the 27th minute, and then missed two clear-cut chances with headers that were misdirected.

284: v **Wales,** Wembley, 31.5.77. England lost 1–0

| Shilton | Neal | Mills | Greenhoff | Watson | Hughes |
| Keegan* | Channon | Pearson | Brooking (Tueart) | | Kennedy |

Wales scored their first victory in England for forty-two years and their first ever at Wembley. Leighton James netted the only goal of the game from the penalty spot a minute before half-time after Peter Shilton had pulled him down following a mistake by Emlyn Hughes.

285: v **Scotland,** Wembley, 4.6.77. England lost 2–1

| Clemence | Neal | Mills | Greenhoff (Cherry) | Watson | Hughes* |
| Francis T. | Channon[1] | Pearson | Talbot | Kennedy (Tueart) | |

Goals in each half by Gordon McQueen and Kenny Dalglish pushed England to defeat and for the first time they lost consecutive matches at Wembley. Mike Channon's consolation goal came from the penalty spot 3 minutes from the end of a game in which Scotland were always the more productive and enterprising side.

286: v **Brazil,** Rio de Janeiro, 8.6.77. Drew 0–0

Clemence	Neal	Cherry	Greenhoff	Watson	Hughes
Keegan*	Francis T.	Pearson (Channon)	Wilkins (Kennedy)	Talbot	

England could and should have been three goals clear at half-time if they had taken their chances. Brazil were equally careless in front of goal in the second half, during which acting manager Les Cocker sent on substitutes Ray Kennedy and Mike Channon to put new life into a tiring team. A sequence of saves by Ray Clemence and three off-the-line clearances by Trevor Cherry stopped the Brazilians from snatching victory.

287: v **Argentina,** Buenos Aires, 12.6.77. Drew 1–1

Clemence	Neal	Cherry	Greenhoff (Kennedy)	Watson	Hughes
Keegan*	Channon	Pearson[1]	Wilkins	Talbot	

Trevor Cherry, with two teeth knocked out by a punch, was unluckily sent off with the culprit Bertoni in the 82nd minute. It was Bertoni who had equalised a 3rd-minute goal by Stuart Pearson when he scored with a curling free-kick in the 15th minute. The game became bogged down in midfield, with England unable to penetrate Argentina's in-depth defence. Emlyn Hughes cleared off the goal-line in the closing moments.

288: v **Uruguay,** Montevideo, 15.6.77. Drew 0–0

Clemence	Neal	Cherry	Greenhoff	Watson	Hughes
Keegan*	Channon	Pearson	Wilkins	Talbot	

Don Revie's last match was notable in that it marked the completion of England's first ever undefeated tour of South America, but the game itself was best forgotten. Uruguay showed interest only in defending their goal, and England's tired players could not work up the energy to find a way through. They finished the tour with only one goal to show for all their effort in three matches. Then came the bombshell news that Revie was deserting to the Arabs. Enter Ron Greenwood.

Ron Greenwood's teams and match highlights

289: v Switzerland, Wembley, 7.9.77. Drew 0-0

Clemence	Neal	Cherry	McDermott	Watson	Hughes*
Keegan	Channon (Hill)	Francis T.	Kennedy	Callaghan (Wilkins)	

Ron Greenwood, appointed in a caretaker capacity, called up seven of the players who had helped Liverpool win the European Cup. His first England selection included veteran Ian Callaghan, who was winning his first cap since the third match of the 1966 World Cup finals eleven years and forty-nine days earlier. But Greenwood's hopes for an instant team rapport were not realized, and England struggled to contain a lively Swiss team. Only a succession of fine saves by Ray Clemence prevented England from going down to an embarrassing defeat.

290: v Luxembourg, Luxembourg, 12.10.77. England won 2–0

Clemence	Cherry	Watson (Beattie)	Hughes*	Kennedy[1]	Callaghan
McDermott (Whymark)	Wilkins	Francis T.	Mariner[1]	Hill	

England needed a goal rush to breathe life into their hopes of qualifying for the 1978 World Cup finals, but they were too anxious and continually snatched at the chances they created. A 30th-minute goal by Paul Mariner and an injury-time goal by Ray Kennedy lifted England to their first victory in seven matches, but it was too little too late.

291: v Italy, Wembley, 16.11.77. England won 2–0

Clemence	Neal	Cherry	Wilkins	Watson	Hughes*
Keegan[1] (Francis T.)	Coppell	Latchford (Pearson)	Brooking[1]	Barnes	

Kevin Keegan inspired England's World Cup victory over Italy, a magnificent win that clinched the full-time manager's job for Greenwood. Keegan headed in a Trevor Brooking pass in the 11th minute, and combined again with Brooking 9 minutes from the end when his brilliant through ball was coolly steered wide of goalkeeper Dino Zoff. Greenwood's boldness in playing Steve Coppell and Peter Barnes as wide men was rewarded with some entertaining and incisive old-fashioned wing play. Now England counted the cost of their missed chances against Luxemburg. Italy were left needing just a 1–0 victory at home against Luxemburg to clinch the place in the World Cup finals. They won 3–0.

292: v West Germany, Munich, 22.2.78. England lost 2–1

Clemence	Neal	Mills	Wilkins	Watson	Hughes*
Keegan (Francis T.)		Coppell	Pearson[1]	Brooking	Barnes

A disputed goal 4 minutes from the end robbed England of a deserved draw against the World Cup holders. England had led from late in the first half when Stuart Pearson beat Sepp Maier with a looping header from a Steve Coppell cross. Hamburg-based Keegan ran himself to the edge of exhaustion in his attempts to make the game safe, and had to be replaced by Trevor Francis. It was Germany's substitute, Ronnie Worm, who equalized shortly after coming on in the 75th minute. The previous evening he had scored after being sent on as a substitute in the 'B' international against England. In the closing moments Dave Watson was adjudged to have fouled Burgsmuller, and while England were still forming their defensive wall, Rainer Bonhof smacked a free-kick low into the net.

293: v Brazil, Wembley, 19.4.78. Drew 1–1

Corrigan	Mills	Cherry	Greenhoff	Watson	Currie
Keegan*[1]	Coppell	Latchford	Francis T.	Barnes	

Brazil, a goal up in 10 minutes through Gil, abandoned their silky smooth samba football for uncompromising tactics that led to five of their players being booked. England missed a hatful of chances to equalize before Kevin Keegan earned a merited draw with a Brazilian-style free-kick that he bent round the defensive wall.

294: v Wales, Cardiff, 13.5.78. England won 3–1

Shilton	Mills*	Cherry (Currie[1])	Greenhoff	Watson	Wilkins
Coppell	Francis T.	Latchford[1] (Mariner)		Brooking	Barnes[1]

Two spectacular goals in the last eight minutes – a 35-yard rifle shot from Tony Currie followed by a rising drive from the edge of the penalty area by Peter Barnes – gave England a winning start to the Home Championship. Currie had come on as a substitute for Trevor Cherry, who was carried off with a fractured collarbone in the 16th minute. Bob Latchford gave England an 8th-minute lead before limping off to be replaced by Paul Mariner. Wales equalized through Dwyer during a long spell of dominance in the second half before Currie and Barnes stepped on to the scoring stage.

295: v Northern Ireland, Wembley, 16.5.78. England won 1–0

Clemence	Neal[1]	Mills	Wilkins	Watson	Hughes 1
Currie	Coppell	Pearson	Woodcock	Greenhoff	

Phil Neal scored his first goal for England seconds before half-time to break the resistance of a brave Northern Ireland team for whom goal-keeper Jim Platt was in outstanding form. The two best chances of the second half both fell to Dave Watson, who was twice denied goals by the brilliance of Platt.

296: v Scotland, Hampden Park, 20.5.78. England won 1–0

Clemence	Neal	Mills	Currie	Watson	Hughes* (Greenhoff)
Wilkins	Coppell[1]	Mariner (Brooking)		Francis T.	Barnes

Scotland were given a miserable send-off to the World Cup finals in Argentina when England beat them, although a draw would have been a fairer reflection of the play. The Scots had long periods of possession but could make little impact against an England defence in which Dave Watson was a pillar of strength. Scotland disputed the deciding goal in the 83rd minute. They claimed that goalkeeper Alan Rough was fouled by Trevor Francis when he dropped a cross from Peter Barnes. Steve Coppell fired the loose ball into the net to clinch the Home Championship for England.

297: v Hungary, Wembley, 24.5.78. England won 4–1

Shilton	Neal[1]	Mills	Wilkins	Watson (Greenhoff)	Hughes*
Keegan	Coppell (Currie[1])		Francis T.[1]	Brooking	Barnes[1]

England, with Kevin Keegan and Trevor Brooking pulling the Hungarian defence apart, rushed into a 3–0 lead inside the first 35 minutes through Peter Barnes, a Phil Neal penalty and a Trevor Francis header. Hungary had their best moments immediately after half-time and pulled a goal back through Nagy before Tony Currie finished them off with a crashing shot from the edge of the area in the 73rd minute.

298: v Denmark, Copenhagen, 20.9.78. England won 4–3

Clemence	Neal[1]	Mills	Wilkins	Watson	Hughes*
Keegan[2]	Coppell	Latchford[1]	Brooking	Barnes	

Kevin Keegan headed two goals from well-directed free-kicks only to see the Danes allowed to pull level with two goals inside 5 minutes against a less than disciplined England defence. Bob Latchford directed a header against a post and Keegan also hit the woodwork as both teams played all-out attacking football in what coach Don Howe later described as 'the most exciting international match I've ever seen'. England regained the lead through a disputed goal by Bob Latchford after the break and Phil Neal made it 4–2 before the Danes forced a third goal in the dying moments of a pulsating European championship qualifying match.

299: v Republic of Ireland, Dublin, 25.10.78. Drew 1–1

Clemence	Neal	Mills	Wilkins	Watson (Thompson)	Hughes*
Keegan	Coppell	Latchford¹	Brooking	Barnes (Woodcock)	

Bob Latchford headed an early goal with the help of a deflection in this second European championship qualifier, but England became disjointed after centre-half Dave Watson went off with an injury in the 21st minute. Steve Coppell, continually running the Irish defence into disarray, smacked a shot against the bar and Kevin Keegan headed wide when well placed, before Gerry Daly hooked in an equalizer.

300: v Czechoslovakia, Wembley, 29.11.78. England won 1–0

Shilton	Anderson	Cherry	Thompson	Watson	Wilkins
Keegan*	Coppell¹	Woodcock (Latchford)	Currie	Barnes	

Steve Coppell scored the only goal of the match on a frozen pitch that ruined the game as a spectacle. The Czechs coped with the conditions better and deserved at least a draw against an overworked England defence in which Peter Shilton was at his majestic best. Viv Anderson created history by becoming the first black player to be capped by England.

301: v Northern Ireland, Wembley, 7.2.79. England won 4–0

Clemence	Neal	Mills	Currie	Watson¹	Hughes*
Keegan¹	Coppell	Latchford²	Brooking	Barnes	

Kevin Keegan was irrepressible after bravely heading England into an early lead in the face of a strong challenge from goalkeeper Pat Jennings. He then laid on the first of Bob Latchford's two goals with an accurate cross, and back headed a Trevor Brooking corner on to Dave Watson for the fourth goal.

302: v Northern Ireland, Belfast, 19.5.79. England won 2–0

Clemence	Neal	Mills*	Thompson	Watson¹	Wilkins
Coppell¹	McDermott	Latchford	Currie	Barnes	

Dave Watson and Steve Coppell each scored in the first 15 minutes to kill off the Northern Ireland challenge in this return European championship qualifying match. England missed the prolific partnership that had been developing between Kevin Keegan and Trevor Brooking, and they lacked the drive and direction that had put them so in command against the Irish at Wembley three months earlier.

303: v **Wales**, Wembley, 23.5.79. Drew 0–0

| Corrigan | Cherry | Sansom | Wilkins (Brooking) | Watson | Hughes* |
| Keegan (Coppell) | | Currie | Latchford | McDermott | Cunningham |

England created enough chances to have won comfortably, but their finishing was weak and wayward. Kenny Sansom played in the first of his eighty-six international matches, making him the most capped England full-back of all time. West Bromwich Albion winger Laurie Cunningham also made his début.

304: v **Scotland**, Wembley, 26.5.79. England won 3–1

| Clemence | Neal | Mills | Thompson | Watson | Wilkins |
| Keegan*[1] | Coppell[1] | Latchford | Brooking | Barnes[1] | |

Scotland took a 26th-minute lead through John Wark as they put England on the rack in the first half and it was against the run of play when Peter Barnes equalized. A couple of magnificent saves by Ray Clemence lifted England's confidence and they bossed the second half, with goals from Steve Coppell and Kevin Keegan giving them the Home Championship.

305: v **Bulgaria**, Sofia, 6.6.79. England won 3–0

| Clemence | Neal | Mills | Thompson | Watson[1] | Wilkins |
| Keegan*[1] | Coppell | Latchford (Francis T.) | Brooking | Barnes[1] | (Woodcock) |

England played with tremendous fervour despite suffocating heat-wave conditions. The Bulgarians threatened to take an early lead when Ray Clemence pushed a header by Borisov against a post, but then Kevin Keegan scored after combining with Trevor Brooking. England clinched victory early in the second-half of this European championship qualifier with two headed goals in a minute, first by Dave Watson and then Peter Barnes.

306: v **Sweden**, Stockholm, 10.6.79. Drew 0–0

| Shilton | Anderson | Cherry | McDermott (Wilkins) | Watson | Hughes* |
| Keegan | Currie (Brooking) | | Francis T. | Woodcock | Cunningham |

In a match dominated by defences, Emlyn Hughes came closest to scoring in the first half when he raced 60 yards before unleashing a shot that rattled the Swedish crossbar. Ron Greenwood made nine changes for a game staged to mark the seventy-fifth anniversary of the Swedish FA, and only two splendid saves by Peter Shilton stopped the Swedes from celebtrating the milestone with a victory.

307: v Austria, Vienna, 13.6.79. England lost 4–3

Shilton (Clemence)	Neal	Mills	Thompson	Watson	Wilkins[1]
Keegan*[1]	Coppell[1]	Latchford (Francis T.)	Brooking	Barnes (Cunningham)	

England had just a Kevin Keegan goal to show at half-time in reply to three first-half goals by the Austrians in a match littered with defensive errors. Goals by Steve Coppell and Ray Wilkins brought England battling back to 3–3, only for them to lose to a late goal headed past substitute goalkeeper Ray Clemence by Pezzey following a free-kick. It was England's first setback since the 2–1 defeat by West Germany back in February, 1978.

308: v Denmark, Wembley, 9.9.79. England won 1–0

Clemence	Neal	Mills	Thompson	Watson	Wilkins
Coppell	McDermott	Keegan*[1]	Brooking	Barnes	

England took an important step towards qualifying for the final stages of the European championship finals with this narrow win over the Danes. Kevin Keegan, shaking off the handicap of a recurring leg injury, scored the only goal of the match with a left-foot volley after a driving right-wing run by Phil Neal. Greenwood settled for a 4–3–3 formation, with Terry McDermott joining Ray Wilkins and Trevor Brooking in midfield.

309: v Northern Ireland, Belfast, 17.10.79. England won 5–1

Shilton	Neal	Mills	Thompson	Watson	Wilkins
Keegan*	Coppell	Francis T.[2]	Brooking (McDermott)	Woodcock[2+1 o.g.]	

England virtually clinched a place in the European championship finals with this resounding win on a soaking-wet Windsor Park pitch. Both Trevor Francis and Tony Woodcock scored in each half, and the rout was completed in the 70th minute when Chris Nicholl turned a Phil Neal centre into his own net. Northern Ireland's goal came midway through the second half from a Moreland penalty.

310: v **Bulgaria,** Wembley, 22.11.79. England won 2–0

| Clemence | Anderson | Sansom | Thompson* | Watson[1] | Wilkins |
| Reeves | Hoddle[1] | Francis T. | Kennedy | Woodcock | |

Fog caused the first ever postponement of a Wembley international and the twenty-four hour delay meant that Kevin Keegan had to miss the game to return to Hamburg. Phil Thompson took over as skipper, and Kevin Reeves and Glenn Hoddle came in for their international débuts. Dave Watson scored the first goal when he headed in a Hoddle cross in the 8th minute, and it was Hoddle who made his début one to remember with the second match-clinching goal when he side-footed the ball powerfully into the net from 20 yards in the 69th minute.

311: v **Republic of Ireland,** Wembley, 6.2.80. England won 2–0

| Clemence | Cherry | Sansom | Thompson | Watson | Robson |
| Keegan*[2] | McDermott | Johnson (Coppell) | | Woodcock | Cunningham |

A goal in each half by the buzzing Kevin Keegan sank the Irish in this final European championship qualifier. A feature of a generally uninspiring match was the forceful début of West Bromwich Albion midfield player Bryan Robson.

312: v **Spain,** Barcelona, 26.3.80. England won 2–0

| Shilton | Neal (Hughes) | Mills | Thompson | Watson | Wilkins |
| Keegan* | Coppell | Francis T.[1] (Cunningham) | | Kennedy | Woodcock[1] |

England ran the Spanish defence to a nervous breakdown, and they might have had three goals before Tony Woodcock opened the scoring in the 16th minute. Trevor Francis put the seal on a magnificent team performance when he collected a pass from Steve Coppell, outpaced two defenders and beat oncoming goalkeeper Arconada with a perfectly placed cross shot. England would have won by at least five goals but for a procession of superb saves by man-of-the-match Arconada.

313: v **Argentina,** Wembley, 13.5.80. England won 3–1

| Clemence | Neal (Cherry) | Sansom | Thompson | Watson | Wilkins |
| Keegan*[1] | Coppell | Johnson[2] (Birtles) | Woodcock | Kennedy | (Brooking) |

World champions Argentina – including the great Maradona – were often chased off their feet by an England team playing above itself. David Johnson, recalled in place of injured Trevor Francis, scored either side of the half-time interval to give England a 2–0 lead. Maradona, who had decorated the match with a series of explosive runs, was brought down by Kenny Sansom in the 54th minute and Daniel Passarella scored from the penalty spot. Kevin Keegan then showed why he had been voted European Footballer of the Year when he crashed a low shot into the net after combining with Johnson and Coppell to find a way through the Argentine defence.

314: v **Wales,** Wrexham, 17.5.80. England lost 4–1

Clemence	Neal (Sansom)	Cherry	Thompson*	Lloyd	(Wilkins)	Kennedy
Coppell	Hoddle	Mariner[1]	Brooking	Barnes		

Just four days after their triumph over the world champions, England showed their worst side with a loose performance against a Welsh team out to impress their new manager Mike England. Larry Lloyd, recalled to the middle of the England defence after eight years, had a nightmare match. He was booked, injured and substituted after being given a chasing by a lively Welsh forward line in which Leighton James was outstanding. Paul Mariner gave England the lead in the 16th minute, but Wales quickly equalized through Mickey Thomas. Two goals from James and an own goal by Phil Thompson piled on the misery for an England team missing the drive and industry of Kevin Keegan.

315: v **Northern Ireland,** Wembley, 20.5.80. Drew 1–1

Corrigan	Cherry	Sansom	Hughes*	Watson	Wilkins
Reeves (Mariner)		McDermott	Johnson[1]	Brooking	Devonshire

Ron Greenwood made sweeping changes following the demoralizing defeat by Wales, and Alan Devonshire came in for his début. An undistinguished game seemed set for a goalless draw until David Johnson forced the ball into the Irish net in the 81st minute. Northern Ireland equalized just a minute later when substitute Cochrane rammed the ball past the previously redundant Joe Corrigan.

316: v **Scotland,** Hampden Park, 24.5.80. England won 2–0

Clemence	Cherry	Sansom	Thompson*	Watson	Wilkins
Coppell[1]	McDermott	Johnson	Mariner (Hughes)		Brooking[1]

A goal in each half by Trevor Brooking and Steve Coppell lifted England to a victory that put them in good heart for the European championship finals three weeks away. Brooking scored his goal after just 7 minutes, continuing where he had left off as West Ham's goal hero against Arsenal in the FA Cup

Final. It was a Brooking back-heel that set up Coppell's goal in the 75th minute, the Manchester United winger steering the ball home after goalkeeper Alan Rough had parried his first shot.

317: v **Australia,** Sydney, 31.5.80. England won 2–1

Corrigan	Cherry*	Lampard	Talbot	Osman	Butcher	Robson (Greenhoff)
Sunderland (Ward)			Mariner¹	Hoddle¹		Armstrong (Devonshire)

A virtual England 'B' team travelled 'Down Under' to play in a match to celebrate 100 years of football in Australia. Goals from Paul Mariner and Glenn Hoddle gave England a 2–0 half-time lead, and the Australians managed to pull one back through a secondhalf penalty. Ipswich partners Russell Osman and Terry Butcher made their débuts together at the heart of the England defence, and there was also a first cap for Alan Sunderland, who was substituted by another débutant in Peter Ward. Neither player was selected by England again. David Armstrong won the first of his three caps.

318: v **Belgium,** Turin, 12.6.80. Drew 1–1

Clemence	Neal	Sansom	Thompson	Watson	Wilkins¹	Keegan*
Coppell (McDermott)		Johnson (Kennedy)			Woodcock	Brooking

England's opening match in the European championship finals was scarred by a sickening outbreak of hooliganism by a section of their so-called supporters. The violence erupted after the Belgians had struck back with an immediate equalizer to a classic goal in the 22nd minute by Ray Wilkins, who collected a clearance, lobbed the ball over the defence and then ran forward to collect his own pass and to direct a hook shot into the roof of the net. Ceulemans scored following a corner just a minute later, and this triggered widespread fighting on the terraces. The police fired tear gas to try to restore order, and several of the England players were affected and the game had to be temporarily suspended. What had been a keenly competitive match lost its impetus, and England had to be satisfied with a draw. Tony Woodcock looked unlucky to have a goal ruled offside just before the Wilkins strike, but it was sadly a game that would be remembered for the ugly scenes on the terraces rather than the football on the pitch.

319: v **Italy,** Turin, 15.6.80. England lost 1–0

Shilton	Neal	Sansom	Thompson	Watson	Wilkins
Keegan*	Coppell	Birtles (Mariner)		Kennedy	Woodcock

Tardelli settled a polished and peaceful game with one of the goals of the tournament 12 minutes from the end. Graziani powered past Phil Neal before delivering the ball into the path of Tardelli, who beat Shilton with an unstoppable volley at the near post. It had class written all over it and was a worthy winner of a game England often dominated with fast, skilful football that had the disciplined Italian defence stretched near to breaking point. Ray Kennedy came closest to scoring for England when he rifled a second-half shot against a post with Dino Zoff beaten.

320: v **Spain,** Naples, 18.6.80. England won 2–1

Clemence	Anderson (Cherry)	Mills	Thompson	Watson	Wilkins
McDermott	Hoddle (Mariner)		Keegan*	Woodcock[1]	Brooking[1]

England needed a clear two-goal victory over Spain to qualify for the third and fourth play-off. Spain packed the midfield and made it difficult for a much-changed England team to get any rhythm. Trevor Brooking gave England the lead in the 19th minute when he steered the ball over the line from a Ray Wilkins header following a free-kick for one of several fouls on dangerman Kevin Keegan. Ray Clemence conceded a disputed penalty early in the second-half from which Cardenosa scored an equalizer. Six minutes later Spain were awarded a second penalty afer a foul by Dave Watson. Dani beat Clemence but was ordered to retake the spot-kick, and this time the Liverpool goalkeeper made a dramatic save. England lifted their game and had the satisfaction of snatching a deserved victory when the industrious Tony Woodcock steered the ball home after a thumping shot from Terry McDermott had been pushed out.

321: v **Norway,** Wembley, 10.9.80. England won 4–0

Shilton	Anderson	Sansom	Thompson*	Watson	Robson
Gates	McDermott[2]	Mariner[1]	Woodcock[1]	Rix	

Without Keegan, Wilkins, Brooking, Coppell and Trevor Francis, a new-look England attack took a long time to get into its stride in this opening qualifying match for the 1982 World Cup finals. A Terry McDermott goal in the 35th minute calmed jangling nerves, and England finally won comfortably with three goals in the last 33 minutes through Tony Woodcock, a McDermott penalty and a beautiful creation by Paul Mariner, who skilfully deceived three defenders before firing the ball majestically into the net with his left foot. Bryan Robson was a powerhouse in midfield and Eric Gates and Graham Rix made satisfactory débuts.

322: v **Romania,** Bucharest, 15.10.80. England lost 2–1

Clemence	Neal	Sansom	Thompson*	Watson	Robson
Rix	McDermott	Birtles (Cunningham)	Woodcock[1]	Gates (Coppell)	

A controversial penalty decided this game in the 75th minute and dealt a severe blow to England's hopes of qualifying for the World Cup finals. Kenny Sansom angrily protested his innocence after his tackle on Iordanescu had been ruled a foul. The Romanian picked himself up and scored the winning goal from the penalty spot. England had just been getting on top after Tony Woodcock scored in the 66th minute following a neat exchange of passes with Garry Birtles. Romania had their best moments in the first half and scored at the peak of their pressure through Raducanu in the 36th minute.

323: v **Switzerland,** Wembley, 19.11.80. England won 2–1

Shilton	Neal	Sansom	Robson	Watson	Mills*
Coppell	McDermott	Mariner[1]	Brooking (Rix)	Woodcock[1 o.g.]	

England were leading comfortably 2–0 at half-time through goals by Tony Woodcock (a deflected shot) and Paul Mariner, and there was no hint of the way the pendulum of play would swing Switzerland's way in the second half of this crucial World Cup qualifier. Trevor Brooking, who had been dominant in midfield, started feeling the effects of an old injury and when his output dropped England began to struggle to contain a suddenly lively Swiss side. A long period of Swiss pressure was finally rewarded when Pfister drove a scorching shot wide of Peter Shilton, and England clung on desperately for a victory that revived their World Cup hopes.

324: v **Spain,** Wembley, 25.3.81. England lost 2–1

Clemence	Neal	Sansom	Robson	Butcher	Osman
Keegan*	Francis T. (Barnes)	Mariner	Brooking (Wilkins)	Hoddle[1]	

England were on the way to their first home defeat under Ron Greenwood from the moment Satrustegui snatched an early goal following a misunderstanding at the centre of the defence between Ipswich partners Terry Butcher and Russell Osman. A rain-saturated surface seemed to give England greater problems than their opponents, and it was against the run of play when Glenn Hoddle equalized with a blistering volley after a Bryan Robson cross had been blocked in the 27th minute. Spain quickly regained the lead through Zamora, and only their weak finishing prevented them scoring a more emphatic victory.

325: v **Romania,** Wembley, 29.4.81. Drew 0–0

Shilton	Anderson	Sansom	Robson	Watson*	Osman	Wilkins
Brooking (McDermott)		Coppell		Francis		Woodcock

Anxiety anchored the England forwards in front of goal, and they missed vital chances that could have clinched victory in this World Cup qualifying match against their closest group rivals. England's defence generally dominated the Romanian forwards, but there was one amazing escape when Peter Shilton's feet slipped from under him as he reached for a dipping header from Balaci during a rare raid in the 33rd minute. Shilton was lying on the ground as he scooped the ball clear with two Romanian forwards bearing down on him.

326: v **Brazil,** Wembley, 12.5.81. England lost 1–0

Clemence*	Neal	Sansom	Robson	Martin	Wilkins
Coppell	McDermott	Withe	Rix	Barnes	

Peter Withe, making his début in the centre of the shot-shy England attack, came within inches of ending the goal famine in the last minute against Brazil when his header hit the inside of a post before being cleared. An equalizer would have been an injustice to a Brazilian team that played with a lot of their traditional flair, particularly in the 12th minute when Zico outsmarted two England defenders before powering a shot past Ray Clemence. Alvin Martin had a tough baptism in the middle of the defence against Reinaldo, but could be pleased with his display in a heartening England performance that earned an ovation from the Wembley crowd despite another defeat.

327: v **Wales,** Wembley, 20.5.81. Drew 0–0

Corrigan	Anderson	Sansom	Robson	Watson*	Wilkins
Coppell	Hoddle	Withe (Woodcock)	Rix	Barnes	

England's lack of goal power was beginning to eat at their confidence, and they scrambled a draw against a Welsh side buoyed by six successive victories. Crystal Palace striker Ian Walsh missed two glittering opportunities to tie up the game for Wales immediately after half-time.

328: v **Scotland,** Wembley, 23.5.81. England lost 1–0

Corrigan	Anderson	Sansom	Wilkins	Watson* (Martin)	Robson
Coppell	Hoddle	Withe	Rix	Woodcock (Francis T.)	

A 65th minute penalty by Nottingham Forest winger John Robertson won this match for Scotland as England continued their miserable form in front of goal. England argued that they should have had a penalty at the opposite end when substitute Trevor Francis was pulled down by Willie Miller, but the French referee waved play on.

329: v Switzerland, Basle, 30.5.81. England lost 2–1

Clemence	Mills	Sansom		Wilkins	Watson (Barnes)	Osman
Coppell	Robson	Keegan*		Mariner	Francis T. (McDermott[1])	

For nearly 30 minutes England outplayed Switzerland in this World Cup qualifier, and it was totally unexpected when the Swiss suddenly swept into the lead with two goals in a minute. Ron Greenwood attempted a salvage operation by sending on Terry McDermott for Trevor Francis and pushing Kevin Keegan forward into a striker's role. It was McDermott who at last ended England's run of almost eight hours without a goal when he collected a Steve Coppell pass in the 55th minute and buried a shot in the Swiss net. But Switzerland held out under enormous pressure to record their first victory over England for thirty-four years.

330: v Hungary, Budapest, 6.6.81. England won 3–1

Clemence	Neal	Mills		Thompson	Watson	Robson
Coppell	McDermott	Mariner		Brooking[2] (Wilkins)		Keegan*[1]

Only a victory could keep alive England's dwindling chances of qualifying for the World Cup finals, and they dug deep to come up with one of their finest performances under the Greenwood banner. Trevor Brooking gave England an 18th-minute lead, which the Hungarians cancelled out seconds before half-time. It was in the second half that England really turned on the pressure, and they got their reward in the shape of a brilliantly taken goal by Brooking, who drove a rising shot so powerfully after accepting a pass from Kevin Keegan that the ball jammed in the net behind the stanchion. Keegan put the result beyond doubt when he scored from the penalty spot in the 73rd minute after being brought down by a desperate tackle.

331: v Norway, Oslo, 9.9.81. England lost 2–1

Clemence	Neal	Mills		Thompson	Osman	Robson[1]
Keegan*	McDermott	Mariner (Withe)		Francis T.	Hoddle	(Barnes)

After hitting the heights against Hungary, England sunk to an all-time low when they lost to Norway's team of part-time professionals – a defeat that seemed certain to end their World Cup hopes. Bryan Robson gave England a 14th minute lead and a comfortable victory looked well within reach, but the Norwegians battled back to snatch a 34th-minute equalizer that gave them the momentum to go on to what was considered their greatest triumph in a football history that had mostly been about taking part. Thorensen took advantage of dithering in the England defence in the 40th minute to force home what proved the match-winning goal. It was a humiliating defeat to rank with the 1950 World Cup loss to the United States.

332: v **Hungary,** Wembley, 18.11.81. England won 1–0

Shilton	Neal	Mills	Thompson	Martin	Robson
Keegan*	Coppell (Morley)		Mariner[1]	McDermott	Brooking

England came back from the dead to clinch a place in the World Cup finals with this nervously constructed victory over Hungary. The door to the finals in Spain was reopened by group favourites Romania making a mess of their final qualifying match, and England needed only a point against Hungary to book their tickets. Paul Mariner scored the vital match-winning goal in the 16th minute, scrambling the ball into the net after a mis-hit shot by Trevor Brooking had confused the Hungarian defenders. Hungary were already assured of their place in the finals, and were content to concentrate on defence and they looked in danger of conceding a second goal only in the final moments when Tony Morley, making his début as a substitute, had his shot well saved by goalkeeper Meszaros.

333: v **Northern Ireland,** Wembley, 23.2.82. England won 4–0

Clemence	Anderson	Sansom	Wilkins[1]	Watson	Foster
Keegan*[1]	Robson[1]	Francis T. (Regis)	Hoddle[1]	Morley	(Woodcock)

Goalkeeper Pat Jennings was picking the ball out of the Irish net after only 44 seconds of his ninetieth international following a typical burst from Bryan Robson. England were experimenting with a sweeper system, Ray Wilkins playing behind the back line of the defence, and there was a lack of rhythm in their play after their dream start. It was not until the second half that they proved their supremacy with goals from Kevin Keegan, Wilkins and Glenn Hoddle. Cyrille Regis replaced the limping Trevor Francis in the 66th minute for his first taste of international football and was only inches wide with a diving header.

334: v **Wales,** Cardiff, 27.4.82. England won 1–0

Corrigan	Neal	Sansom	Thompson*	Butcher	Robson
Wilkins	Francis T.[1] (Regis)	Withe	Hoddle (McDermott)		Morley

Trevor Francis gave England their first victory over Wales in five matches when he struck a powerful shot high into the net after Bryan Robson had pushed a short free-kick into his path in the 74th minute. Glenn Hoddle had looked the most inventive player on the pitch, and England lost a lot of their poise and control when he limped off early in the second half. Wales were always a threat and goalkeeper Joe Corrigan rescued England with three outstanding saves.

335: v **Holland,** Wembley, 25.5.82. England won 2–0

Shilton*	Neal	Sansom	Thompson	Foster	Robson
Wilkins	Devonshire (Rix)	Mariner1 (Barnes)		McDermott	Woodcock¹

Holland's young experimental team were sunk by two goals in 5 minutes immediately after half-time by Tony Woodcock and Graham Rix. It was Rix, Bryan Robson and Ray Wilkins who bossed the match in midfield, and assured a victory for Ron Greenwood in his last Wembley match as manager.

336: v **Scotland,** Hampden Park, 29.5.82. England won 1–0

Shilton	Mills	Sansom	Thompson	Butcher	Robson
Keegan* (McDermott)	Coppell	Mariner¹ (Francis T.)		Brooking	Wilkins

Old heroes Tom Finney and George Young led the teams out for this 100th meeting between Scotland and England. Paul Mariner's brave header in the 13th minute clinched the Home Championship for England and gave them their third successive victory at Hampden Park.

337: v **Iceland,** Reykjavik, 2.6.82. Drew 1–1

Corrigan	Anderson	Neal*	Watson	Osman	McDermott
Hoddle	Devonshire (Perryman)	Withe	Regis (Goddard¹)		Morley

Ron Greenwood fielded his second-string team from his World Cup squad, and they struggled on a frozen pitch to hold an enthusiastic Iceland team. Paul Goddard, making his début as a substitute for injured Cyrille Regis, cancelled out Iceland's 23rd-minute lead when he ran on to a precise pass from Glenn Hoddle and steered the ball home in the 69th minute. It was Goddard's only cap, and he found his way into the record books by becoming the only England player to score while playing less than a full match. Steve Perryman also won his only cap as a substitute.

338: v **Finland,** Helsinki, 3.6.82. England won 4–1

Clemence	Mills	Sansom	Thompson	Martin	Robson² (Rix)
Coppell (Francis T.)	Wilkins	Brooking (Woodcock)	Keegan*	Mariner²	

A goal apiece in each half by Paul Mariner and Bryan Robson gave England their sixth victory in six months and sent them into the World Cup finals in a quietly confident mood. The match was staged to celebrate Finland's seventy-fifth anniversary, and the outplayed Finns had the consolation of a penalty goal in the 80th minute.

339: v **France,** World Cup, Bilbao, 16.6.82. England won 3–1

Shilton	Mills*	Sansom (Neal)	Thompson	Butcher	Robson²
Coppell	Wilkins	Mariner¹	Francis T.	Rix	

England had a dream send-off to the World Cup finals when Bryan Robson scored the fastest goal in the history of the tournament. He struck in just 27 seconds, lashing the ball left-footed past a startled French goalkeeper afer Terry Butcher had headed on a quickly taken Steve Coppell throw from the right. France recovered from this shattering start to equalize after 25 minutes, but England raised their pace despite scorching heat in the second half, and the switch by Ron Greenwood of Graham Rix to a left-sided role in midfield proved a tactical master-stroke. Rix, playing in place of the injured Trevor Brooking, enjoyed his new freedom and England took full control when Robson headed in his second goal in the 67th minute. Paul Mariner underlined England's supremacy with a close-range shot following a defensive mix-up. It was the fifth successive international in which the Ipswich striker had found the net.

340: v **Czechoslovakia,** World Cup, Bilbao, 20.6.82. England won 2–0

Shilton	Mills*	Sansom	Thompson	Butcher	Robson
Coppell (Hoddle)	Wilkins	Francis T.¹	Mariner¹	Rix	

Two fortunate goals in 3 minutes midway through the second half booked England's place in the second phase of the finals. Trevor Francis rammed the ball into the net after Czech goalkeeper Semen had dropped a Ray Wilkins corner, and then Czech defender Barmos diverted the ball into his own net as Francis raced to meet a pass from Paul Mariner. A blow for England was that they now had Bryan Robson joining Kevin Keegan and Trevor Brooking on the injury list.

341: v **Kuwait,** World Cup, Bilbao, 25.6.82. England won 1–0

Shilton	Neal	Mills*	Thompson	Foster	Hoddle
Coppell	Francis T.¹	Mariner	Rix	Wilkins	

A gem of a goal by Trevor Francis was the one highlight of England's third World Cup victory against a Kuwaiti side that battled bravely and with some eye-catching skill. The match-winning goal came in the 27th minute when Mariner back-heeled a Peter Shilton clearance into the path of Francis, who set off on a 30-yard run that he climaxed by sliding the ball past the on-coming goalkeeper.

342: v **West Germany,** World Cup, Madrid, 29.6.82. Drew 0–0

Shilton	Mills*	Sansom	Thompson	Butcher	Robson
Coppell	Francis T. (Woodcock)	Mariner	Rix	Wilkins	

England and West Germany have had some classic confrontations on the football field, but this was not one of them. The Germans decided on a policy of suffocating defence, and the game deteriorated into a midfield muddle. Bryan Robson came closest to scoring for a England with a first-half header that was tipped over the bar by Schumacher, and the subdued, half-fit Rummenigge threatened to win the match with one moment of brilliance when his sniper shot from 25 yards rocked the England crossbar in the closing minutes of a best-forgotten game.

343: v **Spain,** World Cup, Madrid, 5.7.82. Drew 0–0

Shilton	Mills*	Sansom	Thompson	Butcher	Robson
Rix (Brooking)	Francis T.	Mariner	Woodcock (Keegan)	Wilkins	

Ron Greenwood's final game as manager ended in a frustrating draw with the host country and a sad exit from the World Cup, although unbeaten in the tournament. England needed two goals to qualify for a semi-final place against France, but were unable to put the vital finishing touch to some excellent approach work that was a good advertisement for the quality football that Greenwood has always believed in. Greenwood finished his reign with a rare gamble against a Spanish team determined not to be beaten. He sent Kevin Keegan and Trevor Brooking on in the 63rd minute for their first World Cup action, and the double substitution so nearly brought reward. Keegan headed wide from the best chance of the match and Brooking had a rasping shot well saved. Exit Ron Greenwood. Enter Bobby Robson, who had been named as England's next manager during the World Cup finals.

Bobby Robson's teams and match highlights

344: v Denmark, Copenhagen, 22.9.82. Drew 2-2

Shilton	Neal	Sansom	Wilkins*	Osman	Butcher
Morley	Robson	Mariner	Francis²	Rix (Hill)	

Jesper Olsen stopped Bobby Robson celebrating a victory in his first match when he conjured a spectacular last-minute goal that gave Denmark a thoroughly deserved draw in this European championship qualifier. Olsen outwitted three England defenders in a jinking run before guiding the ball wide of Peter Shilton, who had performed minor miracles keeping out the talented Danish forwards. Trevor Francis had given England a 7th minute lead, but they were then forced on the defensive and it was thanks mainly to the acrobatics of Shilton that the Danes had to wait more than an hour before they finally got an equalizer through a Hansen penalty. Francis scored his second goal 10 minutes from the final whistle with a hooked shot that restored England's lead and looked like being the winner until Olsen's moment of magic. Ricky Hill became Robson's first new cap when he came on as substitute for Tony Morley in the 83rd minute. A major surprise was that Robson had decided to kick off his reign without Kevin Keegan, whose international career ended after sixty-three caps.

345: v West Germany, Wembley, 13.10.82. England lost 2–1

Shilton	Mabbutt	Sansom	Thompson	Butcher	Wilkins*
Hill	Regis (Blissett)	Mariner (Woodcock¹)	Armstrong (Rix)	Devonshire	

England had the better of the first-half during which new cap Gary Mabbutt hit a post with a fierce cross shot, but the Germans took control when Pierre Littbarski came on as substitute just twenty-four hours after helping Germany beat England 3–2 in an Under-21 international in Bremen. Karl-Heinz Rummenigge ended brave resistance by England's overworked defence in the 72nd minute when he delicately chipped the ball over Peter Shilton, and shortly after he held off a tackle from Terry Butcher as he swept the ball into the net from a Littbarski cross. Tony Woodcock scored for England 4 minutes from the end with a shot that went in off the bar. Luther Blissett came on as a substitute in the 80th minute for his first taste of international football.

346: v Greece, Salonika, 17.11.82. England won 3–0

Shilton	Neal	Sansom	Thompson	Martin	Robson*
Lee[1]	Mabbutt	Mariner	Woodcock[2]	Morley	

Tony Woodcock, playing in borowed boots, put England on the way to a first victory under Robson with a goal in the second minute, and he made it 2–0 in the 64th minute of this European championship qualifier. 5 minutes later Sammy Lee made his début memorable when he crashed the ball into the net after Bryan Robson had transferred a Woodcock free-kick into his path. Lee and Gary Mabbut were exceptional in midfield in place of injured Ray Wilkins and Glenn Hoddle on a rain-saturated surface.

347: v Luxemburg, Wembley, 15.12.82. England won 9–0

Clemence	Neal[1]	Sansom	Lee	Butcher	Martin
Robson*	Mabbutt (Hoddle[1])	Blissett[3]	Woodcock[1]	Coppell[1] (Chamberlain[1])	[1 o.g.]

England struggled to find their rhythm in the goalless first 20 minutes of this European championship qualifier, but the floodgates opened with a Luxemburg own goal. A minute later Steve Coppell headed in a Bryan Robson cross and Tony Woodcock and Luther Blissett made it 4–0 by half-time. The first 20 minutes of the second half were, as in the first half, barren, but then England stepped up the pace and Blissett completed his hat-trick and substitutes Mark Chamberlain and Glenn Hoddle found the net before, in the final seconds, Phil Neal netted the ninth goal to equal the haul when England – including Bobby Robson – beat Luxemburg in 1960.

348: v Wales, Wembley, 23.2.83. England won 2–1

Shilton*	Neal[1]	Statham	Lee	Martin	Butcher[1]
Blissett	Mabbutt	Mariner	Cowans	Devonshire	

Phil Neal scored from the penalty spot in the 78th minute to end a bold victory bid by Wales on an ice-bound pitch. Ian Rush had given Wales a 14th-minute lead, and was just a coat of paint away from making it 2–0 nine minutes later when his shot struck a post. Terry Butcher equalized 6 minutes before half-time following a quickly taken free-kick by Gordon Cowans who, along with Derek Statham, was making his début. Neal slotted his penalty home just four days after missing a vital spot-kick for Liverpool in an FA Cup tie.

349: v Greece, Wembley, 30.3.83. Drew 0–0

Shilton*	Neal	Sansom	Lee	Martin	Butcher
Coppell	Mabbutt	Francis T.	Woodcock (Blissett)	Devonshire (Rix)	

England were frustrated by a Greek team that came only to defend in this European championship return match. Trevor Francis was the one England forward to play with any penetration, and he might have had a hat-trick before he was subdued by some spiteful tackles. The match was a sad milestone for Steve Coppell, whose international career ended after forty-two caps because of a serious knee injury. After-match quotes by Bobby Robson about Alan Devonshire were taken out of context, and he had to contact the West Ham player to tell him that he had not meant to make him the so-called 'scapegoat' for England's dismal performance.

350: v Hungary, Wembley, 27.4.83. England won 2–0

Shilton*	Neal	Sansom	Lee	Martin	Butcher
Mabbutt	Francis T.[1]	Withe[1]	Blissett	Cowans	

Goals in each half from Trevor Francis and Peter Withe sank a skilful Hungarian team and strengthened England's position at the top of their European championship qualifying group. Francis was always a handful for the Hungarian defence, and Withe topped a powerhouse performance with a cracking goal in the 70th minute when he chested down a long pass from Sammy Lee and rifled in an unstoppable cross shot. Action man Withe had to go to hospital for treatment to a fractured cheekbone and a broken thumb.

351: v Northern Ireland, Belfast, 28.5.83. Drew 0–0

Shilton*	Neal	Sansom	Hoddle	Butcher	Roberts
Mabbutt	Blissett (Barnes J.)	Withe	Cowans	Francis T.	

John Barnes, making his début as a substitute for Luther Blissett, threatened to end the deadlock in the final seconds but goalkeeper Pat Jennings managed to block his close-range shot. Robson also introduced Graham Roberts to international football and he almost turned the ball into his own net in the 28th minute, Peter Shilton saving the day by diving across goal to punch the ball against a post. Glenn Hoddle had his first full game for Robson after a succession of injuries.

352: v Scotland, Wembley, 1.6.83. England won 2–0

Shilton	Neal	Sansom	Lee	Roberts	Butcher
Robson*[1] (Mabbutt)	Francis T.	Withe (Blissett)	Hoddle	Cowans[1]	

Bryan Robson gave England the lead in the 13th minute with a carbon copy of the goal he scored in the opening seconds of the World Cup, forcing the ball into the net from close range after Terry Butcher headed on a Kenny Sansom throw. Robson limped off with a groin injury 10 minutes later, but England continued to dominate in midfield and schemer Gordon Cowans turned scorer in the 54th minute to clinch victory and the British championship. Sammy Lee and Trevor Francis each had 'goals' disallowed.

353: v **Australia,** Sydney, 12.6.83. Drew 0–0

Shilton*	Thomas	Statham (Barnes J.)	Williams	Osman	Butcher
Barham	Gregory	Blissett (Walsh)		Francis T.	Cowans

354: v **Australia,** Brisbane, 15.6.83. England won 1–0

Shilton*	Neal	Statham (Williams)	Barham	Osman	Butcher
Gregory	Francis T.	Walsh[1]	Cowans	Barnes J.	

355: v **Australia,** Melbourne, 19.6.83. Drew 1–1

Shilton* (Spink)	Neal (Thomas)	Pickering	Lee	Osman	Butcher
Gregory	Francis T.[1]	Walsh (Blissett)		Cowans	Barnes J.

Bobby Robson inherited this 'Down Under' tour, and went there reluctantly with what was virtually an England 'B' team and it was a controversial issue that full caps were awarded. Australia missed the chance to turn the games into a soccer showpiece, and defended grimly and often brutally in all three matches. A crowd of 14,000 saw England struggle through a goalless first game in Sydney, and there were just 10,000 to watch Paul Walsh score the only game of the match three days later in Brisbane. A Phil Neal own goal cancelled out a Trevor Francis goal in the third match in front of 20,000 spectaors in Melbourne in the final game of a tour that Robson described as 'of little value to anybody, and nothing like the sort of preparation we needed for the European championships'. Mark Barham, Steve Williams, Danny Thomas, John Gregory, Nick Pickering and Nigel Spink were, along with Walsh, the new full caps, and not one of them was still in the frame for England when the 1986 World Cup build-up started.

356: v **Denmark,** Wembley, 21.9.83. England lost 1–0

Shilton	Neal	Sansom	Wilkins*	Osman	Butcher
Francis T.	Lee (Blissett)	Mariner	Gregory	Barnes J. (Chamberlain)	

A first-half Allan Simonsen penalty decided this European championship qualifier on a soaking-wet pitch and gave Bobby Robson what he described as 'the blackest day of my career'. England disputed the penalty that was awarded when the ball bounced up and struck Phil Neal on the hand. The midfield trio of Sammy Lee, John Gregory and Ray Wilkins failed to function together, and England did not deserve to take a point from the Danes, who were always the more inventive and industrious team. The England players were jeered off and a section of the crowd turned on Robson as he made the long, lonely walk back to the dressing-room.

357: v **Hungary,** Budapest, 12.10.83. England won 3–0

| Shilton | Gregory | Sansom | Lee[1] | Martin | Butcher |
| Robson* | Blissett (Withe) | | Mariner[1] | Hoddle[1] | Mabbutt |

Bryan Robson and Glenn Hoddle were recalled to the midfield, and they were the tandem team that gave England a decided edge over the Hungarians. Hoddle scored an early goal to settle England down, and created the third goal for Paul Mariner after Sammy Lee had made it 2–0 with a 20-yard drive. The victory meant England were still just about breathing in the European championship.

358: v **Luxemburg,** Luxemburg, 16.11.83. England won 4–0

| Clemence | Duxbury | Sansom | Lee | Martin | Butcher[1] |
| Robson*[2] | Hoddle | Mariner[1] | Woodcock (Barnes J.) | | Devonshire |

Just before the kick-off England heard the news that Denmark had beaten Greece 2–0 to clinch the place in the European championship finals, so it was something of an anti-climax as they went into action against Luxemburg. Skipper Bryan Robson refused to allow chins to drop, and he was the main motivator as England cruised to a comfortable victory. Robson scored two of the goals, with Bobby Robson's former Ipswich faithfuls Terry Butcher and Paul Mariner netting a goal each.

359: v **France,** Paris, 29.2.84. England lost 2–0

| Shilton | Duxbury | Sansom | Lee (Barnes J.) | Roberts | Butcher |
| Robson* | Stein (Woodcock) | | Walsh | Hoddle | Williams |

Two second-half goals by Michel Platini gave France a victory that was earned in midfield where they were always a thought and a deed ahead of an experimental England side for whom Luton partners Brian Stein and Paul Walsh failed to find their club form. France went on to win the European championship in the summer, so there was no disgrace for the

England team. The disgrace came off the pitch where hooligans among England's followers again ran riot.

360: v Northern Ireland, Wembley, 4.4.84. England won 1–0

Shilton	Anderson	Kennedy	Roberts	Butcher	Lee
Wilkins	Robson*	Rix	Francis T.	Woodcock[1]	

A Tony Woodcock goal won the match for England at the start of a Home Championship series that was being abandoned after 102 years. Northern Ireland might easily have got at least a draw if the central strikers had made more of the many chances created for them by winger Ian Stewart. Alan Kennedy won the first of his two caps at left-back.

361: v Wales, Wrexham, 2.5.84. England lost 1–0

Shilton	Duxbury	Kennedy	Lee	Martin (Fenwick)	Wright
Wilkins*	Gregory	Walsh	Woodcock	Armstrong (Blissett)	

Two youngsters, Mark Wright and Mark Hughes, had mixed fortunes in their international débuts. Hughes outjumped Wright to head a superb winning goal for Wales. Terry Fenwick came on as substitute for Alvin Martin in the 80th minute for the first of his twenty caps. The *Sun* reacted to the defeat by offering readers 'Robson Out/Clough In' lapel badges.

362: v Scotland, Hampden Park, 26.5.84. Drew 1–1

Shilton	Duxbury	Sansom	Wilkins	Roberts	Fenwick
Chamberlain (Hunt)	Robson*	Woodcock[1] (Lineker)	Blissett	Barnes J.	

Bobby Robson responded to all the criticism by reverting to the 4–2–4 system in which he had been a key man for England as a player a quarter of century earlier. For the midfield role he shared with Johnny Haynes, he called in Manchester United partners Bryan Robson and Ray Wilkins, and for his old-style wingers he selected Mark Chamblerlain and John Barnes. Loose marking let McGhee in for an early goal that was cancelled out by a spectacular 36th-minute equalizer from the edge of the box by Tony Woodcock. Peter Shilton kept England in the match with a series of marvellous saves, and the manager could feel satisfied with his bold experiment at the final whistle. A young striker called Gary Lineker won his first cap when he substituted for injured Tony Woodcock in the 73rd minute.

363: v USSR, Wembley, 2.6.84. England lost 2–0

Shilton	Duxbury	Sansom	Wilkins	Roberts	Fenwick
Robson*	Chamberlain	Francis T. (Hateley)	Blissett	Barnes J.	(Hunt)

'Robson out' chants echoed around Wembley after England had gone down to second half goals from Russian substitutes Gotsanov and Protasov. The first goal could be traced to an unfortunate error by Mike Duxbury – an excellent club player who seemed jinxed the moment he pulled on an England shirt. It was a clumsy, uncoordinated performance by England, brightened only by the entrance on to the international stage of Portsmouth centre-forward Mark Hateley, who brought life to the England attack when he substituted for Trevor Francis. Steve Hunt also came on as a substitute for the second successive match to complete an England career that lasted just 50 minutes in total.

364: v **Brazil,** Rio de Janeiro, 10.6.84. England won 2–0

Shilton	Duxbury	Sansom	Wilkins	Watson	Fenwick
Chamberlain	Robson*	Hateley[1]	Woodcock (Allen)		Barnes J.[1]

John Barnes scored one of the all-time great England goals to inspire this remarkable victory over Brazil just a week after the team had been booed off at Wembley. Terry Fenwick and Mark Hateley combined to feed the ball out to Barnes on the left wing in the last minute of the first half. He set off on a zig-zagging 35-yard run, outsmarting four defenders on the way and then wrong-footing two outstanding players in Costa and Junior, before virtually walking the ball into the net. It was an incredible goal that had 'made-in-Brazil' written all over it, and it was such a confidence boost-er for England that they more than held their own in the second half after Peter Shilton's brilliance had helped curb an attempted fight back by the Brazilians. It was Barnes who set up the second knock-out goal in the 65th minute when his cross to the far post was headed so powerfully by Mark Hateley that goalkeeper Roberto Costa could only help the ball across the line. Clive Allen came on for his début in the 76th minute in place of the tiring Tony Woodcock, and with his first touch almost set up a third goal for Bryan Robson, who sent the ball inches wide of a post. It was Brazil's first home defeat for more than a quarter of a century, and reward for Bobby Robson's courage in sticking to a 4–2–4 formation in the land where the system was born. Norwich centre-half Dave Watson won the first of his twelve caps in place of appendicitis-victim Graham Roberts.

365: v **Uruguay,** Montevideo, 13.6.84. England lost 2–0

Shilton	Duxbury	Sansom	Wilkins	Watson	Fenwick	Robson*
Chamberlain	Hateley	Allen (Woodcock)		Barnes J.		

Urguguay led from the eighth minute through an angrily disputed penalty after winger Acosta fell over Mark Hateley's outstretched leg. England made and missed half a dozen scoring chances before Cabrera wrapped it up with a cleverly created second half goal just as it looked as if England would take full command. A draw would have been a fairer reflection of the play.

366: v Chile, Santiago, 17.6.84. Drew 0–0

Shilton	Duxbury	Sansom	Wilkins	Watson	Fenwick
Robson*	Chamberlain (Lee)		Hateley	Allen	Barnes J.

Despite unleashing more than twenty shots at goal, England could not find the back of the net in a totally one-sided game. Chilean goalkeeper Rojas made half a dozen unbelievable saves, and also enjoyed a charmed life when the ball hit him when he was stretched on the ground on four occasions. Clive Allen came off at the end of his second full international wondering how he had managed to miss at least a hat-trick of goals. Bryan Robson gave a magnificent captain's performance, and continually won the ball in midfield to set up England's avalanche of attacks.

367: v East Germany, Wembley, 12.9.84. England won 1–0

Shilton	Duxbury	Sansom	Williams	Wright	Butcher	Robson*[1]
Wilkins	Mariner (Hateley)		Woodcock (Francis T.)			Barnes J.

Bobby Robson made a double substitution in the second half when he sent on Mark Hateley and Trevor Francis for Paul Mariner and Tony Woodcock, and within a minute England at last broke down the massed East German defence. The goal was an all-Manchester United affair, with Bryan Robson volleying in a cross from his clubmate Ray Wilkins. In a match that was a warm-up for the start of the 1986 World Cup qualifying campaign, England had one scare when East German forward Streich, playing his 100th international, smacked a 25-yard shot against a post.

368: v Finland, Wembley, 17.10.84. England won 5–0

Shilton	Duxbury (Stevens)	Sansom[1]	Williams	Wright	Butcher
Robson*[1] (Chamberlain)	Wilkins	Hateley[2]	Woodcock[1]	Barnes J.	

Mark Hateley excited the Wembley spectators with an exhibition of old-fashioned centre-forward play, powering his way through the Finnish defence for two goals in this opening 1986 World Cup qualifier. Bryan Robson and Tony Woodcock were also on the mark, and in the closing moments Kenny Sansom made it 5–0 with his one and only goal in eighty-six international appearances. Gary Stevens made his début as substitute for injured Mick Duxbury.

369: v Turkey, Istanbul, 14.11.84. England won 8–0

| Shilton | Anderson[1] | Sansom | Williams (Stevens) | Wright | Butcher |
| Robson*[3] | Wilkins | Withe | Woodcock[2] | (Francis T.) | Barnes J.[2] |

Bryan Robson became the first England captain since Vivian Woodward back in 1909 to score a hat-trick as Turkey were steam-rollered to defeat in this World Cup qualifier. John Barnes and Tony Woodcock collected two goals apiece, and Viv Anderson scored the first of his two goals for England.

370: v Northern Ireland, Belfast, 27.2.85. England won 1–0

| Shilton | Anderson | Sansom | Stevens | Martin | Butcher |
| Steven | Wilkins* | Hateley[1] | Woodcock (Francis T.) | | Barnes J. |

England took another step towards the 1986 World Cup finals with this hard-earned victory in the mud of Windsor Park. Mick Quinn headed against the English crossbar and Terry Butcher cleared off the goal-line from Norman Whiteside and Gerry Armstrong before Mark Hateley settled the issue with a second-half goal after Butcher had hammered a Pat Jennings clearance into his path. Trevor Steven won the first of his thirty caps.

371: v Republic of Ireland, Wembley, 26.3.85. England won 2–1

| Bailey | Anderson | Sansom | Steven[1] | Wright | Butcher |
| Robson* | (Hoddle) | Wilkins | Hateley (Davenport) | Lineker[1] (Waddle) | |

Gary Lineker scored the first of his international goals and Trevor Steven got his name on the England scoresheet for the first time against a Republic of Ireland team that battled every inch of the way. Their reward for all their industry came in the closing stages when Liam Brady became the first player to score against England in nearly nine hours following an error by goalkeeper Gary Bailey in his début match. Chris Waddle and Peter Davenport were also introduced to international football for the first time.

372: v Romania, Bucharest, 1.5.85. Drew 0–0

| Shilton | Anderson | Sansom | Steven | Wright | Butcher | Robson* |
| Wilkins | Mariner (Lineker) | | Francis T. | Barnes J. (Waddle) | | |

England retained top place in their World Cup qualifying group with a creditable draw that might easily have been a victory if Bryan Robson's header from a John Barnes free-kick had not hit a post, and if Paul Mariner had steadied himself before missing the best chance of the match. Peter Shilton and Viv Anderson were outstanding in the hard-worked England defence.

373: v **Finland,** Helsinki, 22.5.85. Drew 1–1

| Shilton | Anderson | Sansom | Steven (Waddle) | Fenwick | Butcher |
| Robson* | Wilkins | Hateley[1] | Francis T. | Barnes J. | |

Finland shocked England with an early goal and might have gone 2–0 up but for Terry Butcher clearing the ball off the goal-line with Peter Shilton beaten. Mark Hateley equalized 5 minutes into the second half, but England were unable to force a winner against a spirited Finnish team that hung on for a deserved World Cup point.

374: v **Scotland,** Hampden Park, 25.5.85. England lost 1–0

| Shilton | Anderson | Sansom | Hoddle (Lineker) | Fenwick | Butcher |
| Robson* | Wilkins | Hateley | Francis T. | Barnes J. (Waddle) | |

Graeme Souness got the better of Bryan Robson in the battle for midfield supremacy, and he inspired Scotland to their first victory over the auld enemy at Hampden since 1976. There were thirty-four goal attempts in all, twenty of them coming from England, but the only one that found its way into the net came from full-back Richard Gough in the 68th minute of this first contest for the Sir Stanley Rous Cup. It was England's first defeat in nine matches, but the *Daily Mirror* ran a front-page headline that screamed 'Robson Must Go!'

375: v **Italy,** Mexico City, 6.6.85. England lost 2–1

| Shilton | Stevens | Sansom | Steven (Hoddle) | Wright | Butcher |
| Robson* | Wilkins | Hateley[1] | Francis T. (Lineker) | Waddle (Barnes J.) | |

This opening match in the 'Little World Cup' was staged in the wake of the Heysel Stadium tragedy in which thirty-eight spectators died during rioting just before the Juventus–Liverpool European Cup Final. Players from both sides showed tremendous character in what was a difficult game for everybody involved, and a 1–1 draw looked the likely satisfactory outcome until the Mexican referee amazed even the Italians by awarding them an 88th-minute penalty from which Altobelli scored the winning goal. Peter Shilton was beaten by a shot that swerved in the thin air for Italy's first goal that was quickly cancelled out by Mark Hateley. In the last seconds England had an obvious penalty turned down when Gary Lineker was brought down when shaping to shoot.

376: v **Mexico,** Mexico City, 9.6.85. England lost 1–0

Bailey   Anderson   Sansom   Hoddle (Dixon)   Fenwick   Watson

Robson*   Wilkins (Reid) Hateley   Francis T.   Barnes J. (Waddle)

Peter Reid and Kerry Dixon were sent on for their first caps as substitutes as England tired in the high altitude. Luis Flores had given Mexico the lead with a shot that went in off the post, and then England celebrated what they were convinced was an equalizer from Viv Anderson. But the referee awarded the Mexicans a disputed free-kick when their goalkeeper had collapsed dramatically after Anderson's header had powered into the net. It was the first time since 1959 that an England team had lost three successive matches.

377: v **West Germany,** Mexico City, 12.6.85. England won 3–0

Shilton   Stevens   Sansom   Hoddle   Wright   Butcher

Robson*[1] (Bracewell)   Reid   Dixon[2]   Lineker (Barnes J.)   Waddle

The Germans made the mistake of not getting themselves properly acclimatized, and they were run to the edge of exhaustion in the second half as England stepped up the pace. Kerry Dixon had an exceptional first full game in an England shirt, scoring twice in the second half after laying on the first goal for Bryan Robson in the first half. Four minutes before half-time Peter Shilton played a vital part in an outstanding team display when he saved a Brehme penalty.

378: v **USA,** Los Angeles, 16.6.85. England won 5–0

Woods   Anderson   Sansom (Watson)   Hoddle (Steven[1])   Fenwick   Butcher

Robson* (Reid)   Bracewell   Dixon[2]   Lineker[2]   Waddle (Barnes J.)

Kerry Dixon and Gary Lineker scored two goals apiece against a gallant but outclassed United States team. Lineker's first goal was memorable. He chested down a pass from Glenn Hoddle, swivelled round and volleyed an unstoppable right-foot shot into the net. Glenn Hoddle had a penalty saved, and Trevor Steven scored the fifth and final goal after his Everton clubmate Paul Bracewell had acrobatically knocked the ball into his path. Bracewell was getting his first full outing after playing as a substitute against West Germany, and Bobby Robson awarded a first cap to goalkeeper Chris Woods.

379: v Romania, Wembley, 11.9.85. Drew 1–1

Shilton	Stevens	Sansom	Reid	Wright	Fenwick
Robson*	Hoddle[1]	Hateley	Lineker (Woodcock)	Waddle	(Barnes J.)

Romania's talented Gheorghe Hagi hit the woodwork twice in this World Cup qualifier before Glenn Hoddle calmed England's nerves with a beautifully constructed goal after he had run on to a free-kick from Kenny Sansom. Camataru equalized in the second half with the England defenders standing still, appealing for a handling offence that escaped the notice of the referee.

380: v Turkey, Wembley, 16.10.85. England won 5–0

Shilton	Stevens	Sansom	Hoddle	Fenwick	Wright
Wilkins	Robson*[1] (Steven)	Lineker[3]	Hateley (Woodcock)		Waddle[1]

England played with bite and pace for an hour during which Gary Lineker rattled in a hat-trick and Bryan Robson and Chris Waddle got in on the scoring act against a weak Turkish defence. But they lost their momentum when Robson went off with a pulled hamstring, and though the victory confirmed England's qualification for the World Cup finals, Bobby Robson was less than happy with his team's performance.

381: v Northern Ireland, Wembley, 13.11.85. Drew 0–0

Shilton	Stevens	Sansom	Hoddle	Fenwick	Wright
Bracewell	Wilkins*	Dixon	Lineker	Waddle	

Goalkeeper Pat Jennings celebrated his world record 113th cap with magnificent saves that prevented Glenn Hoddle, Kerry Dixon and Gary Lineker from scoring for England. The point from the goalless game clinched a place in the World Cup finals for Northern Ireland as runners-up in the group to England, who would go to Mexico as the only undefeated European team in the qualifying matches. England argued that they should have had a penalty when defender Alan McDonald handled during a goalmouth scramble, but the referee awarded a corner-kick.

382: v Egypt, Cairo, 29.1.86. England won 4–0

Shilton (Woods)   Stevens   Sansom   Fenwick   Wright   Steven[1] (Hill)

Wilkins*   Cowans[1]   Wallace[1]   Hateley   Lineker (Beardsley) [1 o.g.]

England were flattered by the 4–0 scoreline, and the Egyptians might have salvaged a draw but for the safe hands of Peter Shilton. Club calls meant that Bobby Robson was unable to field several of his World Cup players, and he gave first caps to Danny Wallace and Peter Beardsley. It was Wallace's one and only international appearance, and he marked it with a goal. Gordon Cowans and Trevor Steven were both on the scoresheet, and England were given help by an own goal.

383: v Israel, Rammat Gan, 26.2.86. England won 2–1

Shilton (Woods)   Steven   Sansom   Hoddle   Martin   Butcher

Robson*[2]   Wilkins   Beardsley   Dixon (Woodcock)   Waddle (Barnes J.)

'Captain Courageous' Bryan Robson, back following his hamstring injury, scored both England goals including a penalty after Israel had taken a shock early lead. His first goal was a right foot volley after 50 minutes following a perfect pass by Glenn Hoddle, and he scored the winner from the penalty spot in the closing minutes after former Liverpool player Avi Cohen had punched his header off the goal-line.

384: v USSR, Tbilisi, 26.3.86. England won 1–0

Shilton   Anderson   Sansom   Hoddle   Wright   Butcher

Cowans (Hodge)   Wilkins*   Beardsley   Lineker   Waddle[1] (Steven)

The Russians missed a first-half penalty and were beaten for the first time in eighteen matches by a classic 67th-minute strike by Chris Waddle. It was a goal created in Newcastle, with Peter Beardsley chasing a long ball to the corner by his fellow Geordie Waddle, who raced in to the middle to meet the return pass at the far post and hammer it into the net. Steve Hodge came on for the first of his twenty-four caps.

385: v Scotland, Wembley, 23.4.86. England won 2–1

Shilton   Stevens M.G.   Sansom   Hoddle[1] (Reid)   Watson   Butcher[1]

Wilkins*   Francis T.   Hateley   Hodge (Stevens G.A.)   Waddle

First-half goals from Terry Butcher and Glenn Hoddle gave England the edge in a fiercely fought match for the Sir Stanley Rous Cup. Scotland got back into the game when Graeme Souness scored from the penalty spot after Terry Butcher had upended Charlie Nicholas, but the England defence held out for a confidence-boosting victory before their World Cup journey to Mexico.

386: v **Mexico,** Los Angeles, 17.5.86. England won 3–0

Shilton   Anderson   Sansom   Hoddle   Fenwick   Butcher

Robson* (Stevens G.A.) Wilkins (Steven) Hateley² (Dixon) Beardsley¹ Waddle (Barnes J.)

A convincing victory over World Cup hosts Mexico in a warm-up match was spoilt by the sight of skipper Bryan Robson going off with a dislocated shoulder. Mark Hateley gave England an early 2–0 lead with two magnificent headers, and the third victory-clinching goal was Peter Beardsley's first for England.

387: v **Canada,** Burnaby, 24.5.86. England won 1–0

Shilton (Woods)   Stevens   Sansom   Hoddle   Martin   Butcher

Wilkins* (Reid)   Hodge   Hateley¹   Lineker (Beardsley)   Waddle (Barnes J.)

Gary Lineker damaged a wrist so badly that it was feared he would miss the World Cup in this final tuning-up game before the finals. Mark Hateley scored the only goal of a scrappy game against opponents who were out of their depth, but determined not to let England get into any sort of rhythm. Steve Hodge was the pick of the England players, and with luck might have had a hat-trick.

388: v **Portugal,** World Cup, Monterrey, 3.6.86. England lost 1–0

Shilton   Stevens   Sansom   Hoddle   Fenwick   Butcher

Robson* (Hodge)   Wilkins   Hateley   Lineker   Waddle (Beardsley)

A rare defensive blunder by Kenny Sansom led to Carlos Manuel scoring the winning goal for Portugal in the second half of a disappointing World Cup opener. Gary Lineker played with his sprained wrist strapped, and Bryan Robson came off after 75 minutes to protect his shoulder. England created enough chances to have won the match comfortably, but they lacked finishing finesse.

389: v Morocco, World Cup, Monterrey, 6.6.86. Drew 0–0

| Shilton | Stevens | Sansom | Hoddle | Fenwick | Butcher |

Robson* (Hodge)　Wilkins　Hateley (Stevens G.A.)　Lineker　Waddle

England's World Cup turned into a nightmare in the space of 5 minutes just before half-time when first Bryan Robson was taken off with a recurrence of his shoulder injury, and then acting captain Ray Wilkins was sent off for throwing the ball at the referee in protest at an offside decision. The ten men of England battled with enormous energy and spirit in the second half and could feel satisfied with their point

390: v Poland, World Cup, Monterrey, 11.6.86. England won 3–0

Shilton*　Stevens　Sansom　Hoddle　Fenwick　Butcher

Steven　Reid　Lineker³ (Dixon)　Beardsley (Waddle)　Hodge

Gary Lineker scored all three goals in the first half to put England on the way to an exhilarating victory and into the second round of the World Cup finals. Bobby Robson was forced to make changes because of injuries and the Ray Wilkins suspension, and Lineker looked more comfortable playing in a 4–2–4 formation.

391: v Paraguay, World Cup, Mexico City, 18.6.86. England won 3–0

Shilton*　Stevens　Sansom　Hoddle　Martin　Butcher　Steven

Reid (Stevens G.A.)　Lineker²　Beardsley¹ (Hateley)　Hodge

After surviving some early scares, England took command with a first-half goal by Gary Lineker. Peter Beardsley netted the second goal while Lineker was off the pitch receiving treatment after being elbowed in the throat, and it was Lineker who clinched England's place in the quarter-finals with his fifth goal of the tournament after combining with Tottenham team-mates Glenn Hoddle and Gary Stevens.

392: v Argentina, World Cup, Mexico City, 22.6.86. England lost 2–1

Shilton*　Stevens　Sansom　Hoddle　Fenwick　Butcher

Steven (Barnes J.)　Reid (Waddle) Lineker¹　Beardsley　Hodge

England were put out of the World Cup by the left hand and the left foot of the modern master, Maradona. Five minutes after half-time the chunky Argentinian jumped with goalkeeper Peter Shilton to meet a dipping cross from the right, and he clearly flicked the ball into the net with his hand ('The hand of God', he later called it). England's protests fell on deaf ears, and 5 minutes later their defence was torn to tatters by an electrifying run by Maradona before he steered the ball past Shilton for a brilliantly engineered and legitimate goal. England showed enormous character by battling back, and Lineker became the tournament's top scorer when he met a John Barnes cross to net his sixth goal of the finals. But it was Argentina, the ultimate champions, who went through to the semi-finals. England quite properly felt cheated.

393: v **Sweden,** Stockholm, 10.9.86. England lost 1–0

| Shilton* | Anderson | Sansom | Hoddle | Martin | Butcher |
| Steven | Wilkins | Hodge | Dixon | Barnes J. (Cottee) | |

It took a 50th-minute goal from Sweden's ace striker Johnny Ekstrom to wake up England, and they raised their game but were unable to translate their dominance into goals. Tony Cottee, substituting for injured John Barnes 7 minutes after Sweden took the lead, went on to win seven England caps but was not on the pitch for the full 90 minutes in any of the matches.

394: v **Northern Ireland,** Wembley, 15.10.86. England won 3–0

| Shilton | Anderson | Sansom | Hoddle | Watson | Butcher |
| Robson* | Hodge | Beardsley (Cottee) | | Lineker[2] | Waddle[1] |

In his first international since the World Cup, Barcelona-based Gary Lineker was quickly back to his scoring form with two goals that helped lift England to victory over Northern Ireland in the opening European championship qualifying match. He scored his first goal in the 33rd minute against a spirited Northern Ireland team that often had the England defence at full stretch. It was not until two goals in two minutes in the closing stages, first by Chris Waddle and then Lineker, that England could feel confident they had stifled the Irish challenge. Lineker considered his match-clinching goal among the best he ever scored for England. He ran on to a perfect through ball from Peter Beardsley and outpaced defender John McClelland before chipping the ball into the net from a tight angle while in full stride.

395: v **Yugoslavia,** Wembley, 12.11.86. England won 2–0

| Woods | Anderson[1] | Sansom | Hoddle | Wright | Butcher* |
| Mabbutt[1] | Hodge (Wilkins) | Beardsley | Lineker | Waddle (Steven) | |

Gary Mabbutt celebrated his recall after three years by giving England the lead in the 21st minute of this European championship qualifier. It was his Tottenham team-mate Glenn Hoddle who monopolized the match from midfield, and he created enough chances for England to have sewn up the match long before Viv Anderson scored the second goal in the 57th minute.

396: v **Spain,** Madrid, 18.2.87. England won 4–2

| Shilton (Woods) | Anderson | Sansom | Hoddle | Adams | Butcher |
| Robson* | Hodge | Beardsley | Lineker⁴ | Waddle (Steven) | |

Gary Lineker made it a memorable fifty-fourth birthday for manager Bobby Robson when he scored all four goals against Spain in a dynamic display of finishing in atrocious, mud-caked conditions in the Bernabeu Stadium. Three weeks earlier he had scored a hat-trick for Barcelona against Real Madrid, and now the combined might of those club defences crumbled before him as he pounced for two goals in each half after Spain had taken an early lead. He headed the first, poached the second and third from close range and powered the fourth from the edge of the penalty area after running on to a pass by his favourite partner Peter Beardsley. Tony Adams, twenty-year-old Arsenal centre-half, became the first player born after the 1966 World Cup triumph to be capped by England.

397: v **Northern Ireland,** Belfast, 1.4.87. England won 2–0

| Shilton (Woods) | Anderson | Sansom | Mabbutt | Wright | Butcher |
| Robson*¹ | Hodge | Beardsley | Lineker | Waddle¹ | |

Bryan Robson put his injury problems behind him and returned to the England team with a typically inspiring performance in this European championship qualifier. He headed the first goal in the 19th minute, and Chris Waddle gave England a comfortable two-goal cushion when he scored 2 minutes before half-time. Chris Woods took over from injured Peter Shilton in the 46th minute.

398: v **Turkey,** Izmir, 29.4.87. Drew 0–0

| Woods | Anderson | Sansom | Mabbutt | Adams | Hoddle |
| Robson* | Hodge (Barnes J.) | Allen C. (Hateley) | Lineker | Waddle | |

Two days before being named Footballer of the Year after his forty-nine goals for Tottenham, Clive Allen was celebrating what he thought was his first goal for England against Turkey in this European championship qual-

ifier. But the referee disallowed it, and there was a further disappointment
for him in his first international match for three years when he was substituted by Mark Hateley. England had expected a shoal of goals, but were
unable to find the target against a disciplined Turkish defence.

399: v **Brazil,** Wembley, 19.5.87. Drew 1–1

Shilton	Stevens	Pearce	Reid	Adams	Butcher
Robson*	Waddle	Beardsley	Lineker[1] (Hateley)		Barnes J.

A diving header by Gary Lineker gave England a first-half lead against a
young, experimental Brazilian team that showed flourishes of the skilful
football that would have pleased their ancestors. It was Lineker's nine-
teenth goal in twenty matches, but this did not save him from being substituted by Mark Hateley as Bobby Robson attempted to expose Brazil's
weakness in the air. Marindinha, later of Newcastle, scored Brazil's deserved equalizer in an exciting Rous Cup match. Stuart Pearce made his international bow at left-back.

400: v **Scotland,** Hampden Park, 23.5.87. Drew 0–0

Woods	Stevens	Pearce	Hoddle	Wright	Butcher
Robson*	Hodge	Hateley	Beardsley	Waddle	

Defences dominated in a drab goalless draw in which both teams wasted
scoring chances. Brazil beat Scotland 2–0 on the same Hampden Park pitch
three days later to take the Rous Cup.

401: v **West Germany,** Dusseldorf, 9.9.87. England lost 3–1

Shilton*	Anderson (Pearce)	Sansom	Hoddle (Webb)	Adams	Mabbutt
Reid	Barnes J.	Beardsley	Lineker[1]	Waddle (Hateley)	

England never recovered after going two goals down in the first half-hour.
Gary Lineker pulled one back before half-time, but Littbarski was again
too much for the England defence and his second goal of the match
clinched a convincing victory for the Germans. Neil Webb became the
1,000th player to be capped by England when coming on as substitute for
Glenn Hoddle in the 64th minute.

402: v **Turkey,** Wembley, 14.10.87. England won 8–0

Shilton	Stevens	Sansom	Steven (Hoddle)	Adams	Butcher
Robson*[1]	Webb[1]	Beardsley[1] (Regis)	Lineker[3]	Barnes J.[2]	

England were two goals up in 8 minutes through John Barnes and Gary Lineker, and both players added a goal each before half-time on a rain-soaked Wembley pitch. Bryan Robson deflected a Neil Webb shot into the Turkish net to make it 5–0 and Peter Beardsley headed the sixth goal before Lineker completed his fourth international hat-trick in the 71st minute. It was Webb, playing in his first full international, who completed the massacre with a rasping volley as England moved to the top of their European championship qualifying table.

403: v **Yugoslavia,** Belgrade, 11.11.87. England won 4–1

Shilton	Stevens	Sansom	Steven	Adams[1]	Butcher
Robson*[1] (Reid)	Webb (Hoddle)	Beardsley[1]	Lineker	Barnes J.[1]	

England won the match and clinched a place in the European championship finals with a dazzling first-half display that produced goals in the opening 25 minutes from Peter Beardsley, John Barnes, Bryan Robson and Tony Adams. The Yugoslavs could not cope with the pace and power of the England attack, and were forced to pull attacking players back in a bid to shore up their beleagured defence. England were coasting to victory when Katanec scored a consolation goal in the 80th minute.

404: v **Israel,** Tel Aviv, 17.2.88. Drew 0–0

Woods	Stevens	Pearce	Webb	Watson	Wright (Fenwick)
McMahon	Allen (Harford)		Beardsley*	Barnes J.	Waddle

Steve McMahon and Mick Harford won their first caps in a match that was in danger of being called off as driving rain turned the ground into a quagmire. The waterlogged pitch made decent football an impossibility, and the game became bogged down in midfield. Peter Beardsley was made captain in place of the absent Bryan Robson.

405: v **Holland,** Wembley, 23.3.88. Drew 2–2

Shilton	Stevens	Sansom	Steven	Adams[1]	Watson (Wright)
Robson*	Webb (Hoddle)	Beardsley (Hateley)	Lineker[1]	Barnes J.	

Gary Lineker scored his twenty-fourth goal in twenty-four games to give England a 14th-minute lead, sliding the ball past the advancing Dutch goalkeeper after controlling a 30-yard pass from Gary Stevens. Ruud Gullit was an inspiration behind a Dutch fightback and they equalized when a cross hit Tony Adams and deflected into the England net. A sparkling Gullit run made the opening for Bosman to give Holland a half-time lead that was cancelled out when Adams made amends for his own goal by heading in a Trevor Steven free-kick.

406: v **Hungary,** Budapest, 27.4.88. Drew 0–0

Woods	Anderson	Pearce (Stevens)	Steven	Adams	Pallister
Robson*	McMahon	Beardsley (Hateley)	Lineker (Cottee)		Waddle (Hoddle)

Gary Pallister, stepping up from Second Division football with Middlesbrough, made an excellent début alongside Tony Adams in an England defence that coped well with a Hungarian attack that promised much more than it finally produced. For goalkeeper Chris Woods, the understudy to Peter Shilton, it was a sixth successive full game in which he had not conceded a goal.

407: v **Scotland,** Wembley, 21.5.88. England won 1–0

Shilton	Stevens	Sansom	Webb	Adams	Watson
Robson*	Steven (Waddle)		Beardsley[1]	Lineker	Barnes J.

This 107th match between England and Scotland and the first staged on a Saturday for seven years was spoiled by crowd trouble outside the ground that led to over 200 arrests. The high spot on the pitch was a beautifully created first-half goal by Peter Beardsley that was enough to give England victory in this Rous Cup match.

408: v **Colombia,** Wembley, 24.5.88. Drew 1–1

Shilton	Anderson	Sansom	McMahon	Adams	Wright	Robson*
Waddle (Hoddle)		Beardsley (Hateley)		Lineker[1]		Barnes J.

Gary Lineker's flicked header from a Chris Waddle right-wing cross went in off a post to give England the lead after 23 minutes in this Rous Cup match. The Colombians were forced to abandon their dour defensive tactics, and the orange-haired Carlos Valderrama started to treat the crowd to his bag of tricks. Escobar equalized for Colombia in the 66th minute with a header that went into the net off the underside of the bar following a corner-kick, but it was not enough to stop England skipper Bryan Robson collecting the Rous Cup.

409: v **Switzerland,** Lausanne, 28.5.88. England won 1–0

Shilton (Woods) Stevens Sansom Webb Adams (Watson) Wright

Robson* (Reid) Steven (Waddle) Beardsley Lineker[1] Barnes J.

A superbly struck second-half goal by Gary Lineker gave England a deserved victory over a disciplined Swiss team in a final warm-up match before the European championship finals.

410: v **Republic of Ireland,** Stuttgart, 12.6.88. England lost 1–0

Shilton Stevens Sansom Webb (Hoddle) Adams Wright

Robson* Waddle Beardsley (Hateley) Lineker Barnes J.

Jack Charlton's 25–1 outsiders took a shock 6th-minute lead through Ray Houghton and then defied all attempts by England to save this opening game in the European championship finals. England put too much responsibility on the shoulders of Gary Lineker, who took a buffeting as he missed a hat-trick of chances before goalkeeper Pat Bonner produced a miracle save to stop him snatching an equalizer.

411: v **Holland,** Dusseldorf, 15.6.88. England lost 3–1

Shilton Stevens Sansom Hoddle Adams Wright

Robson*[1] Steven (Waddle) Beardsley (Hateley) Lineker Barnes J.

Marco Van Basten chose this European championship match to reveal to the world that he had developed into one of the great strikers of modern times. He powered Holland into the lead a minute before half-time, and then returned to the scoring stage after Bryan Robson had given England brief hope with a 54th minute equalizer. As Ruud Gullit pulled the English defence inside out with his clever running and precise passing, Van Basten decided the match with two goals in four minutes to complete a devastating hat-trick that wrecked Peter Shilton's 100th international appearance.

412: v **USSR,** Frankfurt, 18.6.88. England lost 3–1

Woods Stevens Sansom Hoddle Adams[1] Watson

Robson* Steven Lineker (Hateley) McMahon (Webb) Barnes J.

The Russians rushed into a 3rd-minute lead and compounded England's misery by handing them their third successive defeat in the European championship tournament. A Tony Adams goal pulled England level in the 15th minute, but the Russians regained the lead 13 minutes later and wrapped up the game with a third goal 13 minutes from the final whistle. Gary Lineker's lethargic performances were more easily understood when it was diagnosed that he was suffering from hepatitis. Bobby Robson survived another campaign by the tabloid press for his head. Questions were even asked in the House of Commons by MPs who felt new leadership was the answer to England's problems.

413: v **Denmark,** Wembley, 14.9.88. England won 1–0

Shilton (Woods)   Stevens   Pearce   Rocastle   Adams (Walker)   Butcher

Robson*   Webb[1]   Harford (Cottee)   Beardsley (Gascoigne)   Hodge

England's supporters voted against England with their feet and a crowd of only 25,837 turned up at Wembley to see England beat Denmark thanks to a 28th-minute goal by Neil Webb. David Rocastle started his first match for England, and there were two substitutes who would play a big part in England's future – Des Walker after 65 minutes and then, with just 5 minutes to go, a beefy young Geordie called Paul Gascoigne.

414: v **Sweden,** Wembley, 19.10.88. Drew 0–0

Shilton   Stevens   Pearce   Webb   Adams (Walker)   Butcher

Robson*   Beardsley   Waddle   Lineker   Barnes J. (Cottee)

There was a tame start to England's 1990 World Cup campaign when they were held to a goalless draw by a Swedish side that came with the main objective of not getting beaten. England's forwards were all out of touch in front of goal, and even a barnstorming display by skipper Bryan Robson failed to give them the key to victory. Goalkeeper Peter Shilton was unemployed for long periods, but proved an unbeatable barrier when the Swedes suddenly stepped up the pace in the second-half and threatened to dismantle the previously sound England defence.

415: v **Saudi Arabia,** Riyadh, 16.11.88. Drew 1–1

Seaman   Sterland   Pearce   Thomas (Gascoigne)   Adams[1]   Pallister

Robson*   Rocastle   Beardsley (Smith)   Lineker   Waddle (Marwood)

It took a 54th-minute equalizer from Tony Adams to save England from the embarrassment of defeat in a match that many considered was an unnecessary fixture in England's international calendar. Sheffield Wednesday right-back Mel Sterland won his one and only England cap, and Brian Marwood's England career lasted just nine minutes when he followed Arsenal clubmate Alan Smith on as a substitute to bring the Highbury contingent to five players, including goalkeeper David Seaman.

416: v **Greece,** Athens, 8.2.89. England won 2–1

Shilton	Stevens	Pearce	Webb	Walker	Butcher
Robson*[1]	Rocastle	Smith (Beardsley)		Lineker	Barnes J.[1]

England were shaken by a 2-minute penalty goal, but cancelled it out 7 minutes later when John Barnes guided the ball into the net. It took more than an hour for England to find anything approaching fluency, and then they started to pound away at the Greek defence until the inevitable goal came from Bryan Robson in the 79th minute.

417: v **Albania,** Tirana, 8.3.89. England won 2–0

Shilton	Stevens	Pearce	Webb	Walker	Butcher
Robson*[1]	Rocastle	Waddle (Beardsley)		Lineker (Smith)	Barnes J.[1]

A toothless Albanian team failed to trouble Peter Shilton in a World Cup qualifying match that was strangely lacking in passion. England won comfortably enough with a goal in each half by John Barnes and Bryan Robson, but the talk was more of the missed chances and a seventh successive blank match for Gary Lineker.

418: v **Albania,** Wembley, 26.4.89. England won 5–0

Shilton	Stevens (Parker)	Pearce	Webb	Walker	Butcher
Robson*	Rocastle (Gascoigne[1])		Beardsley[2]	Lineker[1]	Waddle[1]

Gary Lineker ended a goal famine that had lasted nearly a year when he headed past the seventeen-year-old Albanian goalkeeper in the 5th minute of this return World Cup qualifier. It was Lineker who laid on the second and third goals for his usual provider Peter Beardsley. Then substitute Paul Gascoigne lit up the intenational stage by setting up a goal for his fellow Geordie Chris Waddle before conjuring a magical goal of his own in the 88th minute, ghosting past two defenders and firing a low shot into the far corner of the net. It was a taste of things to come.

419: v **Chile,** Wembley, 23.5.89. Drew 0–0

Shilton	Parker	Pearce	Webb	Walker	Butcher
Robson*	Gascoigne	Clough	Fashanu (Cottee)		Waddle[1]

An experimental England team featuring new caps Nigel Clough and John Fashanu struggled to break down a resolute Chilean defence. There was a graveyard atmosphere at Wembley for this Rous Cup encounter, with a tube train strike helping to keep the attendance down to 15,628. Fashanu, the first Wimbledon player to be capped by England, limped off after 70 minutes. His only other England appearance would last just half an hour. Nigel Clough's call up completed the first father-and-son double act – following his two-cap dad, Brian – since George Eastham followed George senior into the England team. Paul Parker played his first full game.

420: v **Scotland,** Hampden Park, 27.5.89. England won 2–0

Shilton	Stevens	Pearce	Webb	Walker	Butcher
Robson*	Steven	Fashanu (Bull[1])	Cottee (Gascoigne)		Waddle[1]

Substitutes Steve Bull and Paul Gascoigne had double reason for celebrations as England powered to a 2–0 victory in this Rous Cup match. Bull, the first Third Division player capped since Peter Taylor in 1976, marked his début with an 80th-minute goal to add to Chris Waddle's 20th-minute strike. Gascoigne joined the action 2 minutes before Bull's goal on what was his twenty-second birthday.

421: v **Poland,** Wembley, 3.6.89. England won 3–0

Shilton	Stevens	Pearce	Webb[1]	Walker	Butcher	Robson*
Waddle (Rocastle)		Beardsley (Smith)		Lineker[1]	Barnes J.[1]	

Gary Lineker was in exceptional form, scoring the first goal in the 24th minute and helping to set up vital goals for John Barnes and Neil Webb in the 69th and 82nd minutes. Lineker would have opened the scoring early in this World Cup qualifier but for a cynical foul by the goalkeeper as the England striker prepared to shoot into a gaping net. Peter Shilton equalled Bobby Moore's record collection of 108 England caps in what was his 1,200th first-class match.

422: v **Denmark,** Copenhagen, 7.6.89. Drew 1–1

Shilton (Seaman)	Parker	Pearce	Webb (McMahon)	Walker	Butcher
Robson*	Rocastle	Beardsley (Bull)	Lineker[1]	Barnes J. (Waddle)	

Gary Lineker fired England into the lead in the 29th minute in a match staged to celebrate 100 years of Danish football. Denmark equalized early in the second half, the first goal conceded by Peter Shilton in six matches as he set a new England caps record in his 109th appearance before making way for David Seaman.

423: v **Sweden,** Stockholm, 6.9.89. Drew 0–0

| Shilton | Stevens | Pearce | Webb (Gascoigne) | Walker | Butcher* |
| Beardsley | McMahon | Waddle | Lineker | Barnes J. (Rocastle) | |

England's second goalless draw with Sweden virtually clinched their place in the 1990 World Cup finals. Skipper Terry Bucher was England's bloody hero: he insisted on playing on after having ten stitches inserted into a deep gash on his forehead during the half-time interval. It was a sad game for Neil Webb who limped off with an achilles tendon injury that put him on the sidelines for several months.

424: v **Poland,** Katowice, 11.10.89. Drew 0–0

| Shilton | Stevens | Pearce | McMahon | Walker | Butcher |
| Robson* | Rocastle | Beardsley | Lineker | Waddle | |

Almost sixteen years ago to the day England had drawn with Poland at Wembley in a World Cup match in which only a victory would do. Peter Shilton had been in goal then, and here he was again at the age of forty playing to the peak of his ability as England battled for the point that would guarantee their place in the World Cup finals. Shilton was beaten only once when a 30-yard shot rattled his crossbar in the last minute. Thanks to Shilts, England had completed their six-match qualifying programme without conceding a single goal.

425: v **Italy,** Wembley, 15.11.89. Drew 0–0

| Shilton (Beasant) | Stevens | Pearce (Winterburn) | McMahon (Hodge) | Walker | Butcher |
| Robson* (Phelan) | Waddle | Beardsley (Platt) | Lineker | Barnes J. | |

England stretched their unbeaten run to thirteen matches and nine hours without conceding a goal against the 1990 World Cup hosts and tournament favourites. Bobby Robson experimented by sending on four new caps as second-half substitutes – Dave Beasant, Nigel Winterburn, Mike Phelan and David Platt. Phelan went closest to breaking the scoring deadlock with a 30-yard volley from a punched clearance by goalkeeper Zenga. The ball missed the target by inches in what was Phelan's only international appearance

---

426: v Yugoslavia, Wembley, 13.12.89. England won 2–1

Shilton (Beasant) Parker   Pearce (Dorigo)   Thomas (Platt)   Walker   Butcher

Robson*[2] (McMahon)   Rocastle (Hodge)   Bull   Lineker   Waddle

Bryan Robson scored the fastest goal ever witnessed at Wembley when he headed in a Chris Waddle free-kick after just 38 seconds. It ended more than five hours of goalless football by England and set up what was their 100th win at Wembley. Skoro equalized for Yugoslavia with a snap shot in a rare attack in the 17th minute, and it was Robson who struck the winning goal in the 67th minute after Paul Parker had made an enterprising break down the right wing. Bobby Robson continued his experiments, sending on Dave Beasant, Tony Dorigo, David Platt, Steve McMahon and Steve Hodge as substitutes.

427: v Brazil, Wembley, 28.3.90. England won 1–0

Shilton (Woods)   Stevens   Pearce   McMahon   Walker   Butcher*

Platt   Waddle   Beardsley (Gascoigne)   Lineker[1]   Barnes J.

This was billed as an unoffical World championship because both teams were undefeated in their last fourteen international matches. The game was settled by Gary Lineker nine minutes before half-time when he headed in his thirtieth England goal after John Barnes had flicked on a Peter Beardsley corner from the left. It was England's first home victory against Brazil for thirty-four years. Shilton had to go off for stitches after Des Walker's elbow had hit him in the face, and Chris Woods took over in goal. Muller claimed the ball was over the line when Stuart Pearce made a goalmouth clearance in the 66th minute.

428: v Czechoslovakia, Wembley, 25.4.90. England won 4–2

Shilton (Seaman)   Dixon   Pearce[1] (Dorigo)   Steven   Walker (Wright)

Butcher   Robson* (McMahon)   Gascoigne[1]   Bull[2]   Lineker   Hodge

Paul Gascoigne took hold of this game by the scruff of the neck after the Czechs had startled England by taking an early lead. Gazza flourished all his prodigious skills as he laid on two goals for Steve Bull, another for

Stuart Pearce and then in the final moments added a fourth goal himself with a thumping left-foot shot into the roof of the net.

429: v Denmark, Wembley, 15.5.90. England won 1–0

Shilton (Woods) Stevens Pearce (Dorigo) McMahon (Platt) Walker Butcher*

Hodge Gascoigne Waddle (Rocastle) Lineker[1] (Bull) Barnes J.

A draw would have been a fairer reflection of the play as England stretched their unbeaten run to seventeen internationals. England survived half a dozen scares before Gary Lineker scored the match winner in the 54th minute when he rammed a Steve Hodge centre into the net off the bar.

430: v Uruguay, Wembley, 22.5.90. England lost 2–1

Shilton Parker Pearce Hodge (Beardsley) Walker Butcher

Robson* Gascoigne Waddle Lineker (Bull) Barnes J.[1]

Uruguay ended England's undefeated run in what was their final Wembley match before the World Cup finals. Peter Shilton was beaten by a powerful header in the first-half and a swerving free-kick in the second-half, the two goals sandwiching an impressive strike by John Barnes following an audacious 50-yard pass by Paul Gascoigne.

431: v Tunisia, Tunis, 2.6.90. Drew 1–1

Shilton Stevens Pearce Hodge (Beardsley) Walker Butcher (Wright)

Robson* Waddle (Platt) Gascoigne Lineker (Bull[1]) Barnes J.

England's final warm-up match before the World Cup finals almost proved too hot for them. Steve Bull saved them from an unnerving defeat with a headed last-minute equalizer. Tunis had taken a shock first-half lead when Hergal accepted a miscued pass from Paul Gascoigne and astonished everybody, particularly Peter Shilton, with a volley from 35 yards. England looked lethargic and hardly in the mood for the World Cup challenge that lay ahead of them.

432: v Republic of Ireland, World Cup, Cagliari, 11.6.90. Drew 1–1

Shilton Stevens Pearce Gascoigne Walker Butcher

Robson* Waddle Beardsley (McMahon) Lineker[1] (Bull) Barnes J.

England could not have got off to a better start to their World Cup campaign when Gary Lineker chested down a Chris Waddle pass and then forced the ball it into the net in the 8 minute. But it was the Irish who grew in stature and confidence as they piled on pressure with a long-ball game that was ugly to the eye but wearing on the limbs and lungs of the overstretched England defenders. Peter Shilton, equalling Pat Jennings' world record of 119 international caps, was beaten in the 68th minute after substitute Steve McMahon, with his first touch of the ball, lost control and watched in anguish as his Merseyside neighbour, Everton's Kevin Sheedy, whipped it off his toes and planted an instant left-foot drive into the net. Nobody could dispute that Ireland deserved their equalizer in a game that was a poor advertisement for British football, but it was cruel luck for McMahon who in a nightmare couple of minutes also managed to get himself booked.

433: v **Holland,** World Cup, Cagliari, 16.6.90. Drew 0–0

Shilton	Parker	Pearce	Wright	Walker	Butcher
Robson* (Platt)		Waddle (Bull)	Gascoigne	Lineker	Barnes J.

England produced a world-class performance using the sweeper system that Bobby Robson had virtually ignored throughout his reign as England manager. The player he chose for the sweeping job was Derby central defender Mark Wright, who was recalled for his first international since England's defeat by Holland in the European Championships. This was the match in which Paul Gascoigne came of age as an international player. He strode around the centre stage as if he owned it, and some of his forward surges and his passes were exceptional in their quality and execution. One twisting turn on the ball when he foxed two Dutch defenders in the second half was out of the Johan Cruyff school of skill. England were always that little bit sharper and hungrier for the ball, and David Platt proved himself made for the World Cup stage when he came on as substitute for injured skipper Bryan Robson. There was a dramatic climax when Stuart Pearce drove a last-minute free kick from out on the right wide of the Dutch defensive wall and straight into the net past diving goalkeeper Hans van Breukelen. Celebration of a winning goal was cut short when the referee made it clear that he had awarded an indirect free kick. The ball could only have missed the fingers of van Breukelen by inches. England came that close to what would have been a richly deserved win.

434: v **Egypt,** World Cup, Cagliari, 21.6.90. England won 1–0

Shilton*	Parker	Pearce	Gascoigne	Walker	Wright1
McMahon	Waddle (Platt)	Bull (Beardsley)		Lineker	Barnes J.

Mark Wright's first goal in international football catapulted England into the second phase of World Cup '90 and slammed shut the door on an Egyptian team that got the deserts their negative approach deserved. Egypt played with just the one ambition of stopping England from scoring, and tried to strangle the life out of the game with aggravating time-wasting tactics. England were reduced to ten men when Wright scored his dramatic goal in the 59th minute. Des Walker was lying on the perimeter of the pitch having treatment to a leg injury when England were awarded a free-kick out near the left touchline half-way into Egypt's half. Paul Gascoigne floated a high kick tantalizingly into the packed Egyptian penalty area. It hung long enough in the air to tempt goalkeeper Ahmed Shubeir off his line, and he was stranded as the tall figure of Wright rose above all around him. He connected with a glancing header and the ball flicked into the net off defender Hesham Yakan.

435: v **Belgium,** World Cup, Bologna, 26.6.90. England won 1–0 (a.e.t.))

Shilton	Parker	Pearce	Wright	Walker	Butcher*
McMahon (Platt[1])	Waddle	Gascoigne		Lineker	Barnes J. (Bull)

David Platt stepped into this full-blooded thriller as a substitute, and with a penalty shoot-out just seconds away he scored a phenomenal first goal for England to lift them into the quarter-finals. The match was played at a furious pace until the intense heat slowed just about everybody down to an exhausted jog in extra time. Enzo Scifo bossed the game in midfield for Belgium and he and the veteran Jan Ceulemans both smacked shots against Peter Shilton's right post. John Barnes had been almost anonymous but was desperately unlucky in the 40th minute when he steered in a cross from Gary Lineker for what looked an excellent goal. A linesman ended England's celebrations by raising the offside flag. With one minute of extra time to go Paul Gascoigne floated a free-kick deep into the penalty area. Platt watched it carefully like a 'plane spotter, and spun round to face the goal as the ball dropped over his shoulder. All in the same movement he volleyed it wide of the Belgian goalkeeper. It would have been rated a classic goal in any football match. In the last minute of a World Cup finals tie it must go down as one of the greatest goals ever scored for England.

436: v **Cameroon,** World Cup, Naples, 1.7.90. England won 3–2 (a.e.t.))

Shilton	Parker	Pearce	Wright	Walker	Butcher* (Steven)
Platt[1]	Waddle	Gascoigne	Lineker[2]		Barnes J. (Beardsley)

Gary Lineker scored two goals from the penalty spot not only to put
England into the World Cup semi-finals but also to rescue them from one
of the most humiliating defeats in their history. The harsh truth is that for
long periods Cameroon played England off the park in a dramatic duel that
was draining both physically and emotionally, and only a mixture of
enormous luck and true grit pulled England through. It was thirty-eight-
year-old Roger Milla who wrote himself into World Cup folklore against
England. The silken skills of substitute Milla were released into the match
at the start of the second half with Cameroon unlucky to be trailing 1–0 to
an excellent goal that had been burgled by David Platt. Paul Gascoigne was
helping out in an overworked defence when he collided with Milla and
conceded a penalty in the 61st minute: Emmanuel Kunde converted the
spot-kick. Four minutes later Milla drew defenders towards him before
threading a pass through to substitute Eugene Ekeke. He sprinted clear, and
then almost casually flicked the ball into the net past Shilton. With 6
minutes to go, Gary Lineker spun in the penalty area and was brought down
by Thomas Libiih. Lineker himself scored from the spot to breathe life back
into England. There was a fresh crisis for England when Mark Wright was
cut and badly dazed as he headed the back of Milla's head. He was treated
for a jagged gash on his forehead, and then bravely played on through extra
time with a huge plaster protecting a wound that later needed seven stitches.
In the 14th minute of extra time Gascoigne pushed a perfect pass through
to Lineker, whose promising run towards goal was halted when goalkeeper
Thomas Nkono pulled him down. Lineker shot his penalty on a straight line
into the net. England had won a memorable match, and created history by
becoming the first English team to reach a World Cup semi-final on foreign
soil.

437: v West Germany, World Cup semi-final, Turin, 4.7.90. Drew 1–1 (a.e.t.)
England lost 4-3 on penalties

Shilton	Parker	Pearce	Wright	Walker	Butcher* (Steven)
Platt	Waddle	Gascoigne	Lineker[1]	Beardsley	

England saved their finest performance of World Cup '90 for this epic
semi-final, but they finished up with empty hands and broken hearts as
West Germany conquered them in a torturous penalty shoot-out. A 1–1
draw after extra time was just about a fair reflection on a masterpiece of a
match. There was just one irritating incident when Thomas Berthold made
a meal of a tackle by Paul Gascoigne in extra time, and Gazza was close to
tears as he collected his second booking of the tournament, which would
have ruled him out of the Final. Gascoigne had been more prominent and
productive in midfield than West German skipper Lothar Matthaus, who

had been rated by many as the best player on view before this match. Peter Shilton was desperately unlucky to concede the first goal of the match in the 59th minute when Brehme's shot deflected off Parker's heel and ballooned freakishly high before coming down first bounce into the back of England's net. Lineker equalized in the 80th minute when he hit the ball in full stride with his left foot to send it under a sliding defender and into the far corner of the net. Both Chris Waddle and Guido Buchwald hammered shots against the post during a thrilling extra-time period before the penalty shoot-out. Shilton elected the right way to dive for every one of the German penalties, but each time he was a fingernail's distance away from making a vital save. Lineker took the first penalty and coolly drilled it home. Brehme made it all square. Then Beardsley netted penalty number two, which was cancelled out by Matthaus with the most ferocious spot-kick of the tournament. David Platt made it 3–2 while Paul Gascoigne looked on from the centre-circle with tears watering his eyes. Riedle brought the scores level again before Stuart Pearce took aim and fired the first blank. He was inconsolable as his low-driven spot-kick cannoned off Illgner's shins. Olaf Thon netted Germany's next penalty, meaning that Chris Waddle had to hit the target to keep alive England's hopes of reaching the final. He had never taken a spot-kick in a major match in his career, and he produced a novice-like effort as he blazed the ball high over the bar. Germany were through to the final, but England went out with honour in a match that was a credit to the World Cup and to football in general.

438: v Italy, World Cup third-place play-off, Bari, 7.7.90. England lost 2–1

Shilton*	Stevens	Dorigo	Parker	Walker	Wright (Waddle)
Platt[1]	Steven	McMahon (Webb)		Lineker	Beardsley

Bobby Robson's last match as England manager and Peter Shilton's final game as England goalkeeper ended in a defeat by Italy that was partly self-inflicted in this play-off for third place. Shilton, captain for the night as he stretched his world-record collection of caps to 125, will remember his farewell performance for all the wrong reasons. The man who had been one of the most reliable players in the history of English football made a calamitous mistake in the 70th minute. He had just taken possession of the ball and elected to roll it along the ground as he looked for an England player to whom he could pass it. Shilts must have been the only person in the stadium who did not see Roberto Baggio loitering alongside him. Shilton virtually placed the ball at Baggio's feet and he exchanged passes with Salvatore Schillaci before dribbling his way across the face of the England goal and scoring with a close-range shot. Ten minutes after

Shilton's error the skilful Tony Dorigo made an enterprising run down the left wing before sending over a measured cross. David Platt, who had been making penetrating bursts into the Italian penalty area throughout the game, powered the ball into the net from 12 yards for one of the best headed goals of the whole tournament. Paul Parker was adjudged to have fouled Salvatore Schillaci when they became tangled in the penalty area in the 84th minute. Schillaci, needing one goal to become the leading marskman of World Cup '90, sent Shilton the wrong way as he drilled in his sixth goal of the finals. England had lost, but their dignity and their pride were still intact. They had done England in general and Bobby Robson in particular proud. Could Graham Taylor go one better and reach the World Cup Final?

Graham Taylor's teams and match highlights

439: v Hungary, Wembley, 12.9.90. England won 1-0

Woods	Dixon	Pearce (Dorigo)	Parker	Walker	Wright
Platt	Gascoigne	Bull (Waddle)	Lineker*[1]	Barnes J.	

Graham Taylor made Gary Lineker captain for his first match as England manager, and it was the new skipper who scored the match-winning goal in the last minute of the first-half. David Platt had a shot beaten out, Paul Gascoigne played the ball back in and Lineker swooped to put the finishing touch from six yards.

440: v Poland, Wembley, 17.10.90. England won 2-0

Woods	Dixon	Pearce	Parker	Walker	Wright
Platt	Gascoigne	Bull (Waddle)	Lineker*[1] (Beardsley[1])	Barnes J.	

A Gary Lineker penalty after his header had been handled on the line gave England the lead in the 40th minute of this opening European championship qualifier. Peter Beardsley, substituting for injured Lineker in the 56th minute, made the points safe with a second goal a minute from time.

441: v Republic of Ireland, Dublin, 14.11.90. Drew 1-1

Woods	Dixon	Pearce	Adams	Walker	Wright
Platt[1]	Cowans	Beardsley	Lineker*	McMahon	

Graham Taylor made the surprise tactical decision to leave out Paul Gascoigne when most people felt that his flair might have made the difference against Jack Charlton's well-drilled Republic of Ireland team in this European championship qualifier. England were flattered by their 1-0 lead when David Platt scored in the 67th minute of a match in which skill took second place to strength, and justice was done when Tony Cascarino equalized in the 79th minute after coming on as a substitute.

442: v **Cameroon,** Wembley, 6.2.91. England won 2-0

Seaman	Dixon	Pearce	Steven	Walker	Wright M.
Robson* (Pallister)	Gascoigne (Hodge)	Wright I	Lineker²		Barnes J.

Cameroon were a delight in the World Cup finals but a bitter disappointment in this friendly match on a frost-bitten Wembley turf. They played a dour defensive game and produced a spate of spiteful tackles including a reckless challenge on Gary Lineker by the goalkeeper that brought a 20th-minute penalty. Lineker scored from the spot to complete a hat-trick of penalties against Cameroon, the first two being converted in the World Cup match in Italy. It was Lineker who turned in a Stuart Pearce corner in the 62nd minute to finish off the Africans. Crystal Palace striker Ian Wright became Graham Taylor's first new cap.

443: v **Republic of Ireland,** Wembley, 27.3.91. Drew 1-1

Seaman	Dixon¹	Pearce	Adams (Sharpe)	Walker	Wright M.
Robson*	Platt	Beardsley	Lineker (Wright I.)		Barnes J.

Lee Dixon's first goal for England in the ninth minute of this European championship return match was cancelled out 18 minutes later by Niall Quinn. Manchester United's exciting young prospect Lee Sharpe was introduced to international football at the start of the second half, but England were lamentable in front of goal against Irish defenders who took no prisoners. Bryan Robson was called up for the first time by Graham Taylor, but he could not galvanize England into winning action.

444: v **Turkey,** Izmir, 1.5.91. England won 1-0

Seaman	Dixon	Pearce	Wise¹	Walker	Pallister
Platt	Thomas (Hodge)	Smith	Lineker*		Barnes J.

Dennis Wise, picked for his first cap despite a poor run of form with Chelsea, silenced the critics of his selection with the crucial winning goal that he scrambled into the Turkish net in the 32nd minute of this European championship qualifier. Geoff Thomas also made his international bow in a largely undistinguished game.

445: v **USSR,** Wembley, 21.5.91. England won 3-1

Woods	Stevens	Dorigo	Wise (Batty)	Parker	Wright M.*
Platt²	Thomas	Smith¹	Wright I. (Beardsley)		Barnes J.

Only 23,789 fans bothered to turn up to see England play Russia in the contrived 'England Challenge Cup', a three-way tournament that also included Argentina. David Platt got England off to a flying start with a 4th-minute goal from the penalty spot, and Alan Smith made it 2-0 12 minutes later. An own goal by Mark Wright gave the Russians brief hope of getting back into the game before Platt finished them off with an 89th-minute strike. David 'Bites Yer Legs' Batty started his international career as a 70th-minute substitute.

446: v **Argentina,** Wembley, 25.5.91. Drew 2-2

Seaman	Dixon	Pearce	Batty	Walker	Wright M.
Platt[1]	Thomas	Smith	Lineker*[1]	Barnes J. (Clough)	

England let a two-goal lead slip in a 4r-minute spell midway through the second-half of a game that was always niggly and bad-tempered, with the Argentinians giving better than they received in the nasty tackles department. Gary Lineker scored in the 15th minute and the energetic David Platt made it 2–0 5 minutes after half-time. Lineker had the hollow honour of collecting the Challenge Cup.

447: v **Australia,** Sydney, 1.6.91. England won 1-0

Woods	Parker	Pearce	Batty	Walker	Wright M.
Platt	Thomas	Clough	Lineker* (Wise)	Hirst (Salako) [1 o.g.]	

448: v **New Zealand,** Auckland, 3.6.91. England won 1-0

Woods	Parker	Pearce	Batty (Deane)	Walker	Barrett
Platt	Thomas	Wise	Lineker*[1]	Walters (Salako)	

449: v **New Zealand,** Wellington, 8.6.91. England won 2-0

Woods	Charles	Pearce*[1]	Wise	Walker	Wright M.
Platt	Thomas	Deane (Hirst[1])	Wright I.	Salako	

Like his predecessor Bobby Robson, Graham Taylor reluctantly inherited a 'Down Under' tour that did little for him apart from provide some fresh scenery. An own goal 5 minutes before half-time gave England victory over Australia in Sydney, and an injury-time goal by Gary Lineker saved blushes in the first match against New Zealand in Auckland. A goal in each half by Stuart Pearce and David Hirst gave England a 2–0 victory in the return match in Wellington. Hirst was one of six players awarded their first caps during the tour, along with John Salako, Earl Barrett, Brian Deane, Mark Walters and Gary Charles.

450: v Malaysia, Kuala Lumpur, 12.6.91. England won 4-2

Woods	Charles	Pearce	Batty	Walker	Wright M.
Platt	Thomas	Clough	Lineker*⁴	Salako	

Gary Lineker produced the second four-goal burst of his international career, taking over from Jimmy Greaves as the second top England scorer of all time and he was now just four goals behind Bobby Charlton's record forty-nine-goal haul. Many people considered this should not have been classified as a full international, but there was no doubting Lineker's ability as a deadly finisher as he found the net in the first, 23rd, 30th and 70th minutes.

451: v Germany, Wembley, 11.9.91. England lost 1-0

Woods	Dixon	Dorigo	Batty	Pallister	Parker
Platt	Steven (Stewart)	Smith	Lineker*	Salako (Merson)	

England created enough chances to be comfortably in command long before Riedle headed West Germany into the lead a minute before half-time. There was much to applaud in England's approach work, but their finishing was feeble. Graham Taylor tried to rectify the situation by sending on new caps Paul Stewart and Paul Merson, but it was the world champions who came closest to scoring in the second half when Lothar Matthaus brought out the best in Chris Woods with a 30-yard drive.

452: v Turkey, Wembley, 16.10.91. England won 1-0

Woods	Dixon	Pearce	Batty	Walker	Mabbutt
Robson	Platt	Smith¹	Lineker*	Waddle	

Alan Smith headed home a Stuart Pearce cross midway through the first half to give England maximum points in this European championship qualifier, but there was little for Graham Taylor to enthuse about. The Turks might easily have salvaged a draw but for a couple of excellent saves by Chris Woods and the intervention of a post when he was beaten by a snap shot from Riza. Bryan Robson made his ninetieth and final appearance in an England shirt that he had always worn with such pride and passion. Injuries had robbed him of at least another twenty caps.

453: v Poland, Poznan, 13.11.91. Drew 1-1

Woods	Dixon	Pearce	Gray (Smith)	Walker	Mabbutt
Platt	Thomas	Rocastle	Lineker*¹	Sinton (Daley)	

Just one scoring chance came Gary Lineker's way in this tough and tense

European championship qualifier and he tucked it away with tremendous style, volleying the ball into the net on the turn in the 77th minute. It equalized a 32nd-minute Polish goal that went into the net off Gary Mabbut. The draw clinched England's place in the European championship finals. Andy Gray, Andy Sinton and Tony Daley won their first caps.

454: v France, Wembley, 19.2.92. England won 2–0

| Woods | Jones | Pearce* | Keown | Walker | Wright M. |
| Webb | Thomas | Clough | Shearer¹ | Hirst (Lineker¹) | |

France came to Wembley hailed as the new wonder team of Europe after a run of nineteen matches without defeat, but they were sent crashing by an England team producing their finest performance since Graham Taylor became manager. Alan Shearer illuminated his début with a well-taken goal a minute before half-time, swivelling to guide the ball into the net after Mark Wright had flicked on a Nigel Clough centre. The goal boosted England's confidence, and they were always looking the superior side in the second-half against a smooth but punchless French team that had not been beaten for three years. Gary Lineker, who had announced that he was retiring from international football after the European championship finals, joined the game as a substitute and collected his forty-seventh goal in the 74th minute to knock the heart out of Michel Platini's highly regarded team. Rob Jones and Martin Keown made their débuts along with Shearer.

455: v Czechoslovakia, Prague, 25.3.92. Drew 2-2

| Seaman | Keown¹ | Pearce* | Rocastle (Dixon) | Walker | Mabbutt (Lineker) |
| Platt | Merson1 | Clough (Stewart) | Hateley | Barnes J. (Dorigo) | |

A much-changed England twice came back from a goal down to force a draw against a talented Czechoslovakian team. It was a match of mistakes in both goal areas, and a particularly unhappy game for Arsenal goal-keeper David Seaman, whose fumbling form led to him losing his number two spot in the European championship squad. Paul Merson and Martin Keown both scored their first goals for England, Merson equalizing in the 28th minute and Keown scoring with a spectacular shot in the 66th minute after an appalling error by Seaman had let the Czechs in for their second goal on the hour.

456: v Commonwealth of Independent States, Moscow, 29.4.92. Drew 2-2

| Woods (Martyn) | Stevens | Sinton (Curle) | Palmer | Walker | Keown |
| Platt | Steven¹ (Stewart) | Shearer (Clough) | Lineker*¹ | Daley | |

Gary Lineker struck his forty-eighth goal in the 14th minute, and then managed to miss a much easier chance that would have brought him level with Bobby Charlton's all-time record. It was to be his final goal in an outstanding England career. The Russians scored at the end of the first half and the beginning of the second, and it was Trevor Steven who saved the match for England with his first international goal for six years in the 72nd minute. Graham Taylor gave first caps to Nigel Martyn, Carlton Palmer and Keith Curle.

457: v **Hungary,** Budapest, 12.5.92. England won 1-0

Martyn (Seaman)	Stevens	Dorigo	Curle (Sinton)	Walker	Keown
Webb (Batty)	Palmer	Merson (Smith)	Lineker* (Wright I.)	Daley [o.g.]	

Graham Taylor fielded sixteen players in what was developing into a bewildering search for his best squad for the European championships in Sweden. Gary Lineker turned goalmaker in the 56th minute when his cross to the far post was forced into the net off a defender by a determined Neil Webb. England's defence had been pulled inside out by the Hungarian forwards in the first half, but they lost their momentum after a series of missed chances.

458: v **Brazil,** Wembley, 17.5.92. Drew 1-1

Woods	Stevens	Dorigo (Pearce)	Palmer	Walker	Keown
Daley (Merson)	Steven (Webb)	Platt[1]	Lineker*	Sinton (Rocastle)	

Gary Lineker, of all people, missed an early penalty and the chance to equal Bobby Charlton's record, and it was an inexperienced Brazilian team that took the lead in the 20th minute through Bebeto after a mistake by Gary Stevens. David Platt snatched an equalizer 10 minutes after half-time as England once again came from behind to save a game.

459: v **Finland,** Helsinki, 3.6.92. England won 2-1

Woods	Stevens (Palmer)	Pearce	Keown	Walker	Wright M.
Platt[2]	Steven (Daley)Webb	Lineker*	Barnes J.	(Merson)	

England's final warm-up match before the European championship finals in Sweden developed into a nightmare, with both John Barnes and Gary Stevens sustaining injuries that knocked them out of the tournament. Yet again England had to come from behind after Finland had taken a 27th-minute lead from a harshly awarded penalty against Trevor Steven. Following a procession of missed chances, David Platt was on target seconds before half-time. It was Platt, recently signed by Juventus from Bari, who scored the winner in the 62nd minute.

460: v **Denmark,** Malmo, 11.6.92. Drew 0–0

Woods	Curle (Daley)	Pearce	Palmer	Walker	Keown
Steven	Platt	Smith	Lineker*	Merson (Webb)	

England were hustled out of their stride by a Danish team surprised to find themselves in the European Championship finals following the barring of war-torn Yugoslavia. Concentrating on quick and incisive counter-attacks, it was Denmark who looked most likely to break the deadlock and England had a lucky escape when a shot from John Jensen struck a post with goalkeeper Chris Woods beaten. The English defence missed the steadying influence of injured Mark Wright, but Carlton Palmer gave a good account of himself against a Danish side in which Brian Laudrup was outstanding as the orchestrator of their attacks. The Danes got better and better as the tournament wore on and finally emerged as the unexpected champions.

461: v **France,** Malmo, 14.6.92. Drew 0–0

Woods	Stevens	Pearce	Palmer	Walker	Keown
Batty	Platt	Shearer	Lineker*	Sinton	

A game that was eagerly awaited fizzled out into a tame draw, with both sides too cautious and frightened of defeat. A Stuart Pearce free-kick from 30 yards shook the French crossbar, and David Platt was inches wide with a diving header. There were few other England scoring chances of note. One of the features of a disappointing game was the struggle for supremacy between deadly French striker Papin and England defender Des Walker. Papin was hardly allowed a kick, but managed one moment of magic when his sudden shot was magnificently saved by Chris Woods.

462: v **Sweden,** Stockholm, 17.6.92. England lost 2-1

Woods	Batty	Pearce	Palmer	Walker	Keown
Daley	Webb	Platt¹	Lineker* (Smith)	Sinton (Merson)	

England's European championship challenge ended with a depressing defeat by Sweden, who were allowed back into the game after David Platt had scored an early goal. Tony Daley missed two opportunities to make the game safe before Sweden gradually took control following the half-time substitution of Anders Limpar by the veteran Johnny Ekstrom and a change of tactics that had England's defenders completedly bewildered. Jan Eriksson headed an equalizer in the 51st minute, and as England struggled to contain the suddenly buoyant Swedes, Graham Taylor made the controversial decision to call off skipper Gary Lineker for Alan Smith. Lineker had fired his final shots for England after eighty caps and still a goal short of Bobby Charlton's all-time record. England, needing a win to book a place in the semi-finals, were being exposed to the perils of panic, and it was the Swedes who conjured the goal that mattered 7 minutes from the end when the gifted Tomas Brolin exchanged passes with Dahlin before firing in the winner.

463: v **Spain,** Santander, 9.9.92. England lost 1-0

Woods   Dixon (Bardsley) (Palmer)   Pearce*   Ince   Walker   Wright M.

White (Merson)   Platt   Clough   Shearer   Sinton (Deane)

England gave a disjointed and punchless performance against a slick Spanish team that deserved victory by a wider margin. It might have been a different story if David White, making his début on the right side of the attack, had converted an early chance created for him by Nigel Clough. Des Walker and Mark Wright looked uncomfortable at the heart of the defence, and their indecision led to Spain's winning goal.

464: v **Norway,** Wembley, 14.10.92. Drew 1-1

Woods   Dixon (Palmer)   Pearce*   Batty   Walker   Adams

Platt[1]   Gascoigne   Wright [1] (Merson)   Shearer   Ince

David Platt maintained the goal-scoring form that had been one of the few bonuses for Graham Taylor as England produced a fighting performance against a vastly improved Norwegian team. Paul Gascoigne stood out on his return to the international stage, and it was his flair and imagination that brought the smile back to the face of English football. A major worry for Taylor was the shot-shy performance from Ian Wright, who was struggling to produce his club form at England level. Tony Adams brought stability to the England defence that was dented only by a surprise long-range shot that earned Norway a flattering draw in this World Cup qualifier.

465: v **Turkey,** Wembley, 18.11.92. England won 4-0

Woods   Dixon   Pearce*[1]   Palmer   Walker   Adams

Platt   Gascoigne[2]   Shearer[1]   Wright I.   Ince

Paul Gascoigne monopolized this World Cup qualifying match with a spectacular solo show, scoring two of the goals and helping to lay on a third.

The outplayed Turks were lucky not to concede at least three more goals as Gascoigne's passes pulled their defence to shreds. Ian Wright combined well with Alan Shearer, and was unfortunate not to break his England goal-scoring duck.

466: v **San Marino,** Wembley, 17.2.93. England won 6-0

Woods	Dixon	Dorigo	Palmer[1]	Walker	Adams
Batty	Gascoigne	Platt*[4]	Ferdinand[1]	Barnes	

Four goals from David Platt lifted England to a satisfactory rather than stunning victory against a mediocre team of part-time professionals who came only to defend in this World Cup qualifier. Platt, an inspiring skipper in place of the injured Stuart Pearce, had the chance to equal the individual England five-goal record but his 88th-minute penalty was superbly saved. Platt's goals came in the 13th, 24th, 67th and 83rd minutes. Carlton Palmer scored with a diving header in the 78th minute and Les Ferdinand marked his international début with England's sixth goal in the 86th minute. Paul Gascoigne was strangely subdued in midfield and John Barnes, recalled after a long injury-forced lay-off, had a personal nightmare with the frustrated England fans jeering and booing him almost every time he touched the ball.

467: v **Turkey,** Izmir, 31.3.93. England won 2–0

Woods	Dixon(Clough)	Sinton	Palmer	Walker	Adams
Platt*[1]	Gascoigne[1]	Barnes	Wright(Sharpe)	Ince	

A 6th-minute goal by David Platt, his tenth in ten internationals, put England on the road to a hard-earned victory in this rough, tough World Cup qualifying match in front of a hostile crowd. England's players had to show tremendous character as the Turkish fans aimed coins, bottles and fireworks at them from the terraces. A looping header by Paul Gascoigne a minute before halftime gave England a commanding lead, which they had to battle to protect against a Turkish team trying to score their first ever goal in eight meetings. Lee Dixon was brutally kicked out of the match and Paul Ince switched from midfield to take his place at right-back, allowing Nigel Clough into the game as a substitute. Tony Adams was a tower of strength in the middle of the England defence, and John Barnes regained his dignity with a battling performance.

468: v **Holland,** Wembley, 28.4.93. England drew 2–2

Woods	Dixon	Keown	Palmer	Walker	Adams
Platt*[1]	Gascoigne(Merson)	Barnes[1]	Ferdinand	Ince	

England squandered a two-goal lead after taking command of this World Cup qualifier with an impressive display of football matching anything previously

produced under Graham Taylor, Barnes scored with a ferocious first-minute
free-kick, and Platt added number two in the 24th minute. Ten minutes later
Dennis Bergkamp scored with a magnificent volley. England were not so
effective after the departure of the injured Gascoigne, and Walker clumsily
conceded a penalty in the 85th minute that was slotted home by Van Vossen.

469: v Poland, Katowice, 29.5.93. England drew 1–1

Woods	Bardsley	Dorigo	Palmer (Wright[1])	Walker	Adams
Platt*	Gascoigne (Clough)		Sheringham	Barnes	Ince

England trailed to a 34th-minute goal following a careless mix-up between
Walker and Barnes. Substitute Ian Wright scored his first goal for England in
nine appearances in the 84th minute to salvage a precious World Cup point.

470: v Norway, Oslo, 2.6.93. England lost 2–0

Woods	Dixon	Pallister	Palmer	Walker (Clough)	Adams
Platt*	Gascoigne	Ferdinand	Sheringham (Wright)		Sharpe

Graham Taylor gambled on playing with three central defenders at the back,
but the players were uncomfortable with the new tactics. Walker was caught
napping when Norway took a 43rd-minute lead through Leonhardsen. Eight
minutes after half-time Walker was outpaced before Bohinen beat Woods at
his near post to seal a humiliating World Cup qualifying match defeat.

471: v United States, Boston, 9.6.93. England lost 2–0

Woods	Dixon	Dorigo	Pallister	Palmer (Walker)	Batty
Ince*	Clough	Ferdinand (Wright)	Barnes	Sharpe	

472: v Brazil, Washington, 13.6.93. England drew 1–1

Flowers	Barrett	Dorigo	Pallister	Walker	Batty (Platt[1])
Sinton	Ince* (Palmer)	Clough	Wright	Sharpe	

473: v Germany, Detroit, 19.6.93. England lost 2–1

Martyn	Barrett	Sinton	Pallister (Keown)	Walker	
Platt*[1]	Ince	Clough (Wright)	Barnes	Sharpe (Winterburn)	Merson

England started their three-match 'US 93' tournament with a degrading 2–0
defeat by the United States. They regained some dignity with a draw against
Brazil thanks to a headed goal by David Platt, who scored with his first touch
after coming on as a half-time substitute. Tim Flowers made an exceptional
début in the England goal. England finished the tournament in bottom place
after losing 2–1 to world champions Germany in a match played indoors on
grass. Platt again scored England's goal, his twelfth in fourteen games. It was
England's sixth match without a win, their worst run for twelve years.